The I Hate the 21st Century READER

The I Hate the 21st Century READER

THE AWFUL, THE ANNOYING, AND THE ABSURD—FROM ETHNIC CLEANSING TO FRANKENSCIENCE

EDITED BY CLINT WILLIS AND NATE HARDCASTLE

THUNDER'S MOUTH PRESS
NEW YORK

THE I HATE THE 21ST CENTURY READER:
The Awful, the Annoying, and the Absurd—from Ethnic Cleansing to Frankenscience

Published by
Thunder's Mouth Press
An Imprint of Avalon Publishing Group, Inc.
245 West 17th St., 11th floor
New York, NY 10011-5300

ISBN-13: 978-1-56025-718-9

Interior design by Paul Paddock

For Benjamin and Karma (our dogs)

CONTENTS

INTRODUCTION

When I was growing up, I occasionally worried about the possibility of dying in a nuclear holocaust. Now I worry about that—but it's down the list, behind death-by-microscopic robot or imprisonment for my political views and just ahead of the possibility that I might live to 130 and then be slaughtered for food.

I also worry that some angry person will get his hands on some hideous new technology and use it to kill the people I love. I worry that the spectacular gap between rich and poor in our country and on our planet will continue to grow, destroying what is left of global democracy and any hope for a stable, prosperous world.

I worry that some new virus will sweep across North America, killing millions of people. I worry that global warming will fuel a new crop of super-hurricanes and that one of them will flood a major American city . . . oh, right, that already happened.

I worry that television and movies and magazines and books and the media in general will continue to suck and that the people who consume that media will continue to tolerate it. I worry that some of my neighbors won't be able to afford to retire.

Nostalgia is often a brutally sentimental exercise, but these days it seems almost justified. True, things *are* better now in some ways—we can beat some types of cancer, and we have nicer cars and so on. And Hitler is dead. Then again, genocide is very much alive, and most cancer patients can't afford health care anyway and all those fucking cars are killing the planet. And George Bush is even stupider than his father, which is some kind of miracle in reverse.

Even the good hiding places are gone. People who were fed up with civilization 50 years ago could go try to climb Mount Everest or move to Alaska. Now Everest is a tourist trap and Alaska is melting. That leaves theme parks like Disney and Las Vegas or (if you're rich enough) East Hampton.

Twenty years ago I interviewed the president of Loyola University in New Orleans. He predicted that New Orleans would eventually become like some cities he'd seen in South America: places where the rich lived behind walls and the poor lived in cardboard shelters propped against those walls. I had spent some time in housing projects around the city, and I believed him—but his prediction would have seemed far-fetched to most folks at the time.

Well, it came true. Of course, no one noticed until Hurricane Katrina ripped off the city's pubic relations façade, which exploited the population's gifts without acknowledging its suffering. And now most people, ashamed at what they see, will try to forget that New Orleans was a sea of misery even before the storm. But forgetting won't make the ugly facts go away.

And here's my point: Katrina was a window not just on the present but also on the future that is taking shape around the planet and within our country's borders. It is future defined by inequality, environmental catastrophe, and violence. And it's mostly our own damn fault.

Americans these days respond to our problems by turning away from them to embrace fantasies about our own strength and goodness. We tell ourselves that we are a freedom-loving, powerful, and wise people. There is some truth to these notions, but we are more often ashamed and frightened. We are ashamed that we let children in this country and abroad die in poverty even as we squander our enormous and often ill-gotten resources in pursuit of empire and comfort. We are frightened because the consequences of our greed are so terrible—and because we cannot escape them no matter how rich we become.

What is to be done? The work begins and ends with awareness: We must acknowledge our mistakes and our problems and begin to address them in a spirit of realism and hope. We must learn to help each other.

Otherwise, we're finished.

—Clint Willis

THE COMING MAYHEM

*with a cartoon by Mr. Fish
and facts*

War is hell, *said Yankee general Tecumseh Sherman, back when armies fought with bayonets, rifles, and cannons. War in the twenty-first century is far worse thanks to new technologies of destruction. True, government-supported militias riding horses and camels club African villagers to death in Sudan, but even they have helicopter support. And while those of us who live in the wealthy nations of the world are generally safe from club-wielding horsemen (except when we play polo), we do have to worry about pissed-off poor people getting hold of the horrifyingly powerful weapons we've developed at horrifying expense to protect ourselves from pissed-off poor people. Nukes are a problem, of course. But that's not the worst of it. . . .*

War of the Future

from TomDispatch.com (4/18/05)

David Morse

A war of the future is being waged right now in the sprawling desert region of northeastern Africa known as Sudan. The weapons themselves are not futuristic. None of the ray-guns, force-fields, or robotic storm troopers that are the stuff of science fiction; nor, for that matter, the satellite-guided Predator drones or other high-tech weapon systems at the cutting edge of today's arsenal.

No, this war is being fought with Kalashnikovs, clubs and knives. In the western region of Sudan known as Darfur, the preferred tactics are burning and pillaging, castration and rape—carried out by Arab militias riding on camels and horses. The most sophisticated technologies deployed are, on the one hand, the helicopters used by the Sudanese government to support the militias when they attack black African villages, and on the other hand, quite a different weapon: the seismographs used by foreign oil companies to map oil deposits hundreds of feet below the surface.

This is what makes it a war of the future: not the slick PowerPoint presentations you can imagine in boardrooms in Dallas and Beijing showing proven reserves in one color, estimated reserves in another, vast subterranean puddles that stretch west into Chad, and south to Nigeria and Uganda; not the technology; just the simple fact of the oil.

This is a resource war, fought by surrogates, involving great powers whose economies are predicated on growth, contending for a finite pool of resources. It is a war straight out of the pages of Michael Klare's book, *Blood and Oil;* and it would be a glaring example of the consequences of our addiction to oil, if it were not also an invisible war.

Invisible?

Invisible because it is happening in Africa. Invisible because our mainstream media are subsidized by the petroleum industry. Think of all the car ads you see on television, in newspapers and magazines. Think of the narcissism implicit in our automobile culture, our suburban sprawl, our obsessive focus on the rich and famous, the giddy assumption that all this can continue indefinitely when we know it can't—and you see why Darfur slips into darkness. And Darfur is only the tip of the sprawling, scarred state known as Sudan. Nicholas Kristof pointed out in a *New York Times* column that ABC News had a total of 18 minutes of Darfur coverage in its nightly newscasts all last year, and that was to the credit of Peter Jennings; NBC had only 5 minutes, CBS only 3 minutes. This is, of course, a micro-fraction of the time devoted to Michael Jackson.

Why is it, I wonder, that when a genocide takes place in Africa, our attention is always riveted on some black American miscreant superstar? During the genocide in Rwanda ten years ago, when 800,000 Tutsis were slaughtered in 100 days, it was the trial of O. J. Simpson that had our attention.

Yes, racism enters into our refusal to even try to understand Africa, let alone value African lives. And yes, surely we're witnessing the kind of denial that Samantha Power documents in *A Problem from Hell: America and the Age of*

Genocide; the sheer difficulty we have acknowledging genocide. Once we acknowledge it, she observes, we pay lip-service to humanitarian ideals, but stand idly by. And yes, turmoil in Africa may evoke our experience in Somalia, with its graphic images of American soldiers being dragged through the streets by their heels. But all of this is trumped, I believe, by something just as deep: an unwritten conspiracy of silence that prevents the media from making the connections that would threaten our petroleum-dependent lifestyle, that would lead us to acknowledge the fact that the industrial world's addiction to oil is laying waste to Africa.

When Darfur does occasionally make the news—photographs of burned villages, charred corpses, malnourished children—it is presented without context. In truth, Darfur is part of a broader oil-driven crisis in northern Africa. An estimated 300 to 400 Darfurians are dying every day. Yet the message from our media is that we Americans are "helpless" to prevent this humanitarian tragedy, even as we gas up our SUVs with these people's lives.

Even Kristof—whose efforts as a mainstream journalist to keep Darfur in the spotlight are worthy of a Pulitzer—fails to make the connection to oil; and yet oil was the driving force behind Sudan's civil war. Oil is driving the genocide in Darfur. Oil drives the Bush administration's policy toward Sudan and the rest of Africa. And oil is likely to topple Sudan and its neighbors into chaos.

The Context for Genocide

I will support these assertions with fact. But first, let's give Sudanese government officials in Khartoum their due. They prefer to explain the slaughter in Darfur as an ancient rivalry between nomadic herding tribes in the north and black African farmers in the south. They deny responsibility for the militias and claim they can't control them, even as they continue to train the militias, arm them, and pay them. They play down their Islamist ideology, which supported Osama bin Laden and seeks to impose Islamic fundamentalism in Sudan and elsewhere. Instead, they portray themselves as pragmatists struggling to hold together an impoverished and backwards country; all they need is more economic aid from the West, and an end to the trade sanctions imposed by the U.S. in 1997, when President Clinton added Sudan to the list of states sponsoring terrorism. Darfur, from their perspective, is an inconvenient anomaly that will go away, in time.

It is true that ethnic rivalries and racism play a part in today's conflict in Darfur. Seen in the larger context of Sudan's civil war, however, Darfur is not an anomaly; it is an extension of that conflict. The real driving force behind the North-South conflict became clear after Chevron discovered oil in southern Sudan in 1978. The traditional competition for water at the fringes of the Sahara was transformed into quite a different struggle. The Arab-dominated government in Khartoum redrew Sudan's jurisdictional boundaries to exclude the oil reserves from southern jurisdiction. Thus began Sudan's 21-year-old North-South civil war. The conflict then moved south, deep into Sudan, into wetter lands that form the headwaters of the Nile and lie far from the historical competition for water.

Oil pipelines, pumping stations, well-heads, and other key infrastructure became targets for the rebels from the South, who wanted a share in the country's new mineral wealth, much of which was on lands they had long occupied. John Garang, leader of the rebel Sudan People's Liberation Army (SPLA), declared these installations to be legitimate targets of war. For a time, the oil companies fled from the conflict, but in the 1990s they began to return. Chinese and Indian companies were particularly aggressive, doing much of their drilling behind perimeters of bermed earth guarded by troops to protect against rebel attacks. It was a Chinese pipeline to the Red Sea that first brought Sudanese oil to the international market.

Prior to the discovery of oil, this dusty terrain had little to offer in the way of exports. Most of the arable land was given over to subsistence farming: sorghum and food staples; cattle and camels. Some cotton was grown for export. Sudan, sometimes still called The Sudan, is the largest country in Africa and one of the poorest. Nearly a million square miles in area, roughly the size of the United States east of the Mississippi, it is more region than nation. Embracing some 570 distinct peoples and dozens of languages and historically ungovernable, its boundaries had been drawn for the convenience of colonial powers. Its nominal leaders in the north, living in urban Khartoum, were eager to join the global economy—and oil was to become their country's first high-value export.

South Sudan is overwhelmingly rural and black. Less accessible from the north, marginalized under the reign of the Ottoman Turks in the nineteenth century, again under the British overlords during much of the twentieth, and now by Khartoum in the north, South Sudan today is almost devoid of schools, hospitals, and modern infrastructure.

Racism figures heavily in all this. Arabs refer to darker

Africans as "*abeed*," a word that means something close to "slave." During the civil war, African boys were kidnapped from the south and enslaved; many were pressed into military service by the Arab-dominated government in Khartoum. Racism continues to find expression in the brutal rapes now taking place in Darfur. Khartoum recruits the militias, called *Janjaweed*—itself a derogatory term—from the poorest and least educated members of nomadic Arab society.

In short, the Islamist regime has manipulated ethnic, racial, and economic tensions, as part of a strategic drive to commandeer the country's oil wealth. The war has claimed about two million lives, mostly in the south—many by starvation, when government forces prevented humanitarian agencies from gaining access to camps. Another four million Sudanese remain homeless. The regime originally sought to impose shariah, or Islamic, law on the predominantly Christian and animist South. Khartoum dropped this demand, however, under terms of the Comprehensive Peace Treaty signed last January. The South was to be allowed to operate under its own civil law, which included rights for women; and in six years, southerners could choose by plebiscite whether to separate or remain part of a unified Sudan. The all-important oil revenues would be divided between Khartoum and the SPLA-held territory. Under a power-sharing agreement, SPLA commander John Garang would be installed as vice president of Sudan, alongside President Omar al-Bashir.

Darfur, to the west, was left out of this treaty. In a sense, the treaty—brokered with the help of the U.S.—was signed at the expense of Darfur, a parched area the size of France. It has an ancient history of separate existence as a kingdom lapping into Chad, separate from the area known today as Sudan. Darfur's population is proportionately more Muslim and less Christian than southern Sudan's, but is mostly black African, and identifies itself by tribe, such as the Fur. (Darfur, in fact, means "land of the Fur.") The Darfurian practice of Islam was too lax to suit the Islamists who control Khartoum. And so Darfurian villages have been burned to clear the way for drilling and pipelines, and to remove any possible sanctuaries for rebels. Some of the land seized from black farmers is reportedly being given to Arabs brought in from neighboring Chad.

Oil and Turmoil

With the signing of the treaty last January, and the prospect of stability for most of war-torn Sudan, new seismographic studies were undertaken by foreign oil companies in April. These studies had the effect of doubling Sudan's estimated oil reserves, bringing them to at least 563 million barrels. They could yield substantially more. Khartoum claims the amount could total as much as 5 billion barrels. That's still a pittance compared to the 674 billion barrels of proven oil reserves possessed by the six Persian Gulf countries—Saudi Arabia, Iraq, the United Arab Emirates, Kuwait, Iran, and Qatar. The very modesty of Sudan's reserves speaks volumes to the desperation with which industrial nations are grasping for alternative sources of oil.

The rush for oil is wreaking havoc on Sudan. Oil revenues to Khartoum have been about $1 million a day, exactly the amount which the government funnels into arms—helicopters and bombers from Russia, tanks from

Poland and China, missiles from Iran. Thus, oil is fueling the genocide in Darfur at every level. This is the context in which Darfur must be understood—and, with it, the whole of Africa. The same Africa whose vast tapestry of indigenous cultures, wealth of forests and savannas was torn apart by four centuries of theft by European colonial powers—seeking slaves, ivory, gold, and diamonds—is being devastated anew by the 21st century quest for oil.

Sudan is now the seventh biggest oil producer in Africa after Nigeria, Libya, Algeria, Angola, Egypt, and Equatorial Guinea.

Oil has brought corruption and turmoil in its wake virtually wherever it has been discovered in the developing world. Second only perhaps to the arms industry, its lack of transparency and concentration of wealth invites kickbacks and bribery, as well as distortions to regional economies.

"There is no other commodity that produces such great profit," said Terry Karl in an interview with Miren Gutierrez, for the International Press Service, "and this is generally in the context of highly concentrated power, very weak bureaucracies, and weak rule of law." Karl is co-author of a Catholic Relief Services report on the impact of oil in Africa, entitled *Bottom of the Barrel.* He cites the examples of Gabon, Angola, and Nigeria, which began exploiting oil several decades ago and suffer from intense corruption. In Nigeria, as in Angola, an overvalued exchange rate has destroyed the non-oil economy. Local revolts over control of oil revenues also have triggered sweeping military repression in the Niger delta.

Oil companies and exploration companies like Halliburton wield political and sometimes military power. In

Sudan, roads and bridges built by oil firms have been used to attack otherwise remote villages. Canada's largest oil company, Talisman, is now in court for allegedly aiding Sudan government forces in blowing up a church and killing church leaders, in order to clear the land for pipelines and drilling. Under public pressure in Canada, Talisman has sold its holdings in Sudan. Lundin Oil AB, a Swedish company, withdrew under similar pressure from human rights groups.

Michael Klare suggests that oil production is intrinsically destabilizing:

> When countries with few other resources of national wealth exploit their petroleum reserves, the ruling elites typically monopolize the distribution of oil revenues, enriching themselves and their cronies while leaving the rest of the population mired in poverty—and the well-equipped and often privileged security forces of these "petro-states" can be counted on to support them.

Compound these antidemocratic tendencies with the ravenous thirst of the rapidly growing Chinese and Indian economies, and you have a recipe for destabilization in Africa. China's oil imports climbed by 33% in 2004, India's by 11%. The International Energy Agency expects them to use 11.3 million barrels a day by 2010, which will be a sizable chunk of global demand. China alone accounted for 40% of last year's increase in global demand.

Keith Bradsher, in a *New York Times* article, "2 Big Appetites Take Seats at the Oil Table," observes:

> As Chinese and Indian companies venture into countries like Sudan, where risk-aversive multinationals have hesitated to enter, questions are being raised in the industry about whether state-owned companies are accurately judging the risks to their own investments, or whether they are just more willing to gamble with taxpayers' money than multinationals are willing to gamble with shareholders' investments.

The geopolitical implications of this tolerance for instability are borne out in Sudan, where Chinese state-owned companies exploited oil in the thick of fighting. As China and India seek strategic access to oil—much as Britain, Japan, and the United States jockeyed for access to oil fields in the years leading up to World War II—the likelihood of destabilizing countries like Sudan rises exponentially.

Last June, following the new seismographic exploration in Sudan and with the new power-sharing peace treaty about to be implemented, Khartoum and the SPLA signed a flurry of oil deals with Chinese, Indian, British, Malaysian, and other oil companies.

Desolate Sudan, Desolate World

This feeding frenzy may help explain the Bush administration's schizophrenic stance toward Sudan. On the one hand, Secretary of State Colin Powell declared in September 2004 that his government had determined that what was happening in Darfur was "genocide"—which appears to have been a pre-election sop to conservative

Christians, many with missions in Africa. On the other hand, not only did the President fall silent on Darfur after the election, but his administration has lobbied quietly against the Darfur Peace and Accountability Act in Congress.

That bill calls for beefing up the African Union peacekeeping force and imposing new sanctions on Khartoum, including referring individual officials to the International Criminal Court (much hated by the administration). The White House, undercutting congressional efforts to stop the genocide, is seeking closer relations with Khartoum on grounds that the regime was "cooperating in the war on terror."

Nothing could end the slaughter faster than the President of the United States standing up for Darfur and making a strong case before the United Nations. Ours is the only country with such clout. This is unimaginable, of course, for various reasons. It seems clear that Bush, and the oil companies that contributed so heavily to his 2000 presidential campaign, would like to see the existing trade sanctions on Sudan removed, so U.S. companies can get a piece of the action. Instead of standing up, the President has kept mum—leaving it to Secretary of State Condoleezza Rice to put the best face she can on his policy of appeasing Khartoum.

On July 8, SPLA leader John Garang was sworn in as vice president of Sudan, before a throng of 6 million cheering Sudanese. President Oman Bashir spoke in Arabic. Garang spoke in English, the preferred language among educated southerners, because of the country's language diversity. Sudan's future had never looked brighter. Garang was a charismatic and forceful leader who wanted a united Sudan. Three weeks later, Garang was killed in a helicopter crash. When word of his death emerged, angry riots broke out in Khartoum, and in Juba, the capital of South Sudan. Men with guns and clubs roamed the streets, setting fire to cars and office buildings. One hundred and thirty people were killed, thousands wounded.

No evidence of foul play in his death has been uncovered, as of this writing. The helicopter went down in rain and fog over mountainous terrain. Nevertheless, suspicions are rampant. SPLA and government officials are calling for calm, until the crash can be investigated by an international team of experts. All too ominously, the disaster recalls the 1994 airplane crash that killed Rwandan president Juvenal Habyarimana, who was trying to implement a power-sharing agreement between Hutus and Tutsis. That crash touched off the explosive Rwandan genocide.

What Garang's death will mean for Sudan is unclear. The new peace was already precarious. His chosen successor, Salva Kiir Mayardit, appears less committed to a united Sudan.

Nowhere is the potential impact of renewed war more threatening than in the camps of refugees—the 4 million Internally Displaced Persons (IDPs) driven from their homes during the North-South civil war, several hundred thousand encamped at the fringes of Khartoum as squatters or crowded into sprawling ghetto neighborhoods. Further west, in Darfur and Chad, another 2.5 million IDPs live in the precarious limbo of makeshift camps, in shelters cobbled together from plastic and sticks—prevented by the Janjaweed from returning to their villages, wholly dependent on outside aid.

In short, Sudan embodies a collision between a failed state and a failed energy policy. Increasingly, ours is a planet whose human population is devoted to extracting what it can, regardless of the human and environmental cost. The Bush energy policy, crafted by oil companies, is predicated on a far different future from the one any sane person would want his or her children to inherit—a desolate world that few Americans, cocooned by the media's silence, are willing to imagine.

FACTS

Portion of the land normally cultivated in Darfur, Sudan, that went unplanted in 2004: ½
(CARE USA)

Minimum percentage of Darfuris who required emergency food assistance in March 2005: 39
(UN World Food Programme)

In the Driver's Seat

from TomDispatch.com (7/6/04)

Tom Engelhardt

Here we are just past our Independence Day, past that moment in memory when the United States was, by active example, a "beacon of freedom" to the world, past the moment in memory when, as Barbara Ehrenreich reminded us in the *New York Times* on July 4, the signers of the Declaration of Independence penned their names to the following line: "And for the support of this Declaration . . . we mutually pledge to each other our Lives, our Fortunes and our sacred Honor." She adds:

> Today, those who believe that the war on terror requires the sacrifice of our liberties like to argue that 'the Constitution is not a suicide pact.' In a sense, however, the Declaration of Independence was precisely that. By signing Jefferson's text, the signers of the declaration were putting their lives on the line. . . . If the rebel American militias were beaten on the battlefield, their ringleaders could expect to be hanged as traitors. They signed anyway, thereby stating to the world that there is something worth more than life, and that is liberty.

Now, let's leap a couple of centuries-plus and consider another group of Americans who signed onto what's looking more and more like an inadvertent (political) suicide pact. Our media washes over us like some mind-cleansing drug, so today, in the shambles of Bush administration Iraq policy, in the wake of Abu Ghraib, just beyond the "transition to Iraqi rule," it's difficult to recall what life was like back when the press was simply a lapdog; CBS's Dan Rather was burbling, "George Bush is the President, he makes the decisions and, you know, as just one American, he wants me to line up, just tell me where"; war was a swift, smiting blow (when was the last time you heard the phrase "shock and awe"?), and we were about to be anointed as the New Rome.

It's hard to remember that we were then ruled by the greatest, and most arrogant, gamblers in our history, men (and a single woman) ready to roll the dice any old time on the fate of the Earth. In the wake of every crumbling pseudo-explanation for the war in Iraq, it's hard to remember just how sweeping their vision actually was or what they had in mind when, not so long after September 11, 2001, they loaded some high-tech Hummer (regular cars being far too retro for them) with explosives and drove out into the world looking for something to blow up. Now that the strategists among them are in decline and the "realists," long left in the lurch, are wheeling and dealing in Iraq and Washington, it's hard to recall the utopian (or dystopian) fantasies they were so intent on imposing on what turned out to be a surprisingly recalcitrant world.

For the nostalgia buffs among you, the increasingly lonely Dick Cheney, who not so long ago imagined himself to be the co-ruler of our energy planet, continues to hoof it around the country reiterating charges of al-Qaeda/Saddam ties on a "best of 2001–2002" Bush administration top-ten tour. But even the man who prided himself on never cracking, no less cracking a smile, has had his public bad moments and temper squalls—and all without a duck, quail, or pheasant in sight to knock out of the skies.

In a bow to the Veep's oldies-but-baddies routine, let's try, for a moment, to recall the strategic thinking that lay behind the shock-and-awe campaign seen 'round the world: From the start, of course, this was an energy administration. After all, how many national security advisers in our history have had an oil tanker named after them? How many vice presidents ran a giant energy company deeply entangled with the U.S. military? The fact is, when it came to energy, like a group of vulgar Marxists with oil on the brain, most of them saw the world quite naturally in terms of energy flows, just the way a doctor might see blood flows as the body's essence.

They identified an "arc of instability" that stretched east-west from the former Yugoslavia to the borders of China and southward into Africa. (It was sometimes also said to include the Andean parts of Latin America.) This "arc," covering significant parts of what once was called the Third World, took in most of the planet's prime, or prospective, oil lands. Even before 9/11 in this vast region, some of which had dropped out of the former Soviet empire, the Bush administration began to plant, or expand, American military bases. The heart of these oil lands lay in the Middle East, a region with—in better times—the world's five leading oil producers.

Post 9/11, the top strategists of this administration followed their President happily into the "war on terror," the wilder among them imagining it as World War IV, the equivalent of, if not World War II, at least the Cold War, and so engendering dreams of another half-century twilit struggle to victory. Endless years of war would release them to act exactly as they pleased. The President (and his speechwriters), dreaming "Good War" dreams from his movie-made childhood, then elevated a pathetic "Axis of Evil" (Iran, Iraq, and North Korea, none of which previously knew of their close relationship) to the role of the Axis powers (Germany, Japan, Italy) in World War II; and so, with an enemy of nation states in hand, far more worthy of a world at war than Osama bin Laden and small groups of fanatic Islamists, they announced a policy of global supremacy not over terrorists, but over all the other nations of our planet, swearing that no future bloc of powers would be allowed to interfere with our benevolent hegemony over the Earth—and of preventive war. We would reserve the right to take out anybody we even thought might sooner or later in some way or another challenge us. A list of up to 60 states believed to "harbor" terrorists was also drawn up. This was a list for a lifetime. And finally, declaring weapons of mass destruction evil, they made it our job to decide who exactly shouldn't have them and to bolster our own nuclear forces in order to prepare for a series of what Jonathan Schell has called anti-proliferation wars. With this trio of policies in their foreign policy quiver, they looked around for some action.

Of course, the neocon strategists of this administration had long been spoiling for, planning for, and dreaming of a second American Gulf War that would take down Saddam Hussein's regime. (Just a peek at the wonderfully named Project for the New American Century website, where they proudly posted their wares, will give you a sense of this.) Assessing the satanic trio that made up the Axis of Evil—a fierce and desperate despotism with a sizeable air force but no fuel to get pilots aloft to practice flying planes; an increasingly embattled and unpopular but combative semi-theocracy; and a country sitting on the world's second largest oil reserves, strung out by three failed wars, twelve years of economic sanctions and periodic bombings, and run by a detested, brutal, increasingly out-of-touch regime with a military that was just a ghost of its former self—they naturally chose the third. It was a grudge rematch to begin with; it looked like a snap (there was little question that Saddam's army, crushed in our first Gulf War, wouldn't last long in a second one); and the assaults of September 11, 2001, had made it a far more sellable commodity (hence, the endless administration linkages of Iraq and al-Qaeda).

Nothing could be worse than Saddam, so Iraq's crushed people would prove both pliable and grateful for their "liberation." (You remember that "cakewalk," and all those flowers to be strewn in our path by joyous Shiites . . .) In return for a Saddam-less life, they would, of course, let us proceed apace with our plans. In an over-armed region, we would drastically downsize their army so that they would need our protection forever, build a string of permanent bases to the tune of billions of dollars (in part to replace those being mothballed in Saudi Arabia), and install a government run by Ahmed Chalabi, the sweet-talking exile with so much useful intelligence so close at hand, who was so deeply beloved by the neocons in the Pentagon and the Veep's office. He would be our satrap in a formally democratic Iraq. It was all so obvious.

And then, of course, there was all that oil. In our desperately over-determined world where the multiple-explanation is the only explanation, the point of all this was never simply to take Iraq's oil, though the neocons did think it would be most useful in reconstructing and running the country on the cheap, as Pentagon Deputy Secretary Paul

Wolfowitz made quite clear numerous times, and still claims. In a world of rising oil desire and potentially limited oil resources, the point was to find ourselves ensconced militarily at the very heart of the Middle East, controlling the taps to the energy veins of the globe, and to do so before any of those future blocs of irritated countries could form to challenge us.

But Iraq wasn't the end of their plans. Not by a long shot. Seen as the region's soft underbelly, Iraq was to be but a pit stop on a long-imagined armed drive through the Middle East—and implicitly the world. (After all, the third member of the Axis of Evil was conveniently located on the other side of the planet.) Iraq was to be the motor for regional change. Once we stood triumphant in our Iraqi bases, Syria would find itself between the pincers of an American Army and Sharon's militarized Israel. The Palestinians would find themselves completely isolated and would be forced to make a humiliating peace of the defeated with an expansive Israel. (Remember, this administration was filled with died-in-the-wool Likudniks who saw themselves delivering long-term safety to an Israel triumphant, while making regional use of the Sharonistas and their skills to help establish that New American Century.)

Iran, another of those grudge-match countries, with American encampments on two of its borders—don't forget our war in Afghanistan here—would be ripe for an Iraqi-style regime change, a bring-back-the-son-of-the-Shah event filled with Orange County Iranians (already promising the same cakewalks and flowers). The Saudis, that giant oil-well of a state, would, of course, be thoroughly intimidated. With NATO well established in the old Eastern Europe preserves of the Soviet Union, American troops flowing into increasingly permanent encampments in its former Central Asian SSRs as well as into a complex of expanding bases in Afghanistan and Pakistan, and with a strengthened American alliance with a right-wing Hindu government in India (also growing ever closer to Israel), impoverished Russia would finally be "contained" along its many-thousand-mile frontier (in a way the Cold Warriors of the twentieth century could only have dreamed of).

Energy-starved China, with its booming economy, seen by many in this administration as our great future competitor and enemy, would be left out in the cold, and the North Koreans would have been safely stowed in the refrigerator, a fit object for mopping up in a second Bush administration. The uppity old Europeans would be put in their place; the new (Eastern) Europeans would be eternally grateful for whatever economic favors and bases we dropped in their laps; the Middle East would be reorganized on a basis favorable to Israel and so to the U.S.; and there would be an American Iraq with, as they so liked to say, "an Iraqi face" and a democratic façade. This was to be a New Rome indeed, not to say an Earth towered over by a single colossus. Pentagon planners talked about our military configuration in the world as our "footprint" as if we were indeed a giant capable of planting only a single vast foot on the planet. (Note that in all this, the war on al-Qaeda played at best a modest role, except as an enemy of convenience that explained everything to a terrified American populace—largely because this vision preceded 9/11 and had next to nothing to do with terrorism.)

By the way, if you consider this vision, you immediately

grasp one of the great, post-war mysteries of Iraq. Now that Iraq policy has crumbled, it's often asked why, given the Powell Doctrine (and the fact that he was, after all, Secretary of State), we never prepared an "exit strategy" for Iraq? Consider, for example, this sentence from a recent *Christian Science Monitor* piece: "Much of the discussion [about future U.S. military doctrine] revolves around the so-called Powell Doctrine of war (explicit objectives, overwhelming use of force, clear exit strategy) versus the 'Rumsfeld Doctrine' (smaller numbers of highly maneuverable ground forces, emphasis on special operations, and high-tech air power)."

What's the difference between the two military strategies? Rumsfeld's was a no-exit strategy. Remember, administration strategists were setting up in Iraq in order to drive elsewhere. They never imagined leaving, just as they never imagined all sorts of other possibilities that didn't go well with their dreams. In this sense, our President embodied our no-exit administration in his rhetoric. Only one party was going to leave town in this showdown on Main Street—the Saddamist enemy, and they were going to exit stone cold and feet first.

For such a vision of the world, gaily decorated with much talk about bringing "democracy" to the benighted, they were ready to take any step imaginable: targeted assassinations (á la Israel), the setting up of an offshore mini-gulag, the torture of those from whom information must be extracted . . . all the dark arts of the world were to be mobilized for that bright dream of benevolent imperial domination. They planned for the worst they could imagine with the worst tools they could dream up. Where they failed was in their inability to imagine the world as it was, not as they wished it to be. In this sense they were both a Feith-based and faith-based administration; and this was why—despite copious prewar planning over at State—the boys from the Pentagon arrived in Iraq largely without Iraqis, Arabic speakers, or much in the way of plans for the country. They had won, hadn't they? They had Chalabi, didn't they? What else could they possibly need?

Starting with Iraqi nationalism, the basics of our planet in the last century, no less the new one, escaped them, but at least one has to grant them the audacity of their vision. It couldn't have been grander—though there was no way for the American public to know much about it, since at no other time in our recent past has the American press been so demobilized. At a time when our leaders were putting together the most expansive of global maps, most of the time you could hardly find a piece of analysis, no less news, in our papers that had two countries in it at the same time.

The administration neocons were utopian fantasists who, if you think of Afghanistan as the first enforced stop on their path to Iraq, and Iraq as the chosen second stop on the way to the larger Middle Eastern region, didn't actually get far along the path they set out for themselves. And here's the almost incomprehensible thing (if you don't consider the history of resistance to imperial power of every sort over the last centuries), they were stopped by a group of ill-armed nobodies, lacking predator drones, tanks, billions in intelligence, access to the globe's emails, or even evidently a central command. They were stopped by relatively small groups of brutes and thugs, fanatics and dead-enders backed by the extraordinary power, the overwhelming desire of everyday Iraqis not to be occupied and ruled by a foreign power or its proxies.

And yet the neocons weren't completely wrong. They imagined Iraq as the motor for reorganizing first the region, then the world—a kind of wild force for change, a chaos machine that would scramble the previous world order in ways advantageous to them. Their only mistake was to believe that the levers of change in that scrambling would remain in their hands. They loosed—to use a classic phrase—the whirlwind and now it seems to be in the process of sweeping them away.

They weren't, of course, much at predictions. None of us are. It's one of those human failings. We can't help ourselves when it comes to predicting, but we're almost always surprised by reality. Still, they were worse at it than most, insistent as they were on imposing their soaring vision on a stubborn reality (exactly the charge long laid to the left). In a sense, of all their dreams, only the permanent bases in Iraq and the no-exit strategy remain, embedding Washington in the heartland of chaos for years to come. Perhaps the moral of their tale might simply be: Be careful what you wish for.

Of all the things they couldn't imagine, the first and foremost—they would have found the thought laughable only a year ago—was that a ragtag Iraqi insurgency would find itself in the driver's seat of some battered sedan, well-packed with munitions, and driving the Bush administration willy-nilly toward disaster.

This is the famed getting-the-toothpaste-back-in-the-tube dilemma, and it's likely to be with us for quite a while. One of the few things the neocons seem to have done successfully is pass on a no-exit catastrophe to whomever. Ending the occupation—I mean the real one—

and withdrawing our troops, these are not live thoughts in much of Washington. In this sense, with Americans already at the 40% mark on withdrawal, the public is way ahead of its leaders who, on both sides of the aisle, seem to be opting for a Vietnam-style response: escalation.

But, as Dr. Seuss might have said, that is not all, oh, no, that is not all. The administration policies that crystallized in the invasion and high-handed occupation of Iraq seem to have set off a process that is reorganizing the world in ways we can't yet fully grasp. Some may be hopeful, some frightening indeed. In Korea and India, the right has already been swept from power. In Italy and possibly Japan, rightist governments totter. In Britain, Blair stands unsteady at the helm as does Howard in Australia, and so on. In the Middle East, this administration has created a border-blurring monster and god knows what will follow. All we can say with any degree of certainty is that it will be ugly, and every day we occupy Iraq under whatever "face" will make it worse.

The Bush people were audacious; they were visionary (and didn't mind telling you so); the only liberty they truly valued was their liberty to do as they damn pleased; they were focused on unilateral global domination of a sort seen at most only a few times in history; they had the mentality of plunderers and didn't hesitate to use fear to herd Americans in the directions they most desired. In the end, they may find themselves alone and vulnerable in a Baghdad-on-the-Potomac of their own making with no Green Zone in sight and chaos in the driver's seat.

Now comes the difficult job of teaching them about democracy.
MR.FISH

FACTS*

Cost of "The Sword," an unmanned robo-soldier equipped with a rifle, machine gun, or rocket launcher: $230,000

Number of these devices the U.S. Army plans to deploy in Iraq: 18

Number of overseas bullet suppliers the U.S. Army contracted with in 2004 and 2005, respectively: 1, 5

Minimum number of bullets the U.S. military purchased for use in 2004: 1,500,000,000

Average number of bullets per Iraqi this represented: 58

* (Picatinny Arsenal/*Harper's* research)

FACTS

Annual cost of all 16 UN peacekeeping missions currently underway: $3,870,000,000
(UN Department of Peacekeeping Operations)

Monthly cost of the U.S. occupation of Iraq: $4,100,000,000
(U.S. Department of Defense)

Average black-market price in Baghdad of a DVD showing the beheading of a foreigner or Iraqi "collaborator": 50 cents
(Richard Beeston)

Factor by which an Iraqi is more likely to die today than in the last year of the Hussein regime: 2.5
(Les Roberts, Johns Hopkins University)

Factor by which the cause of death is more likely to be violence: 58
(Les Roberts)

New, Advanced Technologies Pose Potential Terrorist Risks of Misuse, Expert Tells U.S. Lawmakers

from *Global Security Newswire* (2/3/05)

Mike Nartker

Washington—Terrorists could employ new, advanced technologies to conduct attacks with the potential to cause mass casualties, a U.S. terrorism expert warned lawmakers yesterday.

"There [have] always been small groups and individuals who have threatened societies and nations around the world. The difference today is that advanced technologies, particularly the spread of advanced technologies of mass destruction, are enabling these groups to threaten us in a way that in the past was reserved only to nation states," said Michael Swetnam, chief executive officer and chairman of the Potomac Institute for Policy Studies.

Among those that pose potential risks is biotechnology, which is "even more frightening" than nuclear technology, Swetnam told the House Permanent Select Committee on Intelligence.

"The potential harm from the misuse of biotechnology should frighten everyone in this room, this country, and in fact, everyone in the world," he said in prepared testimony.

"It is conceivable that one could engineer an organism that targets and kills selective segments of the world population," Swetnam said in his prepared remarks. "Those who might wish to commit genocide . . . will be able to create biological weapons that accomplish this dastardly goal without firing a shot."

Swetnam also warned lawmakers about the risks of terrorists using advances in neurotechnology to conduct attacks.

"On the not-too-distant horizon are technologies that will allow us to directly interface computers with the human brain," he said in his prepared testimony. "The ease with which Internet viruses are propagated around the world today causing millions of dollars of damage should forewarn us about a time when cyberwarfare might not only attack and spoof our systems, but might attack and spoof our thinking."

"Moving at an equally rapid pace," Swetnam said, are developments in the field of nanotechnology—the production of microscopic machines and materials. "The potential for harm here is absolutely mind-boggling," he said.

As an example of the possible threat, Swetnam told *Global Security Newswire* after yesterday's hearing that at some point in the future, terrorists may be able to use advances in nanotechnology to develop miniature devices that would enter a person's bloodstream to clog the arteries, resulting in death—in contrast to hopes that such devices could be used to improve cardiovascular health.

While neurotechnology and nanotechnology are relatively new areas of research, Swetnam warned that it might not be too long before terrorists are able to take advantage of them.

"We have probably a decade or two . . . to worry about it," he told *GSN*.

Swetnam warned lawmakers that it is too late to control

the spread of biotechnology information and equipment that may be useful to terrorists.

"It is unlikely that we can come up with any way to control the spread of biotechnology today, and many of the most frightening parts of biotechnology in fact appear to be the kind of technology that will be readily available in almost all parts of the world," he testified.

One concern, according to Swetnam, is that other countries may take the lead in biotechnology research, and potentially provide their work to terrorist groups, since they spend more money on such efforts than does the United States.

"Even though we're investing billions, the world is investing more," he told lawmakers. "The import of this is that, clearly, even though we lead in almost all technologies today, that lead is diminishing, and in the future we are not going to be leading in some of the most critical technologies, for good and for evil, in the world."

Instead of seeking to control the spread of advanced technologies, the United States needs to increase its capabilities to track their distribution, as well as those who may seek to acquire them, Swetnam said. U.S. intelligence, however, is more capable of acquiring information on other countries, he said.

"We have to understand that our first line of defense, the intelligence community, is not yet well configured to either find those individuals, track them, or to track the technology that they're seeking," Swetnam said.

He called for improved uses of information technology to better track various signs of human movement.

"Human beings moving around the world today more and more, in the industrialized world, at least, and more and more in the entire world, leave an electronic signature. And the more that we build a capability to track that signature and find where those human beings are, who they are, through that technology, the more we'll be able to really find and track the bad guys," Swetnam said.

In addition, U.S. intelligence needs to improve its measurement and signatures intelligence (MASINT) capabilities, which could be used to identify emissions associated with biological and chemical development, he said.

"MASINT has been a third sister in the intelligence community for decades and decades. It's time we pulled it out of the closet and gave it a front-row seating," Swetnam said.

FACT

Number of Navy-trained dolphins armed with toxic dart guns missing from Navy facilities following Hurricane Katrina: 36
(*The Guardian*, 9/25/05)

Excerpts from a memo to students at Stuyvesant High School in New York City, October 2001:

There are bad people out there who believe that they will spend all eternity in heaven with seventy-two virgins if they can kill some of us while killing themselves. They really believe that. There are nuts who see Satan, there are an infinite variety of other kinds of nuts and wackos, and you think that you are above wearing an ID card while in school. We are in a war and this is a potential front."

How Do I Look?

from *The Atlantic Monthly* (5/2004)

Robert D. Kaplan

For years I had been borrowing this particular piece of sartorial equipment. Now I felt that I had reached the stage in life where I needed something that fit right, set the appropriate tone, and was hanging in my own closet ready for use. I am not talking about a tuxedo. I am talking about body armor: a vest that holds steel, ceramic, or polyethylene plates for protection against 9 mm, 5.56 mm, and 7.62 mm rounds, and also against various fragmentation devices.

I thought that buying a bulletproof vest and helmet would be simple, but it quickly became complicated—so many choices, so many Web sites, so much conflicting advice from friends. In the early twenty-first century there is a big demand for this type of thing. There are waiting lists for certain vests, and not all sizes are in stock. Just as there are people who attend soirees, company dinners, awards nights, and charity balls, there arc people who find themselves in war zones, and they need to be protected but also to look right.

I was attracted to one Web site, BotachTactical.com, which advertised "Clearance: Great Products at Blowout

Prices." It offered machine-washable Point Blank Concealable Armor with removable panels. Another Web site, BulletProofME.com, offered similar vests to "put the odds back in YOUR favor."

But I didn't want concealable armor that fit under a shirt—I am not a Secret Service agent, a police detective, a convenience-store clerk in a high-crime area, a drug lord, or a Mafioso. I wanted tactical body armor that fits over a shirt or a jacket. And the array of tactical body armor offered on the Internet seemed endless.

Friends in the Marines and the Army Special Forces recommended that I buy a vest and plates that gave Level III or IV protection. With that in mind I found a Military Outer Tactical Vest (OTV) I liked for $790 at Bullet ProofME.com, and an even nicer Paraclete Modular Armor Vest—a "hybrid composite [of] Goldflcx and Spectraflex"—sold by Lightfighter.com for $1,990, with soft-armor panels and Velcro pockets for hard-armor trauma plates.

When it comes to armor plates, you pay for lightness. As one Web site put it, an iron stove will stop a bullet, but who wants to wear an iron stove strapped to his body? Thus nine-pound steel plates cost $110 apiece on Bullet ProofME.com, whereas ceramic plates that weigh only five and a half pounds cost $245 apiece, and "maximum coverage" ceramic plates that weigh 7.9 pounds cost $280. The lightest plates—three pounds—are made of polyethylene, and cost $395 each.

All right, I thought. I'll buy polyethylene. Trouble is, polyethylene can deteriorate when exposed to excessive heat—so don't leave your IBA (Individual Body Armor) in a vehicle cooking in the sun, one seller advised. Well, I had just spent a summer in the southern Philippines and part of an autumn in Afghanistan cooking in the sun. Moreover, the polyethylene plates did not fit inside some of the vests I liked.

There were other decisions, too. Did I need side plates? I remembered hearing a colonel berate a sergeant in Afghanistan for not having side plates. "Do you want to die, son?" the colonel asked. "Well, sir," the sergeant replied, "my first wife is getting one half of my retirement pension and my second wife the other half so it's a good question."

Then I discovered an entire new range of plates, some offering pointblank Level TV protection: if 7.62 mm armor-piercing ammunition hits you twice in the same plate, you are still protected. A single Multi Hit III + Hard Armor Plate costs $1,678.95 at Paraclete armor.com. The top of the line from this Web site was a Level IIIA releasable vest filled with multi-hit plates for $7,300.05, complete with pockets for ammunition, magazines, and explosive devices such as flash bangs.

I also had to choose a color. The vests that interested me came in black, plain tan, smoke green, woodland camouflage, and desert or tricolor camouflage. Black was out of place everywhere I had been. Plain tan attracted me, because it would set me apart as a journalist without being too conspicuous among the desert cammies worn by American troops in Iraq and Afghanistan. Woodland camouflage is the forest green pattern used by the U.S. Army in every theater except the Middle East; I had seen woodland vests used occasionally in the Middle East, though I had never seen desert cammies used in South America or the Pacific. I liked woodland, but smoke green might be an alternative, I thought.

My decision was further complicated by the Marines.

They wear digital cammies in a pattern different from the woodland and tricolor designs of the other services. Would they be offended if I wore woodland?

As with a lot of clothing these days, there were accessory items to consider. Did I want groin protection? Well, why not? The problem was that, as I had learned in the southern Philippines from observing an exercise featuring low-level explosives, groin protectors are cumbersome, albeit useful if something explodes at your feet.

There were other possibilities too. Members of an Army Special Forces team I had encountered in southern Afghanistan didn't like any of the vests on the market, so they ordered ceramic plates from the United States and had an Afghan tailor design vests for them. After all, why not employ and consult the locals, in order to win hearts and minds? I tried on one of the Afghan vests. No, I thought, it wasn't me.

In London, if you have money and you want an expert to make decisions about your dinner jacket, you might go to Savile Row. In the United States for this kind of thing you might go to Fayetteville, North Carolina, outside Fort Bragg, home of the Army Special Forces, or to Jacksonville, North Carolina, home of the Marine base Camp Lejeune.

In Fayetteville, I learned from a friend who has had a lifetime of experience in plainclothes intelligence work overseas that "there are vests and there are vests, and there are plates and there are plates." He warned, "Don't just go buy something over the Internet." He also advised me against buying any plates not made of boron carbide or silicon carbide or not in "tiled array" (if a plate cracks when one bullet hits you, you want the damage isolated to a tile, keeping the rest of the plate intact). Another friend told me that stopping rounds from an AK-47 isn't enough; a plate has to be able to stop armor-piercing bullets, too.

In Afghanistan I had noticed that if body armor is too heavy, you wind up taking it off at every opportunity. And bad things happen when you least expect it. In the end I traded some protection for lightness, figuring that if my body armor was comfortable, I'd wear it more often and be better protected. I bought a ProMAX Tactical Vest for $750, with front and back polyethylene plates. I had been advised that the plates, snug inside the vest, would be protected from the sun for at least a few years. I had asked for tan, but it was sold out in my size, so I settled for desert camouflage. The total package cost $1,540 at BulletProofME.com, an Austin, Texas, firm with great customer service. A helmet and ballistic eyewear (from another Web site) added another $340 to the bill. The helmet was covered in a desert pattern, and the salesman sent along a woodland cover for use outside the Middle East.

Everywhere in my odyssey through the world of body armor, salesmen mentioned satisfied customers. It was the unsatisfied customers I worried about.

FACTS*

Dollar value of global arms sales, 2003: $28.5 billion

Dollar value of global arms sales, 2004: $37 billion

* (*New York Times*, 8/30/05)

Loose Nukes of the West

from the *Washington Post* (5/7/03)

Alan J. Kuperman

Ever since the breakup of the Soviet Union, and especially since the attacks of Sept. 11, 2001, the United States has been trying to control "loose nukes"—the former Eastern Bloc's nuclear materials—to prevent their being stolen or sold to make an atomic bomb. This effort is vital, but its narrow regional focus has obscured an equally pressing danger: the loose nukes of the West. In fact, while Russia has been gradually tightening controls on bomb-grade materials, the United States and Europe have been slackening theirs, and a bill moving rapidly through Congress would roll back protections still further. Unless remedial action is taken, Osama bin Laden may soon have better luck shopping for nuclear bomb material in Western markets than in the former Soviet Union.

A particular vulnerability is posed by civilian commerce in highly enriched uranium. This fissile explosive, which powered the atomic bomb dropped on Hiroshima, is still used at many research and commercial facilities in North America and Europe that lack adequate security forces. If terrorists got hold of a sufficient amount, they could quickly fabricate an atomic bomb using the simplest design. According to the late Manhattan Project physicist Luis Alvarez, "terrorists, if they had such material, would have a good chance of setting off a high-yield explosion simply by dropping one half of the material onto the other half." Just 100 pounds is enough for a Hiroshima-era bomb, while even less is needed for a moderately sophisticated design such as Pakistan's.

Dangerous civilian commerce in bomb-grade uranium persists for two reasons. First, unlike modern nuclear reactors, a few old research facilities in Europe and America still use bomb-grade fuel. Second, pharmaceutical companies in Canada and Europe have rejected safer production methods and still use bomb-grade uranium to produce medical isotopes for hospitals.

Oddly enough, the West confronted this nuclear threat more seriously before the advent of al Qaeda than it does today. In 1978 it started developing technologies to fuel reactors and produce isotopes using much safer, low-enriched uranium, which is unsuitable for weapons. In 1992 a bill by then-Rep. Charles E. Schumer (D-N.Y.), now a senator, was enacted that banned all further exports of bomb-grade uranium, except on an interim basis to facilities in the process of converting to low-enriched uranium.

But a decade later, despite the rise of catastrophic terrorism, pharmaceutical companies and reactor operators are trying to undermine this landmark anti-terrorism law. One culprit is a large new German research reactor that is the West's first in a quarter-century built to use bomb-grade uranium fuel. Located on a vulnerable university campus near Munich, the reactor is slated to require 1.2 tons of such fuel—sufficient for at least a dozen nuclear weapons. President Bill Clinton refused to provide the fuel, but the Germans then struck a deal with Russia. President Bush, rather than discouraging such Russian trafficking, has legitimized it by seeking identical material from Moscow to fuel U.S. nuclear research reactors. The

Germans could convert to safer fuel before starting up their reactor but have refused.

The biggest offender in the pharmaceutical industry is the Canadian isotope producer Nordion, which reneged on an explicit pledge to design its new facilities to eliminate any need for bomb-grade uranium. The Canadians have constructed an isotope plant that will require more highly enriched uranium than any other. Though the lightly guarded Ontario facility is yet to begin commercial operation, it already has stockpiled 200 pounds of highly enriched uranium—enough for at least two nuclear weapons.

Still worse, the foreign pharmaceutical companies are lobbying to repeal the Schumer provision that requires them to gradually convert to low-enriched uranium as a condition for receiving bomb-grade uranium in the meantime. The repeal amendment, sponsored by Rep. Richard Burr (R-N.C.), already has been approved by the House in its new energy bill. In the Senate, it is being pushed toward quick enactment by Kit Bond, a Republican from Missouri, where the overseas isotope producer Mallinckrodt has its corporate home.

The shame is that the foreign pharmaceutical companies could have ceased their reliance on bomb-grade uranium years ago, if they had put as much effort into converting their production processes as they have into lobbying. There is no technical barrier to conversion. The United States has significant leverage on foreign producers, because we are the main source of bomb-grade uranium and the primary consumer of medical isotopes. Several years ago the State Department worked with these companies and the Nuclear Control Institute to draft a pledge under which all producers would agree to convert. Unfortunately, a mid-level official in the Bush administration's Department of Energy spiked the initiative in 2001.

In Iraq the United States has budgeted huge sums and sacrificed American lives in a war premised mainly on preventing terrorists from acquiring weapons of mass destruction. The very least that the pharmaceutical companies and our ally Germany can contribute is to stop undermining U.S. anti-terrorism law. And as the energy bill heads to the Senate floor, Congress must halt the special-interest effort to overturn this vital law.

FACTS

Amount that the 2006 Defense Department budget proposal requests for researching low-yield nuclear weapons: $9,000,000
(Arms Control Association)

Number of years that such research was illegal before Congress repealed the ban in November, 2005: 10
(Arms Control Association)

Number of countries given weapons-grade uranium since the 1950s under the U.S. Atoms for Peace program: 51
(Nuclear Regulatory Commission)

Chance that a Russian scientist says he or she would consider working for North Korea: 1 in 7
(Lawrence Livermore National Laboratories)

Year by which every U.S. nuclear weapon will have reached the end of its original design life: 2014
(Office of Inspector General, U.S. Department of Energy)

MAD MAD MAD MAD SCIENCE

Good scientists ask lots of questions. Lately they've been asking questions like these: Will that tiny black hole we just created eat the planet? And is it a really such a good idea to give that mouse a brain made of human neurons?

Extreme Science!

J. M. Berger

Some headlines just sit there.

"Iraq Death Toll Surpasses (insert number here)"

It's not that the story isn't important, of course. But that one is repetitive and arbitrary—each increment of one hundred cataloged with clinical detachment. You don't feel a need to read the story. You have already absorbed the most important information.

On the other hand, some headlines pop.

"Black Hole-Like Phenomenon Created by Collider"

When I saw that headline on NewScientist.com in the spring of 2005, I stared at it blankly for a moment, and then I read the story.

Then I had to go back to the blank stare.

It seems that one day, scientists at the Relativistic Heavy Ion Collider in Brookhaven, New York, were whacking a selection of tiny particles together, just to see what would happen.

The tiny particles in question were atoms of gold (sans electrons). The accelerator flung these particles toward each other at velocities approaching the speed of light. The expectation was that the gold would be pulverized into even tinier bits of quantum fluff (quarks and gluons).

Under "normal" conditions the process creates a tiny, adorable fireball. This particular day, the process created a tiny, adorable black hole—the great cosmic devourer of worlds that sucks everything into its inescapable maw and grinds it into something even less substantial than cosmic dust.

Now, as you can imagine, there is a long list of disclaimers that must be appended to the description above. Obviously, we haven't been ground into less-than-dust. The New York black hole was tiny. It wasn't like an astronomical black hole. It only lasted for a moment. It didn't suck up the entire earth and exterminate all human life. And the scientists at the Relativistic Heavy Ion Collider would just like you to know that there was never any danger that such a thing might happen.

The problem here, of course, is that it's very easy to say nothing could have gone wrong several weeks after something has already finished not going wrong. Quantum physics is governed by a scientific law known as the Uncertainty Principle. The basic thrust of the Uncertainty Principle is that you can't always be sure what's going to happen in quantum physics. So while it might extremely *unlikely* that a mini–black hole could suddenly grow to giant size and swallow the Earth, it's not quite impossible.

Sadly, this is only the *most recent* occasion on which scientists have decided to roll dice regarding the future of all human existence without bothering to phone humanity first and ask if it would be okay.

Let's set the Wayback Machine for 1947 and the first test of the atomic bomb. Let's go to one of the original witnesses, Gen. Leslie Groves, the military man in charge, who relates this charming anecdote in his memoir, *Now It Can Be Told*:

> I had become a bit annoyed with (head physicist Enrico) Fermi the evening before (the test), when he suddenly offered to take wagers from his fellow

> scientists on whether or not the bomb would ignite the atmosphere, and if so, whether it would merely destroy New Mexico, or destroy the world.

Groves, perhaps to soothe his conscience, chalks Fermi's sporting proposition up to "tension-busting" humor, but there had been serious discussion of this possibility as well as other fun scenarios, like the possibility that the detonation might crack the earth open like a walnut, causing its guts to spill out all over the solar system.

These stories are only the tip of the iceberg, and physics is only part of the problem.

In 2004, scientists at the Mayo Clinic used genetic engineering to create pigs with human blood in their veins. The idea was to breed porcine blood donors, who would eventually eliminate the need for human donors.

The experiment didn't quite go as planned. Instead of cleanly creating a critter that was a pig in every meaningful respect, they ended up with creatures that looked like pigs but genetically fell somewhere in between being pigs and humans.

Instead of just popping out human blood, the people-pigs were shot through with some cells that were porcine, some that were human, and some that were half and half. As if accidentally creating pig-people weren't entirely bad enough, the hybrid cells contained a mutated pig virus similar to HIV which could potentially infect humans.

The list goes on. And on. And on and on and on.

Chimeras—half-human creatures—are all the rage these days. The Shanghai Second Medical University created half-human, half-rabbit embryos in 2003, but mercifully destroyed them after just a couple days' gestation. (At least, that's what they said. For all we know, there could be dozens of rabbit-toddlers sitting around in a lab somewhere practicing on a Speak & Spell.)

Stanford University researchers are already hard at work creating a mouse with human brain cells, a chimera which is created by injecting mouse fetuses with human stem cells collected from aborted fetuses. The researchers, while defensively insisting there is nothing wrong with this research, concede that you could end up with a really smart half-human mouse.

"If the mouse shows human-like behaviors, like improved memory or problem-solving, it's time to stop," the head researcher told newspapers. No kidding. Hey, you know, and this is just a thought, but maybe it would be better to stop *before* that point?

I'm not anti-science. Honest. I love science. I think it's extremely important that we continue to make progress in every area of science.

But when I see stories like these, it makes me think.

I am required by law to obtain a license to go fishing. I am required to formally notify the neighbors and review their objections before I cut the curb in front of my house to put in a driveway. *I am required by law to register my dog.*

Did the Relativistic Heavy Ion Collider notify the neighbors before conducting experiments that are capable of accidentally creating a black hole? Is there a permit required for creating black holes? Is there a Black Hole Commission that reviews cases of accidental black hole creation? Can you have your license revoked for creating a black hole under the influence?

There is an inherent problem in conducting experiments

that could potentially wipe out the human race. There might only be a one-in-a-trillion chance that the Relativistic Heavy Ion Collider could accidentally create a black hole that would instantly devour the Earth. But with one particularly unlucky twist of a quark, everything we know could be gone—and we would never even know why.

What degree of risk is too much when the consequence is potentially the end of all human life? One in a billion? One in a million? One in ten thousand? One in a thousand?

What degree of risk is too much when the consequence is creating a self-aware, intelligence-endowed, half-human, half-animal hybrid? One in a hundred? One in ten?

The U.S. government is obsessed with stem cell research in the abstract because of its implications regarding the abortion debate. But George W. Bush isn't driving a vigorous discussion of the staggering implications raised by half-human chimeras, and other nations have also neglected to examine the issue aggressively. We're busy chasing phantom weapons of mass destruction around the globe, while black holes are spontaneously combusting in our collective backyard.

The president isn't alone in ignoring the risks of extreme science. No one is talking about unexpected black holes. No one is talking about civil rights for intelligent mice and self-aware computers. No one is talking about whether the creators of human-rabbit hybrids have the right to abort their monster-spawn. (I can see the bumper stickers now: "My petri dish, my choice!")

No one is talking about the looming crisis of human-driven evolutionary and ecological change in its whole context all over the world—the broad range of human practices that create pesticide-resistant insects, invasive grasses that choke the life out of indigenous plants, cane toads the size of house cats, undersized fish, shrinking lotus flowers, drug-resistant bacteria and turkeys with breasts so bloated they can't balance well enough to stand upright (deliberately bred that way because Americans prefer white meat).

The media pick out tiny individual slices of the problem for quirky science features. Scientists discuss tiny individual slices of the problem with their highly segregated specialties. Once in a while, someone cuts out a tiny individual slice of the problem and chews on it for a lightweight "think piece" in the Sunday paper.

And still we ignore the broad implications.

It's a miniature black hole or a gigantic cane toad. It's mutant pig viruses or the possibility that global warming might cause an epidemic of earthquakes.

This isn't a collection of different problems. It's all the same problem—humans have learned to alter the world faster than they have learned to understand the consequences of their alterations.

When you experiment with very small effects—whether tampering with genes or creating quarks—sometimes you'll end up with results you didn't expect. The problem of these unintended consequences can only grow as our scientific horizons push further and further into the world of complex systems.

Ironically, the smallest phenomena in science are those most desperately in need of "big picture" thinking. Human beings are clever and determined enough to create tiny black holes. Surely we can create a discussion about unintended consequences. Surely we can create a dialogue about the dangers of "extreme science."

We won't find an easy solution, because the most extreme experiments are also intensely specialized. The task of designing one-size-fits-all guidelines is daunting at best. It may be impossible in the final analysis.

The extraordinary complexity of Planet Earth in the twenty-first century has created a culture of specialists. Just-plain-physicists are still out there, but they're hard to find. Search the universities, and you'll find optical physicists, low-temperature physicists, molecular physicists, superconductivity physicists, acoustic physicists, fluid physicists, elementary particle physicists. Within each specialty you can find dozens of sub-specialties—whether brane theorists or string theorists, savants in wave dynamics or quantum mechanics who politely decline comment on issues outside their backyards.

It's the same everywhere—doctors, lawyers and engineers are already painfully and obviously specialized, but the syndrome is slowly creeping into every other field as well—from computer programmers to auto mechanics, journalists to soldiers, even workers at the coffee counter are now required to memorize and make a dizzying array of proprietary drinks than can only be ordered from certain shops.

Specialization drives progress, obviously, because it empowers people to delve into the minute details of how complex systems—such as the human body—work.

But when all the smart people start specializing, who looks at the big picture?

By default, our society delegates big-picture thinking to politicians. Government is the only institution large enough to encompass all these diverse issues. Within government, specialization runs rampant—its effects only magnified by massive federal bureaucracies which are structurally designed to compartmentalize functions into isolated agencies.

The various agencies only overlap at the executive level—the office of the president. The fallacies of this approach became clear on September 11, 2001, when several key agencies of the federal government utterly failed to work together to protect American lives.

The same failings that plagued national security on that dark day also plague national science. George W. Bush is the self-appointed guardian of the big picture in stem cell research, but even many of his ardent supporters have to admit he doesn't understand the full ramifications of the issue. Does anyone expect him to be more competent in evaluating experiments at the Relativistic Heavy Ion Collider?

We need to find and train people who can take in the big picture. And when we find some, we need to elect them to public office. We need to appoint them to run our universities, and we need to hire them to run our news networks.

This isn't an abstract academic postulate. We're stuck in the middle of a genuine crisis that is slowly but surely approaching a watershed point. The anecdotes above were not plucked from the pages of science fiction—*they are happening now*.

We must start elevating big-picture thinkers to positions where they can make a difference, and we must start *now*.

Otherwise there might not be much of a big picture left to see—only the sad story of a promising race of pig-men whose potential was cut tragically short when their planet was prematurely sucked into oblivion by the birth of a freak neutron star in Long Island.

Of Mice, Men, and In Between

from the *Washington Post* (11/20/04)

Rick Weiss

In Minnesota, pigs are being born with human blood in their veins.

In Nevada, there are sheep whose livers and hearts are largely human.

In California, mice peer from their cages with human brain cells firing inside their skulls.

These are not outcasts from *The Island of Dr. Moreau,* the 1896 novel by H. G. Wells in which a rogue doctor develops creatures that are part animal and part human. They are real creations of real scientists, stretching the boundaries of stem cell research.

Biologists call these hybrid animals chimeras, after the mythical Greek creature with a lion's head, a goat's body and a serpent's tail. They are the products of experiments in which human stem cells were added to developing animal fetuses.

Living Test Beds

Chimeras are allowing scientists to watch, for the first time, how nascent human cells and organs mature and interact—not in the cold isolation of laboratory dishes but inside the bodies of living creatures. Some are already revealing deep secrets of human biology and pointing the way toward new medical treatments.

But with no federal guidelines in place, an awkward question hovers above the work: How human must a chimera be before more stringent research rules should kick in?

The National Academy of Sciences, which advises the federal government, has been studying the issue and hopes to make recommendations by February. Yet the range of opinions it has received so far suggests that reaching consensus may be difficult.

During one recent meeting, scientists disagreed on such basic issues as whether it would be unethical for a human embryo to begin its development in an animal's womb, and whether a mouse would be better or worse off with a brain made of human neurons.

"This is an area where we really need to come to a reasonable consensus," said James Battey, chairman of the National Institutes of Health's Stem Cell Task Force. "We need to establish some kind of guidelines as to what the scientific community ought to do and ought not to do."

Beyond Twins and Moms

Chimeras (ki-MER-ahs)—meaning mixtures of two or more individuals in a single body—are not inherently unnatural. Most twins carry at least a few cells from the sibling with whom they shared a womb, and most mothers carry in their blood at least a few cells from each child they have borne.

Recipients of organ transplants are also chimeras, as are the many people whose defective heart valves have been replaced with those from pigs or cows. And scientists for years have added human genes to bacteria and even to farm animals—feats of genetic engineering that allow those critters to make human proteins such as insulin for use as medicines.

"Chimeras are not as strange and alien as at first blush they seem," said Henry Greely, a law professor and ethicist at Stanford University who has reviewed proposals to create human-mouse chimeras there.

But chimerism becomes a more sensitive topic when it involves growing entire human organs inside animals. And it becomes especially sensitive when it deals in brain cells, the building blocks of the organ credited with making humans human.

In experiments like those, Greely told the academy last month, "there is a nontrivial risk of conferring some significant aspects of humanity" on the animal.

Greely and his colleagues did not conclude that such experiments should never be done. Indeed, he and many other philosophers have been wrestling with the question of why so many people believe it is wrong to breach the species barrier.

Does the repugnance reflect an understanding of an important natural law? Or is it just another cultural bias, like the once widespread rejection of interracial marriage?

Many turn to the Bible's repeated invocation that animals should multiply "after their kind" as evidence that such experiments are wrong. Others, however, have concluded that the core problem is not necessarily the creation of chimeras but rather the way they are likely to be treated.

Imagine, said Robert Streiffer, a professor of philosophy and bioethics at the University of Wisconsin, a human-chimpanzee chimera endowed with speech and an enhanced potential to learn—what some have called a "humanzee."

"There's a knee-jerk reaction that enhancing the moral status of an animal is bad," Streiffer said. "But if you did it, and you gave it the protections it deserves, how could the animal complain?"

Unfortunately, said Harvard political philosopher Michael J. Sandel, speaking last fall at a meeting of the President's Council on Bioethics, such protections are unlikely.

"Chances are we would make them perform menial jobs or dangerous jobs," Sandel said. "That would be an objection."

A Research Breakthrough

The potential power of chimeras as research tools became clear about a decade ago in a series of dramatic experiments by Evan Balaban, now at McGill University in Montreal. Balaban took small sections of brain from developing quails and transplanted them into the developing brains of chickens.

The resulting chickens exhibited vocal trills and head bobs unique to quails, proving that the transplanted parts of the brain contained the neural circuitry for quail calls. It also offered astonishing proof that complex behaviors could be transferred across species.

No one has proposed similar experiments between, say, humans and apes. But the discovery of human embryonic stem cells in 1998 allowed researchers to envision related experiments that might reveal a lot about how embryos grow.

The cells, found in 5-day-old human embryos, multiply

prolifically and—unlike adult cells—have the potential to turn into any of the body's 200 or so cell types.

Scientists hope to cultivate them in laboratory dishes and grow replacement tissues for patients. But with those applications years away, the cells are gaining in popularity for basic research.

The most radical experiment, still not conducted, would be to inject human stem cells into an animal embryo and then transfer that chimeric embryo into an animal's womb. Scientists suspect the proliferating human cells would spread throughout the animal embryo as it matured into a fetus and integrate themselves into every organ.

Such "humanized" animals could have countless uses. They would almost certainly provide better ways to test a new drug's efficacy and toxicity, for example, than the ordinary mice typically used today.

But few scientists are eager to do that experiment. The risk, they say, is that some human cells will find their way to the developing testes or ovaries, where they might grow into human sperm and eggs. If two such chimeras—say, mice—were to mate, a human embryo might form, trapped in a mouse.

Not everyone agrees that this would be a terrible result.

"What would be so dreadful?" asked Ann McLaren, a renowned developmental biologist at the University of Cambridge in England. After all, she said, no human embryo could develop successfully in a mouse womb. It would simply die, she told the academy. No harm done.

But others disagree—if for no other reason than out of fear of a public backlash.

"Certainly you'd get a negative response from people to

have a human embryo trying to grow in the wrong place," said Cynthia B. Cohen, a senior research fellow at Georgetown University's Kennedy Institute of Ethics and a member of Canada's Stem Cell Oversight Committee, which supported a ban on such experiments there.

How human?

But what about experiments in which scientists add human stem cells not to an animal embryo but to an animal fetus, which has already made its eggs and sperm? Then the only question is how human a creature one dares to make.

In one ongoing set of experiments, Jeffrey L. Platt at the Mayo Clinic in Rochester, Minnesota, has created human-pig chimeras by adding human-blood-forming stem cells to pig fetuses. The resulting pigs have both pig and human blood in their vessels. And it's not just pig blood cells being swept along with human blood cells; some of the cells themselves have merged, creating hybrids.

It is important to have learned that human and pig cells can fuse, Platt said, because he and others have been considering transplanting modified pig organs into people and have been wondering if that might pose a risk of pig viruses getting into patient's cells. Now scientists know the risk is real, he said, because the viruses may gain access when the two cells fuse.

In other experiments led by Esmail Zanjani, chairman of animal biotechnology at the University of Nevada at Reno, scientists have been adding human stem cells to sheep fetuses. The team now has sheep whose livers are up to 80 percent human—and make all the compounds human livers make.

Zanjani's goal is to make the humanized livers available to people who need transplants. The sheep portions will be rejected by the immune system, he predicted, while the human part will take root.

"I don't see why anyone would raise objections to our work," Zanjani said in an interview.

Mice and men

Perhaps the most ambitious efforts to make use of chimeras come from Irving Weissman, director of Stanford University's Institute of Cancer/Stem Cell Biology and Medicine. Weissman helped make the first mouse with a nearly complete human immune system—an animal that has proved invaluable for tests of new drugs against the AIDS virus, which does not infect conventional mice.

More recently his team injected human neural stem cells into mouse fetuses, creating mice whose brains are about 1 percent human. By dissecting the mice at various stages, the researchers were able to see how the added brain cells moved about as they multiplied and made connections with mouse cells.

Already, he said, they have learned things they "never would have learned had there been a bioethical ban."

Now he wants to add human brain stem cells that have the defects that cause Parkinson's disease, Lou Gehrig's disease and other brain ailments—and study how those cells make connections.

Scientists suspect that these diseases, though they manifest themselves in adulthood, begin when something goes wrong early in development. If those errors can be found, researchers would have a much better chance of designing useful drugs, Weissman said. And those drugs could be tested in the chimeras in ways not possible in patients.

Now Weissman says he is thinking about making chimeric mice whose brains are 100 percent human. He proposes keeping tabs on the mice as they develop. If the brains look as if they are taking on a distinctly human architecture—a development that could hint at a glimmer of humanness—they could be killed, he said. If they look as if they are organizing themselves in a mouse brain architecture, they could be used for research.

So far this is just a "thought experiment," Weissman said, but he asked the university's ethics group for an opinion anyway.

"Everyone said the mice would be useful," he said. "But no one was sure if it should be done."

THE NEW DEATH

with a cartoon by Mr. Fish
and facts

The good news is that people in wealthy countries may start living much, much longer. The bad news is that this could create problems ranging from dire poverty to ultraviolent revolution that will make us wish we were dead. Then again, a host of terrible plagues may kill us before any of this happens. That is already happening in Africa, which does not suffer from a longevity problem—far from it!—but does have an orphan problem.

The Coming Death Shortage

from *The Atlantic Monthly* (5/05)

Charles C. Mann

Anna Nicole Smith's role as a harbinger of the future is not widely acknowledged. Born Vickie Lynn Hogan, Smith first came to the attention of the American public in 1993, when she earned the title Playmate of the Year. In 1994 she married J. Howard Marshall, a Houston oil magnate said to be worth more than half a billion dollars. He was eighty-nine and wheelchairbound; she was twenty-six and quiveringly mobile. Fourteen months later Marshall died. At his funeral the widow appeared in a white dress with a vertical neckline. She also claimed that Marshall had promised half his fortune to her. The inevitable litigation sprawled from Texas to California and occupied batteries of lawyers, consultants, and public-relations specialists for more than seven years.

Even before Smith appeared, Marshall had disinherited his older son. And he had infuriated his younger son by lavishing millions on a mistress, an exotic dancer, who then died in a bizarre face-lift accident. To block Marshall senior from squandering on Smith money that Marshall junior regarded as rightfully his, the son seized control of his father's assets by means that the trial judge later said were so "egregious," "malicious," and "fraudulent" that he regretted being unable to fine the younger Marshall more than $44 million in punitive damages.

In its epic tawdriness the Marshall affair was natural fodder for the tabloid media. Yet one aspect of it may soon seem less a freak show than a cliché. If an increasingly influential group of researchers is correct, the lurid spectacle of intergenerational warfare will become a typical social malady.

The scientists' argument is circuitous but not complex. In the past century U.S. life expectancy has climbed from forty-seven to seventy-seven, increasing by nearly two thirds. Similar rises happened in almost every country. And this process shows no sign of stopping: according to the United Nations, by 2050 global life expectancy will have increased by another ten years. Note, however, that this tremendous increase has been in *average* life expectancy—that is, the number of years that most people live. There has been next to no increase in the *maximum* lifespan, the number of years that one can possibly walk the earth—now thought to be about 120. In the scientists' projections, the ongoing increase in average lifespan is about to be joined by something never before seen in human history: a rise in the maximum possible age at death.

Stem-cell banks, telomerase amplifiers, somatic gene therapy—the list of potential longevity treatments incubating in laboratories is startling. Three years ago a multi-institutional scientific team led by Aubrey de Grey, a theoretical geneticist at Cambridge University, argued in a widely noted paper that the first steps toward "engineered negligible senescence"—a rough-and-ready version of immortality—would have "a good chance of success in mice within ten years." The same techniques, de Grey says, should be ready for human beings a decade or so later. "In ten years we'll have a pill that will give you twenty years," says Leonard Guarente, a professor of biology at MIT. "And then there'll be another pill after that. The first hundred-and-fifty-year-old may have already been born."

Critics regard such claims as wildly premature. In March ten respected researchers predicted in the *New England Journal of Medicine* that "the steady rise in life expectancy during the past two centuries may soon come to an end," because rising levels of obesity are making people sicker. The research team leader, S. Jay Olshansky, of the University of Illinois School of Public Health, also worries about the "potential impact of infectious disease." Believing that medicine can and will overcome these problems, his "cautious and I think defensibly optimistic estimate" is that the average lifespan will reach eighty-five or ninety—in 2100. Even this relatively slow rate of increase, he says, will radically alter the underpinnings of human existence. "Pushing the outer limits of lifespan" will force the world to confront a situation no society has ever faced before: an acute shortage of dead people.

The twentieth-century jump in life expectancy transformed society. Fifty years ago senior citizens were not a force in electoral politics. Now the AARP is widely said to be the most powerful organization in Washington. Medicare, Social Security, retirement, Alzheimer's, snowbird economies, the population boom, the golfing boom, the cosmetic-surgery boom, the nostalgia boom, the recreational-vehicle boom, Viagra—increasing longevity is entangled in every one. Momentous as these changes have been, though, they will pale before what is coming next.

From religion to real estate, from pensions to parent-child dynamics, almost every aspect of society is based on the orderly succession of generations. Every quarter century or so children take over from their parents—a transition as fundamental to human existence as the rotation of the planet about its axis. In tomorrow's world, if the optimists are correct, grandparents will have living grandparents; children born decades from now will ignore advice from people who watched the Beatles on *The Ed Sullivan Show*. Intergenerational warfare—the Anna Nicole Smith syndrome—will be but one consequence. Trying to envision such a world, sober social scientists find themselves discussing pregnant seventy-year-olds, offshore organ farms, protracted adolescence, and lifestyles policed by insurance companies. Indeed, if the biologists are right, the coming army of centenarians will be marching into a future so unutterably different that they may well feel nostalgia for the long-ago days of three score and ten.

The oldest *in vitro* fertilization clinic in China is located on the sixth floor of a no-star hotel in Changsha, a gritty flyover city in the south-central portion of the country. It is here that the clinic's founder and director, Lu Guangxiu, pursues her research into embryonic stem cells.

Most cells *don't* divide, whatever elementary school students learn—they just get old and die. The body subcontracts out the job of replacing them to a special class of cells called stem cells. Embryonic stem cells—those in an early-stage embryo—can grow into any kind of cell: spleen, nerve, bone, whatever. Rather than having to wait for a heart transplant, medical researchers believe, a patient could use stem cells to grow a new heart: organ transplant without an organ donor.

The process of extracting stem cells destroys an early-stage embryo, which has led the Bush administration to place so many strictures on stem-cell research that scientists complain it has been effectively banned in this country. A visit to Lu's clinic not long ago suggested that ultimately Bush's rules won't stop anything. Capitalism won't let them.

During a conversation Lu accidentally brushed some papers to the floor. They were faxes from venture capitalists in San Francisco, Hong Kong, and Stuttgart. "I get those all the time," she said. Her operation was short of money—a chronic problem for scientists in poor countries. But it had something of value: thousands of frozen embryos, an inevitable by-product of *in vitro* fertilizations. After obtaining permission from patients, Lu uses the embryos in her work. It is possible that she has access to more embryonic stem cells than all U.S. researchers combined.

Sooner or later, in one nation or another, someone like Lu will cut a deal: frozen embryos for financial backing. Few are the stem-cell researchers who believe that their work will not lead to tissue-and-organ farms, and that these will not have a dramatic impact on the human lifespan. If Organs 'R Us is banned in the United States, Americans will fly to longevity centers elsewhere. As Steve Hall wrote in *Merchants of Immortality*, biotechnology increasingly resembles the software industry. Dependence on venture capital, loathing of regulation, pathological secretiveness, penchant for hype, willingness to work overseas—they're all there. Already the U.S. Patent Office has issued 400 patents concerning human stem cells.

Longevity treatments will almost certainly drive up medical costs, says Dana Goldman, the director of health economics at the RAND Corporation, and some might drive them up significantly. Implanted defibrillators, for example, could constantly monitor people's hearts for signs of trouble, electrically regulating the organs when they miss a beat. Researchers believe that the devices would reduce heart-disease deaths significantly. At the same time, Goldman says, they would by themselves drive up the nation's health-care costs by "many billions of dollars" (Goldman and his colleagues are working on nailing down how much), and they would be only one of many new medical interventions. In developed nations antiretroviral drugs for AIDS typically cost about $15,000 a year. According to James Lubitz, the acting chief of the aging and chronic-disease statistics branch of the CDC National Center for Health Statistics, there is no a priori reason to suppose that lifespan extension will be cheaper, that the treatments will have to be administered less frequently, or that their inventors will agree to be less well compensated. To be sure, as Ramez Naam points out in *More Than Human*, which surveys the prospects for "biological enhancement," drugs inevitably fall in price as their patents expire. But the same does not necessarily hold true for medical procedures: heart bypass operations are still costly, decades after their invention. And in any case there will invariably be newer, more effective, and more costly drugs. Simple arithmetic shows that if 80 million U.S. senior citizens were to receive $15,000 worth of treatment every year, the annual cost to the nation would be $1.2 trillion—"the kind of number," Lubitz says, "that gets people's attention."

The potential costs are enormous, but the United States is a rich nation. As a share of gross domestic product the cost of U.S. health care roughly doubled from 1980 to the present, explains David M. Cutler, a health-care economist at Harvard. Yet unlike many cost increases, this one signifies that people are better off. "Would you rather have a heart attack with 1980 medicine at the 1980 price?" Cutler asks. "We get more and better treatments now, and we pay more for the additional services. I don't look at that and see an obvious disaster."

The critical issue, in Goldman's view, will be not the costs per se but determining who will pay them. "We're going to have a very public debate about whether this will be covered by insurance," he says. "My sense is that it won't. It'll be like cosmetic surgery—you pay out of pocket." Necessarily, a pay-as-you-go policy would limit access to longevity treatments. If high-level anti-aging therapy were expensive enough, it could become a perk for movie stars, politicians, and CEOs. One can envision Michael Moore fifty years from now, still denouncing the rich in political tracts delivered through the next generation's version of the Internet—neural implants, perhaps. Donald Trump, a 108-year-old multibillionaire in 2054, will be firing the children of the apprentices he fired in 2004. Meanwhile, the maids, chauffeurs, and gofers of the rich will stare mortality in the face.

Short of overtly confiscating rich people's assets, it would be hard to avoid this divide. Yet as Goldman says, there will be "furious" political pressure to avert the worst inequities. For instance, government might mandate that insurance cover longevity treatments. In fact, it is hard to imagine any democratic government foolhardy enough *not* to guarantee access to those treatments, especially when the old are increasing in number and political clout. But forcing insurers to cover longevity treatments would only change the shape of the social problem. "Most everyone will want to take [the treatment]," Goldman says. "So that jacks up the price of insurance, which leads to more people uninsured. Either way, we may be bifurcating society."

Ultimately, Goldman suggests, the government would probably end up paying outright for longevity treatments: an enormous new entitlement program. How could it be otherwise? Older voters would want it because it is in their interest; younger ones would want it because they, too, will age. "At the same time," he says, "nobody likes paying taxes, so there would be constant pressure to contain costs."

To control spending, the program might give priority to people with healthy habits; no point in retooling the genomes of smokers, risk takers, and addicts of all kinds. A kind of reverse eugenics might occur, in which governments would freely allow the birth of people with "bad" genes but would let nature take its course on them as they aged. Having shed the baggage of depression, addiction, mental retardation, and chemical-sensitivity syndrome, tomorrow's legions of perduring old would be healthier than the young. In this scenario moralists and reformers would have a field day.

Meanwhile, the gerontocratic elite will have a supreme weapon against the young: compound interest. According to a 2004 study by three researchers at the London Business School, historically the average rate of real return on stock markets worldwide has been about five percent. Thus a twenty-year-old who puts $10,000 in the market in 2010 should expect by 2030 to have about $27,000 in real terms—a tidy increase. But that happy forty-year-old will be in the same world as septuagenarians and octogenarians who began investing their money during the Carter administration. If someone who turned seventy in 2010 had invested $10,000 when he was twenty, he would have about $115,000. In the same twenty-year period during which the young person's account grew from $10,000 to $27,000, the old person's account would grow from $115,000 to $305,000. Inexorably, the gap between them will widen.

The result would be a tripartite society: the very old and very rich on top, beta-testing each new treatment on themselves; a mass of the ordinary old, forced by insurance into supremely healthy habits, kept alive by medical entitlement; and the diminishingly influential young. In his novel *Holy Fire* (1996) the science-fiction writer and futurist Bruce Sterling conjured up a version of this dictatorship-by-actuary: a society in which the cautious, careful centenarian rulers, supremely fit and disproportionately affluent if a little frail, look down with ennui and mild contempt on their juniors. Marxist class warfare, upgraded to the biotech era!

In the past, twenty- and thirty-year-olds had the chance of sudden windfalls in the form of inheritances. Some economists believe that bequests from previous generations have provided as much as a quarter of the start-up capital for each new one—money for college tuitions, new houses, new businesses. But the image of an ingénue's getting a leg up through a sudden bequest from Aunt Tilly will soon be a relic of late-millennium romances.

Instead of helping their juniors begin careers and families, tomorrow's rich oldsters will be expending their disposable income to enhance their memories, senses, and immune systems. Refashioning their flesh to ever higher levels of performance, they will adjust their metabolisms on computers, install artificial organs that synthesize smart drugs, and swallow genetically tailored bacteria and viruses that clean out arteries, fine-tune neurons, and repair broken genes. Should one be reminded of H. G. Wells's *The Time Machine*, in which humankind is divided into two species, the ethereal Eloi and the brutish, underground-dwelling Morlocks? "As I recall," Goldman told me recently, "in that book it didn't work out very well for the Eloi."

When lifespans extend indefinitely, the effects are felt throughout the life cycle, but the biggest social impact may be on the young. According to Joshua Goldstein, a demographer at Princeton, adolescence will in the future evolve into a period of experimentation and education that will last from the teenage years into the mid-thirties. In a kind of *wanderjahr* prolonged for decades, young people will try out jobs on a temporary basis, float in and out of their parents' homes, hit the Europass-and-hostel circuit, pick up extra courses and degrees, and live with different people in different places. In the past the transition from youth to adulthood usually followed an orderly sequence: education, entry into the labor force, marriage, and parenthood. For tomorrow's thirtysomethings, suspended in what Goldstein calls "quasi-adulthood," these steps may occur in any order.

From our short-life-expectancy point of view, quasi-adulthood may seem like a period of socially mandated fecklessness—what Leon Kass, the chair of the President's Council on Bioethics, has decried as the coming culture of "protracted youthfulness, hedonism, and sexual license." In Japan, ever in the demographic forefront, as many as one out of three young adults is either unemployed or working part-time, and many are living rent-free with their parents. Masahiro Yamada, a sociologist at Tokyo Gakugei University, has sarcastically dubbed them *parasaito shinguru*, or "parasite singles." Adult offspring who live with their parents are common in aging Europe, too. In 2003 a report from the British Prudential financial-services group awarded the 6.8 million British in this category the mocking name of "kippers"—"kids in parents' pockets eroding retirement savings."

To Kass, the main cause of this stasis is "the successful pursuit of longer life and better health." Kass's fulminations easily lend themselves to ridicule. Nonetheless, he is in many ways correct. According to Yuji Genda, an economist at Tokyo University, the drifty lives of parasite singles are indeed a by-product of increased longevity, mainly because longer-lived seniors are holding on to their jobs. Japan, with the world's oldest population, has the highest percentage of working senior citizens of any developed nation: one out of three men over sixty-five is still on the job. Everyone in the nation, Genda says, is "tacitly aware" that the old are "blocking the door."

In a world of 200-year-olds "the rate of rise in income and status perhaps for the first hundred years of life will be almost negligible," the crusty maverick economist Kenneth Boulding argued in a prescient article from 1965. "It is the propensity of the old, rich, and powerful to die that gives the young, poor, and powerless hope." (Boulding died in 1993, opening up a position for another crusty maverick economist.)

Kass believes that "human beings, once they have attained the burdensome knowledge of good and bad, should not have access to the tree of life." Accordingly, he has proposed a straightforward way to prevent the problems of youth in a society dominated by the old: "resist the siren song of the conquest of aging and death." Senior citizens, in other words, should let nature take its course once humankind's biblical seventy-year lifespan is up. Unfortunately, this solution is self-canceling, since everyone who agrees with it is eventually eliminated. Opponents, meanwhile, live on and on. Kass, who is sixty-six, has another four years to make his case.

Increased longevity may add to marital strains. The historian Lawrence Stone was among the first to note that divorce was rare in previous centuries partly because people died so young that bad unions were often dissolved by early funerals. As people lived longer, Stone argued, divorce became "a functional substitute for death." Indeed, marriages dissolved at about the same rate in 1860 as in 1960, except that in the nineteenth century the dissolution was more often due to the death of a partner, and in the twentieth century to divorce. The corollary that children were as likely to live in households without both biological parents in 1860 as in 1960 is also true. Longer lifespans are far from the only reason for today's higher divorce rates, but the evidence seems clear that they play a role. The prospect of spending another twenty years sitting across the breakfast table from a spouse whose charm has faded must have already driven millions to divorce lawyers. Adding an extra decade or two can only exacerbate the strain.

Worse, child-rearing, a primary marital activity, will be even more difficult than it is now. For the past three decades, according to Ben J. Wattenberg, a senior fellow at the American Enterprise Institute, birth rates around the world have fallen sharply as women have taken advantage of increased opportunities for education and work outside the home. "More education, more work, lower fertility," he says. The title of Wattenberg's latest book sums up his view of tomorrow's demographic prospects: *Fewer.* In his analysis, women's continuing movement outside the home will lead to a devastating population crash—the mirror image of the population boom that shaped so much of the past century. Increased longevity will only add to the downward pressure on birth rates, by making childbearing even more difficult. During their twenties, as Goldstein's quasi-adults, men and women will be unmarried and relatively poor. In their thirties and forties they will finally grow old enough to begin meaningful careers—the worst time to have children. Waiting still longer will mean entering the maelstrom of reproductive technology, which seems likely to remain expensive, alienating, and prone to complications. Thus the parental paradox: increased longevity means *less* time for pregnancy and child-rearing, not more.

Even when women manage to fit pregnancy into their careers, they will spend a smaller fraction of their lives raising children than ever before. In the mid-nineteenth century white women in the United States had a life expectancy of about forty years and typically bore five or six children. (I specify Caucasians because records were not kept for African-Americans.) These women literally spent more than half their lives caring for offspring. Today U.S. white women have a life expectancy of nearly eighty and bear an average of 1.9 children—below replacement level. If a woman spaces two births close together, she may spend only a quarter of her days in the company of offspring under the age of eighteen. Children will become ever briefer parentheses in long, crowded adult existences. It seems inevitable that the bonds between generations will fray.

Purely from a financial standpoint, parenthood has always been a terrible deal. Mom and Dad fed, clothed, housed, and educated the kids, but received little in the way of tangible return. Ever since humankind began acquiring property, wealth has flowed from older generations to younger ones. Even in those societies where children herded cattle and tilled the land for their aged progenitors, the older generation consumed so little and died off so quickly that the net movement of assets and services was always downward. "Of all the misconceptions that should be banished from discussions of aging," F. Landis MacKellar, an economist at the International Institute for Applied Systems Analysis, in Austria, wrote in the journal *Population and Development Review* in 2001, "the most persistent and egregious is that in some simpler and more virtuous age children supported their parents."

This ancient pattern changed at the beginning of the twentieth century, when government pension and social-security schemes spread across Europe and into the Americas. Within the family parents still gave much more than they received, according to MacKellar, but under the new state plans the children in effect banded together outside the family and collectively reimbursed the parents. In the United States workers pay less to Social Security than they eventually receive; retirees are subsidized by the contributions of younger workers. But on the broadest level financial support from the young is still offset by the movement of assets within families—a point rarely noted by critics of "greedy geezers."

Increased longevity will break up this relatively equitable arrangement. Here concerns focus less on the super-rich than on middle-class senior citizens, those who aren't surfing the crest of compound interest. These people will face a Hobson's choice. On the one hand, they will be unable to retire at sixty-five, because the young would end up bankrupting themselves to support them—a reason why many would-be reformers propose raising the retirement age. On the other hand, it will not be feasible for most of tomorrow's nonagenarians and centenarians to stay at their desks, no matter how fit and healthy they are.

The case against early retirement is well known. In economic jargon the ratio of retirees to workers is known as the "dependency ratio," because through pension and Social Security payments people who are now in the work force funnel money to people who have left it. A widely cited analysis by three economists at the Organization for Economic Cooperation and Development estimated that in 2000 the overall dependency ratio in the United States was 21.7 retirees for every 100 workers, meaning (roughly speaking) that everyone older than sixty-five had five younger workers contributing to his pension. By 2050 the dependency ratio will have almost doubled, to 38 per 100; that is, each retiree will be supported by slightly more than two current workers. If old-age benefits stay the same, in other words, the burden on younger workers, usually in the form of taxes, will more than double.

This may be an underestimate. The OECD analysis did not assume any dramatic increase in longevity, or the creation of any entitlement program to pay for longevity care. If both occur, as gerontological optimists predict, the number of old will skyrocket, as will the cost of maintaining them. To adjust to these "very bad fiscal effects," says the OECD economist Pablo Antolin, one of the report's coauthors, societies have only two choices: "raising the retirement age or cutting the benefits." He continues, "This is arithmetic—it can't be avoided." The recent passage of a huge new prescription-drug program by an administration and Congress dominated by the "party of small government" suggests that benefits will not be cut. Raising the age of retirement might be more feasible politically, but it would lead to a host of new problems—see today's Japan.

In the classic job pattern, salaries rise steadily with seniority. Companies underpay younger workers and overpay older workers as a means of rewarding employees who stay at their jobs. But as people have become more likely to shift firms and careers, the pay increases have become powerful disincentives for companies to retain employees in their fifties and sixties. Employers already worried about the affordability of older workers are not likely to welcome calls to raise the retirement age; the last thing they need is to keep middle managers around for another twenty or thirty years. "There will presumably be an elite group of super-rich who would be immune to all these pressures," Ronald Lee, an economic demographer at the University of California at Berkeley, says. "Nobody will kick Bill Gates out of Microsoft as long as he owns it. But there will be a lot of pressure on the average old person to get out."

In Lee's view, the financial downsizing need not be

inhumane. One model is the university, which shifted older professors to emeritus status, reducing their workload in exchange for reduced pay. Or, rather, the university *could* be a model: age-discrimination litigation and professors' unwillingness to give up their perks, Lee says, have largely torpedoed the system. "It's hard to reduce someone's salary when they are older," he says. "For the person, it's viewed as a kind of disgrace. As a culture we need to get rid of that idea."

The Pentagon has released few statistics about the hundreds or thousands of insurgents captured in Afghanistan and Iraq, but one can be almost certain that they are disproportionately young. Young people have ever been in the forefront of political movements of all stripes. University students protested Vietnam, took over the U.S. embassy in Tehran, filled Tiananmen Square, served as the political vanguard for the Taliban. "When we are forty," the young writer Filippo Marinetti promised in the 1909 *Futurist Manifesto*, "other younger and stronger men will probably throw us in the wastebasket like useless manuscripts—we want it to happen!"

The same holds true in business and science. Steve Jobs and Stephen Wozniak founded Apple in their twenties; Albert Einstein dreamed up special relativity at about the same age. For better and worse, young people in developed nations will have less chance to shake things up in tomorrow's world. Poorer countries, where the old have less access to longevity treatments, will provide more opportunity, political and financial. As a result, according to Fred C. Iklé, an analyst with the Center for Strategic and International Studies, "it is not fanciful to imagine a new cleavage opening up in the world order." On one side would be the "'bioengineered' nations," societies dominated by the "becalmed temperament" of old people. On the other side would be the legions of youth—"the protagonists," as the political theorist Samuel Huntington has described them, "of protest, instability, reform, and revolution."

Because poorer countries would be less likely to be dominated by a gerontocracy, tomorrow's divide between old and young would mirror the contemporary division between rich northern nations and their poorer southern neighbors. But the consequences might be different—unpredictably so. One assumes, for instance, that the dictators who hold sway in Africa and the Middle East would not hesitate to avail themselves of longevity treatments, even if few others in their societies could afford them. Autocratic figures like Arafat, Franco, Perón, and Stalin often leave the scene only when they die. If the human lifespan lengthens greatly, the dictator in Gabriel García Márquez's *The Autumn of the Patriarch*, who is "an indefinite age somewhere between 107 and 232 years," may no longer be regarded as a product of magical realism.

Bioengineered nations, top-heavy with the old, will need to replenish their labor forces. Here immigration is the economist's traditional solution. In abstract terms, the idea of importing young workers from poor regions of the world seems like a win-win solution: the young get jobs, the old get cheap service. In practice, though, host nations have found that the foreigners in their midst are stubbornly . . . foreign. European nations are wondering whether they really should have let in so many Muslims. In the United States, traditionally hospitable to migrants, bilingual education is under attack and the southern border is increasingly locked down. Japan, preoccupied by *Nihonjinron* (theories of "Japaneseness"), has always viewed immigrants with suspicion if not hostility. Facing potential demographic calamity, the Japanese government has spent millions trying to develop a novel substitute for immigrants: robots smart and deft enough to take care of the aged.

According to Ronald Lee, the Berkeley demographer, rises in life expectancy have in the past stimulated economic growth. Because they arose mainly from reductions in infant and child mortality, these rises produced more healthy young workers, which in turn led to more productive societies. Believing they would live a long time, those young workers saved more for retirement than their forebears, increasing society's stock of capital—another engine of growth. But these positive effects are offset when increases in longevity come from old people's neglecting to die. Older workers are usually less productive than younger ones, earning less and consuming more. Worse, the soaring expenses of entitlement programs for the old are likely, Lee believes, "to squeeze out government expenditures on the next generation," such as education and childhood public-health programs. "I think there's evidence that something like this is already happening among the industrial countries," he says. The combination will force a slowdown in economic growth: the economic pie won't grow as fast. But there's a bright side, at least potentially. If the fall in birth rates is sufficiently vertiginous, the number of people sharing that relatively smaller pie may shrink fast enough to let everyone have a bigger piece. One effect of the longevity-induced "birth dearth" that Wattenburg fears, in other words, may be higher per capita incomes.

For the past thirty years the United States has financed its budget deficits by persuading foreigners to buy U.S. Treasury bonds. In the nature of things, most of these foreigners have lived in other wealthy nations, especially Japan and China. Unfortunately for the United States, those other countries are marching toward longevity crises of their own. They, too, will have fewer young, productive workers. They, too, will be paying for longevity treatments for the old. They, too, will be facing a grinding economic slowdown. For all these reasons they may be less willing to finance our government. If so, Uncle Sam will have to raise interest rates to attract investors, which will further depress growth—a vicious circle.

Longevity-induced slowdowns could make young nations more attractive as investment targets, especially for the cash-strapped pension-and-insurance plans in aging countries. The youthful and ambitious may well follow the money to where the action is. If Mexicans and Guatemalans have fewer rich old people blocking their paths, the river of migration may begin to flow in the other direction. In a reverse brain drain, the Chinese coast guard might discover half-starved American postgraduates stuffed into the holds of smugglers' ships. Highways out of Tijuana or Nogales might bear road signs telling drivers to watch out for *norteamericano* families running across the blacktop, the children's Hello Kitty backpacks silhouetted against a yellow warning background.

Given that today nobody knows precisely how to engineer major increases in the human lifespan, contemplating these issues may seem premature. Yet so many scientists believe that some of the new research will pay off, and that lifespans will stretch like taffy, that it would be shortsighted not to consider the consequences. And the potential changes are so enormous and hard to grasp that they can't be understood and planned for at the last minute. "By definition," says Aubrey de Grey, the Cambridge geneticist, "you live with longevity for a very long time."

We Are Not Immune

from *Harper's* (7/04)

Ronald J. Glasser

Death is inevitable, but not disease. The difference may be as simple as washing our hands or keeping the wastes of industrialized farming out of the water supply, but it is often much more complicated. Bacteria and viruses are no mean adversaries, nor are they easily defeated. If we fail to be watchful or to protect those most at risk, a public-health catastrophe is inevitable, and yet somewhere within the span of the last thirty years the idea of the common good has disappeared from our national consciousness, giving way to the misconception that we no longer need concern ourselves with the welfare of our fellow citizens. It is a dangerous conceit, and it leads us toward a future infected with unprecedented and unnecessary disease.

We have grown not so much complacent as narcotized, lulled into a sense of security by the almost daily pronouncements from corporate medicine and the pharmaceutical industry of ever better drugs and more "breakthrough" treatments. The spectacular progress of twentieth-century medicine, most recently the sequencing of the human genome, sponsors the widespread fancy that disease might someday be conquered, that genetic manipulation or nanotechnology or some other science-fiction marvel might bring with it a cure for death. Long forgotten are the days when the loss of a child to diphtheria or whooping cough or yellow fever was a commonplace event, the days before widespread vaccination and government safety and health regulations; we no longer remember life before publicly funded sewage-treatment plants and the passage of the clean-air and -water acts. Public health is often invisible and unremarked when it works well; when it fails, our neighbors sicken and die.

A public-health system is only as strong as its weakest link; an epidemic enforces, in the most rigorous fashion, the American credo that all men are created equal. If we allow one segment of our society to suffer and perish from preventable disease, little stands in the way of collective doom. Yet today, 44 million people in the United States are without health insurance; those who can afford to pay for it generally receive inferior treatment, despite the fact that Americans spend $1.4 trillion annually for their health care. Public-health departments across the country have never recovered from decades of cutbacks, despite injections of funding in response to specific emergencies such as AIDS or the threat of bioterrorism. Purchases of newer and more reliable diagnostic-testing equipment have been deferred; technical staff and other employees needed to support epidemiologic and testing programs have been downsized; vital on-site bacteriological and viral laboratories have been closed and the testing outsourced to the lowest bidder or simply abandoned. State and local early-childhood services, prenatal care, immunization campaigns for the poor, alcohol-abuse and smoking-awareness campaigns, monitoring programs for lead and arsenic levels, as well as HIV/AIDS treatment programs, have been curtailed as health departments shift around available monies and reassign what few permanent staff members they have left in an attempt to keep the most critical programs in operation. Prevention becomes secondary to simply keeping people alive. Nor must we concern ourselves simply with the state of American public health; as distances collapse and human populations grow ever more mobile, so also new and deadly diseases (among them Ebola and the Marburg virus) find their way across deserts and oceans. AIDS took decades to escape its origins in central Africa; we should not expect the next simian retrovirus to take so long. SARS made its way from Asia to Toronto in a matter of weeks.

Medical historians describe the last few decades as the age of "the emerging plagues." Overpopulation, poverty, ecological devastation and global climate change, chemical pollution and industrial agriculture—all of these factors conspire to create the conditions for unprecedented death by infectious disease. Between 1977 and 1994, twenty-nine previously unknown human pathogens emerged, and it is estimated, moreover, that we have identified only 1 percent of the bacteria and 4 percent of the viruses on the planet. Tuberculosis, a disease that should have disappeared decades ago, has reemerged as an epidemic, and drug-resistant strains continue to spread throughout our cities.

In 1995, 1.7 million American patients contracted hospital-spread infections; 88,000 of these patients died; 70 percent of the infections were drug-resistant. Each year an estimated 76 million Americans fall ill to food-borne illnesses resulting in approximately 325,000 hospitalizations and 5,000 deaths. Influenza infects 10 to 20 percent of the U.S. population every year and kills 36,000; a virulent avian flu could kill millions. Such numbers, a mere sampling of those available, paint a grim portrait, and the view does not improve if we narrow the perspective.

During a two-week period in 1993 one of Milwaukee's two water-treatment plants malfunctioned. This waterworks supplied treated drinking water directly from Lake Michigan to at least half the population of Milwaukee and nine of its suburbs. The investigation that eventually followed revealed unprecedented increases in the density levels of the supposedly treated water during that two-week period. The gauges designed for continuous measurement of water purity had clearly not been functioning properly for periods as long as eight to twelve hours at a time. The precise reason for the failure remains obscure, but what is clear is that no alarms went off, no backup systems were brought online, and no one noticed the increases in turbidity that led to the largest waterborne epidemic ever to occur in the United States.

Within days of the plant's malfunction and continuing for an additional month, more than 403,000 people in the Milwaukee area developed fever, vomiting, and diarrhea. One hundred people died. The cause of the illness was Cryptosporidium, a single-celled microorganism that survives in bodies of standing water and has been known as a cause of diarrhea, abdominal cramping, nausea, vomiting, and fever since the 1970s. There is no medical treatment for the infection, and in otherwise healthy individuals the disease is usually self-limiting, though in a minority of cases the disease can lead to weeks of disability. In patients on immunosuppressive medications, those undergoing chemotherapy, or those with AIDS, the infection can be ruthless, unrelenting, and fatal.

The seriousness of Cryptosporidium in an immune-suppressed patient became clear at the beginning of the AIDS epidemic when physicians first found this strange and unexpected parasite in the blood and bone marrows of infected patients. Knowing that the organism was basically a disease of herd animals, the doctors contacted the preeminent expert on Cryptosporidium in the department of agriculture at the University of Iowa. When the professor was asked how infected sheep were treated, he hesitated. "There is no treatment," he answered. "We shoot them."

There are well over 1,400 documented microorganisms that can infect humans, of which fully one half first caused disease in animals. Cryptosporidium made the transfer to humans through the contamination of surface waters by runoff from farmlands and drainage ditches. Unfortunately, the cysts that spread the infection are highly resistant to chlorine and even remain viable in the laboratory after exposures to full-strength household bleaches. You can't kill the Cryptosporidium cysts, and while alive they remain astonishingly infectious. Disease has been known to occur through ingestion of as few as thirty cysts, and experimental data have shown that even a single cyst can pass on the disease to uninfected sheep as well as to humans. The only means of prevention for a contaminated water supply are filters of less than one micron placed within water-purification systems that physically remove the millions of heavy, dense cysts before they reach the household taps of public water supplies.

The failure of the main safety and backup gauges in Milwaukee was clearly a disaster, but the most unnerving aspect of the Wisconsin epidemic was not the astronomical numbers of affected people or even the deaths; it was the fact that, in the midst of the worsening epidemic, it was not the federal government or any state or local health department or surveillance program or emergency-room database or managed-health-care reporting system that alerted the public that an epidemic was in progress. It was a pharmacist, who happened to notice unusual sales of over-the-counter diarrhea medication. The local media reported the outbreak days before the health department took action, almost a week after the alarm was first raised.

The outbreak of Cryptosporidium in Milwaukee was more than the simple malfunction of a few gauges in a midsized American city; to those concerned about the nation's ability to treat its people and control disease, it was a clear sign that our infectious-disease and medical surveillance and prevention programs were no longer working. Although the Milwaukee disaster was unusual for its size, waterborne outbreaks of disease are not uncommon. The Centers for Disease Control maintains a database on the subject, but the statistics are not very reliable because they depend on the voluntary reporting of state and local health officials. Some states choose not to make these reports; some states do not even have active disease-surveillance systems. But local failures can often have far broader consequences, as we learned from the 1999 outbreak of the West Nile virus in New York City. Mosquito surveillance and control was a local budget casualty that led to a national epidemic, and by last year West Nile had appeared in every state but Washington, Oregon, Alaska, and Hawaii; 14,163 people are known to have been infected and 564 have died. The discovery in 2002 that the virus was transmitted via organ transplantation, and possibly by blood transfusion, has led to fears that the national blood supply could be contaminated. Testing for West Nile raises the cost of blood by $4 to $7 a unit. And even as the virus spreads across the continent, federal funding is being cut; in 2004 the Mosquito Abatement for Safety and Health Act received zero funding, and none has been requested for 2005.

The United States has no single agency responsible for public health and thus no coherent policy. As Laurie Garrett suggests in her monumental study, *Betrayal of Trust: The Collapse of Global Public Health,* it is no exaggeration to say that we simply lack a public-health system per se; what we do have is best described as "a hodgepodge of programs, bureaucracies, and failings."

The great public-health victories of the nineteenth and early twentieth centuries over yellow fever, cholera, encephalitis, smallpox, puerperal fever, and a host of other infectious diseases were largely the result of preventive measures enacted by visionary public officials: improved sanitation and nutrition (safe water and food, decent housing, paved streets, sewers), vigorous powers of quarantine to prevent contagion, mosquito control and the installation of window glass, and the creation of vaccination programs. Few advances were as important as the realization that merely washing one's hands could prevent the spread of disease. Life expectancy in the eighteenth century for an average male was about thirty years; by the early 1970s, it was seventy-five years. And as Garrett points out, most of that progress occurred prior to the invention of antibiotics, and "less than 4 percent of the total improvement in life expectancy since the 1700s can be credited to twentieth century advances in medical care." Ironically, the medical revolutions of the twentieth century have contributed to our overconfident and complacent neglect of the public-health infrastructure. We spend vast sums to lengthen the lives of terminally ill patients by a few days and refuse to make modest investments that would prevent millions of needless illnesses and deaths.

The peculiar dynamics of American politics, with its periodic spasms of irrational antigovernment hysteria, have ensured that few effective public-health policies fail to attract powerful political enemies, enemies that more often than not have succeeded in weakening the agencies charged by Congress with the responsibility for the health and well-being of the American people. Not even the CDC is immune from the virus of partisan politics; despite an overwhelming medical consensus, the agency has refused to take a position on the use of condoms to prevent AIDS and has curtailed the printing or distribution of any data on the control or treatment of sexually transmitted diseases that might offend the most conservative Christians. In response to political pressure from the NRA and threats from Congress to withhold funding, the CDC has also discontinued its definitive research documenting the public-health costs of handguns.

The Food and Drug Administration presents the same self-defeating pattern of regulatory behavior. In May of this year, the agency refused to approve a morning-after contraceptive pill for over-the-counter use, even after its own expert advisory panel recommended it. Far worse is the degree to which the FDA panders to its industrial constituency. Drugs receive approval without adequate testing; the agency dithers when patients begin to die; eventually it turns out that adverse findings were ignored or suppressed. Often more concerned for the well-being of the pharmaceutical industry than for the health of American citizens, the FDA challenges states that seek to purchase cheaper Canadian drugs for their citizens and ignores the ongoing concentration of drug and vaccine production into the hands of fewer and larger companies, which has led to greater consumer costs and vaccine shortages. The agency has shown no inclination to pressure manufacturers into adopting new technologies that would allow the timely and safe development of new vaccines in response to emerging diseases. Not too long ago the FDA supported the pharmaceutical industry's wish to give antidepressant drugs to children despite the agency's own finding that such drugs might cause them to commit suicide.

Faced with alarming outbreaks of food-borne illness, the Department of Agriculture has refused to enforce the use of any of the more definitive and reliable, though admittedly more costly, bacterial tests of meat and meat products to replace the pathetically ineffective "poke and sniff" test used in all government-monitored and -approved slaughterhouses and meat-processing plants. E. coli, salmonella, listeria, shigella have all caused outbreaks of disease. What is astonishing is not that a million pounds of hamburger can be contaminated from one infected cow but that the federal government demands only "voluntary" recalls. Confronted with proof that mad cow disease has infected the American food supply, the agency has prohibited the routine testing of American cattle for the disease, using the newly available tests only in obviously diseased animals and then allowing the animals to be slaughtered and put into the food supply before the results of those tests are available. The USDA has dismissed the recommendations of some of the nation's most prominent professors of agriculture and veterinary medicine to institute a more rigorous and scientific method of testing for this disease, usually citing as an excuse the meat industry's concern that any testing will add an additional three to five cents a pound to consumer prices. The USDA is not so much a regulatory agency as it is an arm of the meat-industry lobby.

Americans, we know, pay too much for their health care, and compared with other countries we receive a very poor return on our investment. The reasons are many, but they are not hard to understand: in essence, we have tended historically to view health care as a commodity like any other. But health is not a product; it is a public good. The evidence is clear that even when viewed through the reductive lens of purely economic self-interest, market-based, entrepreneurial medicine is a failure. Healing people after they fall ill is vastly more expensive than preventing the illness in the first place: every dollar spent preventing diphtheria, for instance, saves $27; every dollar spent on measles, mumps, and rubella saves $23. Yet policymakers have consistently preferred the most expensive and least efficient models of health care, proving once again that the apostles of privatization are motivated not by hard-nosed economics but by an incoherent ideology that is little more than a brittle mask concealing the most irrational species of self-interest.

For the last quarter century, especially after the election of Ronald Reagan and his declaration that government itself is the problem that afflicts us, the public-health infrastructure of this country has been eviscerated. Between 1981 and 1993, public-health expenditures declined by 25 percent as a proportion of overall health spending; in 1992, less than 1 percent of all American health-care spending was devoted to public health. That trend has continued, even after the anthrax attacks of 2001, when politicians suddenly realized how vulnerable the nation was to biological attack.

Since then, it is true, the federal government has appropriated about $2 billion for bioterrorism response, an undertaking that if it were actually carried out would necessarily involve improving the public-health infrastructure. In theory, the bioterrorism money is channeled through the CDC, which distributes it to the states, which in turn disperse money to local health departments. Superficially, the gains are impressive: the CDC's budget for "public health preparedness and response for bioterrorism" increased from $49.9 million in 2001 to $918 million in 2002 and $870 million in 2003. Yet strangely enough, state and local public-health budgets have continued to decline. Public-health laboratories in California could lose 20 percent of their funding this year; the Alabama Department of Public Health expects to fire 250 people and to close regional labs and cut back on its flu-vaccination programs. State funding for AIDS prevention in Massachusetts has been cut by 40 percent over the last two years. Larimer County, Colorado, where last summer 500 people contracted the West Nile virus, received $100,000 in federal funds but lost $700,000 in state money. Overall, thirty-two states cut their public-health budgets between fiscal years 2002 and 2003. Michigan cut its spending by 24 percent, Massachusetts by 23 percent, and Montana, which received more federal bioterror money per capita than New York, cut its public-health budget by 19 percent. Many states, facing huge budget deficits, apparently took the federal money and simply cut their own appropriations. This should come as no surprise: in 2003 the states collectively faced a $66 billion shortfall, and in 2004 state deficits are estimated to be $78 billion. Federal investment will do no good if state politicians, struggling to cope with the economic effects of other federal policies, use those funds to reduce their own deficits.

The Trust for America's Health (TFAH), a nonprofit group that monitors public-health policy, in December released a comprehensive study of what the state health departments have accomplished with their "increased" funding. TFAH found that only twenty-four states had spent at least 90 percent of their 2002 bioterror funds, and only seventeen states had passed at least 50 percent of the money along to local health departments. Much of the money is mired in bureaucracy. A February GAO report revealed that the states were not much better prepared for bioterrorism (and by extension, a natural epidemic) than they were in 2001.

Of course, state health departments can hardly be blamed for their inability to correct a quarter century of neglect with what amounts to a mere $2,000 for every staffed hospital bed in America. Bioterrorism funds are being used simply to keep the lights on, and no one who has carefully observed the Bush Administration would expect it to follow through with its promises to rebuild the public-health system. In fact, the President's 2005 budget proposal calls for a $105 million decrease in state and local bioterrorism funding. The new budget also cuts $1.1 billion from the "Function 550" account, which finances disease-prevention programs and other public-health initiatives, and the federal Public Health Improvements Programs were cut by 64 percent.

Secretary of Health and Human Services Tommy Thompson has claimed that preparing for bioterrorism will enable the government to respond to influenza and other infectious diseases; in fact, the reverse is true. Bioterrorism is a remote threat and a massive attack is very unlikely, but it captures the imagination of weak-minded politicians and a populace raised on movies starring Bruce Willis. The truly imminent biological threat, which all public-health experts agree will inevitably strike, is an influenza pandemic. The 1918 pandemic killed 550,000 Americans and 30 million worldwide. A virulent flu would thus be much worse than a bioterrorism attack, and it would strike every part of the country more or less simultaneously. These facts are well known and understood, yet TFAH found that only thirteen states have a plan or at least a draft of a plan to confront an influenza pandemic. Amazingly, the CDC itself has yet to release a federal plan for such a pandemic; nor does the CDC require states to report flu cases or even flu deaths.

Every year influenza epidemics emerge from areas such

as the Guangdong region of China, where large populations of farmers, pigs, and poultry share their species' various strains of the influenza virus. When multiple strains of the virus infect the same host, they begin to share genes, creating new mutations; when a new strain emerges for which humans have no immunity, a pandemic can occur.

In response to a 1997 avian influenza outbreak that began to infect humans but stopped short, for some reason, of becoming an epidemic, the World Health Organization significantly expanded its flu-prevention activities and set up its Global Agenda for Influenza Surveillance and Control, a program whose four main objectives are to monitor the spread of influenza in animals and humans, to identify each year's newest infective strain, to accelerate global pandemic awareness, and to increase usage and speed development of an effective vaccine. Each year the WHO surveillance program puts its infectious-disease teams along with its worldwide network of more than one hundred laboratories on alert, hoping to detect outbreaks before they spread around the globe. Such generalized surveillance is difficult and expensive, but the danger of emerging infections and the continuing influenza threat have left the world health community with little choice.

In February 2003 the WHO issued a report about a group of patients with severe influenza in Hong Kong. The index case was a physician from Guangdong province in China. A global alert was soon issued concerning similar illnesses in Singapore and Hanoi. The WHO sent Dr. Carlo Urbani, an Italian infectious-disease specialist, to Hanoi to investigate. Urbani swiftly determined that the disease was something unusual and that it was highly contagious and virulent. Unlike influenza, which always begins with a runny nose, waves of generalized aches and pains, and weakness, followed by days of fever and an increasing cough before the onset of pneumonia, this disease progressed almost immediately to severe pneumonia, respiratory collapse, and, for many, death. We now know that these alerts were describing the SARS outbreak, which nearly became a global pandemic. Working closely with the Vietnamese authorities, Urbani and other specialists from the WHO, the CDC, and Doctors Without Borders were able to contain the disease in Hanoi, though tragically Urbani himself contracted SARS and died in a makeshift isolation ward in Bangkok. It was not long before the disease spread to Toronto. By late March, 6,800 people there had already been quarantined, with another 5,200 health-care staff working "in quarantine" at facilities that public-health officials had quickly set aside for treating suspected SARS cases. In the United States public-health officials were simply holding their breath and hoping for the best. Not only have cutbacks stripped rural areas of their hospitals and clinics but even the major cities now lack the number of acute-care and infectious-disease beds—not to mention the nursing staff, technicians, and isolation units—to deal with a bad year of influenza much less a full-fledged disease with what appeared to be the staggering demands of SARS.

What happened next was unprecedented: researchers quickly determined that the disease was caused by a new type of virus and very rapidly isolated the cause as a previously unknown coronavirus that had apparently jumped from an animal species to humans. It was not lost on the world's infectious-disease experts that what had taken physicians and scientists almost four years in the case of AIDS was accomplished for SARS in less than four months. It is no exaggeration to say that the billions of dollars so reluctantly pushed into viral research as a result of the efforts of AIDS activists in the 1980s and 1990s enabled the WHO to quickly find the cause of another viral plague. And it was the ability to share accurate information in real time via email and the Internet that allowed the WHO to hold the disease in check.

In the midst of all the tracking of potential contacts, the increased hospitalizations, the thousands of people in quarantine, the disease simply vanished at virtually the same time all over the world. Coronaviruses thrive in cold weather, and, like influenza, they spread during the winter months, which accounts for the yearly outbreaks of colds and upper-respiratory infections. The realization that SARS is a cold-weather virus is troubling, because it means that there has been no real victory, only a reprieve. It has to be assumed that SARS is still out there waiting for another winter.

The lesson of the SARS outbreak was that preparation, surveillance, and decisive action from public officials can prevent epidemics. The WHO response was exemplary—training, staffing, equipment, and funding were all in place, ready for an emergency—but we still lack a truly global early-warning system. In the United States we continue to be without an effective national warning system. As *Lancet* editor Richard Horton writes in *Health Wars*, his scathing critique of contemporary medicine, "No single agency—CDC, WHO, the military, or a nongovernmental organization (such as Médecins Sans Frontières)—

currently has the resources, staff, or equipment to act as a rapid-response strike force during a civilian health emergency." If SARS had come to the United States, there is little hope that it could have been contained.

Today, we are no better prepared for a SARS epidemic than we were before. "Homeland security," curiously interpreted to exclude the most plausible and deadly threats facing our population, has remained the priority. The massive smallpox immunization program in 2002 was little more than a distraction and waste of precious funds. Meanwhile, we are afflicted with a government that has waged war all across the world to avenge the deaths of 3,000 terror victims, far fewer than die of influenza in a mild year; a government that insists on spending $50 billion to build a missile-defense system that does not work, a military-industrial make-work project designed to meet a threat that does not exist. The war in Iraq consumes almost $4 billion a month, twice the amount we have largely squandered on bioterrorism since 2001. We have grown so foolish and so incompetent that perhaps we do not deserve to survive. Perhaps it is simply time to die.

The Next Plague?

from *The Atlantic Monthly* (6/05)

Michael Slenske

From last December to this writing, the disease known to epidemiologists as H5N1 avian flu infected twenty-eight people in Vietnam, killing fourteen. On the scale of global catastrophe that may not sound like a lot. But World Health Organization officials worry that a worldwide outbreak could kill as many as seven million. Human populations have proved particularly susceptible to new flu pandemics every twenty to thirty years, as flu strains mutate and overcome built-up immunities. The most recent major flu pandemic petered out in 1972, so we may be overdue. Here are some noteworthy disease outbreaks through history.

1. **Pneumonic plague.** Since last December there have been some 300 suspected cases of—and at least sixty-one deaths from—pneumonic plague in eastern Congo. This is the largest plague outbreak since 1920, when more than 9,000 Manchurians succumbed.

2. **Severe acute respiratory syndrome.** SARS first appeared in China in November of 2002, and was soon recognized as a coronavirus that caused high fevers and fatal pneumonia. Over the course of the next eight months the disease infected more than 8,000 people and killed 774 in twenty-six countries.

3. **West Nile virus.** Although outbreaks of this mosquito-borne encephalitis were identified as early as 1937, in

Uganda, West Nile didn't reach the United States until the summer of 1999, when it infected sixty-two people and killed seven in New York City. Since then more than 15,000 American cases—and more than 500 deaths—have been reported to the Centers for Disease Control.

4. Ebola virus. Nearly two decades after Ebola—which can turn organs into virus-ridden slime in less than a week—took the lives of 600 people in Zaire and Sudan, in 1976, it resurfaced in Zaire, infecting 316 people and killing 245 from May to July of 1995. Fifty of the victims were hospital staffers treating the outbreak.

5. Hong Kong flu. Sweeping across the Pacific from Hong Kong in early 1968, the disease reached the United States by September of that year and went on to kill 34,000 Americans in six months. Outbreaks of this strain recurred in 1970 and 1972, and may have produced a million fatalities worldwide—despite the fact that another flu eleven years earlier (see #6) is believed to have built up global resistance to the disease.

6. Asian flu. First identified by health officials in East Asia in February of 1957, this influenza traveled to the United States that summer and spread through classrooms nationwide, even though a vaccine was introduced in August of that year. The flu claimed 70,000 American lives, and a million worldwide, before dissipating in March of 1958.

7. Spanish flu. After coursing through the trenches of World War I in 1918—accounting for half of all GI deaths during the war—this bug was carried across the globe by homebound soldiers. By some estimates it infected a billion people (about half the world's population), killing 20 million to 50 million in just one year. Most victims of "la Grippe" were healthy adults aged twenty to fifty.

8. **Yellow fever.** Thousands of Philadelphia residents, including President George Washington, fled their city (then the nation's capital) in 1793, after seeing scores of infected people turn yellow and vomit blood. The fever—which killed 5,000 people (10 percent of Philadelphia's population at the time)—returned to the city in subsequent years, though not on the scale of the '93 epidemic.

9. **Black Death.** Although it is generally thought to have been transmitted from rodents to human beings, some scholars believe that the Black Death was actually a person-to-person disease. It ravaged Europe from 1347 to 1352, killing around 25 million people—nearly a third of the Continent's population.

And you tell your friends, it isn't Mad Cow Disease anymore. It's Beyond-Pissed-Off-Make-A-Fucking-Salad-And-Leave-Us-The-Fuck-Alone Disease! Got it?
MR. FISH

Fake Medicine

J. M. Berger

'Kids are different today'
I hear ev'ry mother say
Mother needs something today to calm her down
And though she's not really ill
there's a little yellow pill . . .

It's been forty years since the Rolling Stones first warned us about relying on pills to get us through the ordinary problems of life. Today the song sounds like a prophecy.

Consider a 2005 study by Case Western Reserve University School of Medicine, which found that 20 to 30 percent of American males suffer from the terrible disorder of premature ejaculation (PE). With calculated scientific precision, the study defined PE as the act of shooting one's wad within the first two minutes of intercourse. The most obvious implication of all this was is that premature ejaculation is a medical disorder.

But there is no disease called "premature ejaculation." Look it up.

Not only is there no such thing as a "premature ejaculation" disorder, but there is no known medical condition which causes premature ejaculation. Hair loss is not a medical condition, for instance, but it can be a symptom of an underlying disease. Not so premature ejaculation. Zero. Nothing. Nada.

So if premature ejaculation is not a medical condition in itself, and it's not a symptom of any known medical condition, then why would the venerable Case Western Reserve University School of Medicine perform this study?

You will probably not be surprised to learn that the study—which was covered by straight-faced news outlets as "science"—was commissioned by the pharmaceutical industry. The "premature ejaculation" study was bought and paid for by Alza Corp. and Johnson & Johnson Pharmaceutical Services as part of a campaign to pressure the Food and Drug Administration into approving a new drug for the "medical condition" of premature ejaculation.

"So what's the harm?" you might ask, especially if your pistol has been on a hair trigger lately. "Premature ejaculation is an embarrassing and emotionally painful experience which affects quality of life. Why shouldn't doctors treat it with a drug?" You already know the answer: *it isn't a medical condition.*

Men have been prematurely ejaculating for approximately all of human history. Sometimes it happens when you're tired, sometimes it happens when you're overly excited, sometimes it happens because you've got "stuff on your mind," sometimes it happens because you're just a selfish jerk.

In almost every instance, the "disorder" of premature ejaculation can be "cured" by changing the behavior of the ejaculator—using slower strokes during intercourse, pausing when "the moment" is too close at hand, masturbating an hour to two before having sex, or thinking about baseball during a crucial juncture. There are even advanced disciplines devoted to prolonging "the act," such as Tantric Yoga and the many splendiferous techniques outlined in the Kama Sutra.

Calling "premature ejaculation" a medical disorder and

treating it with drugs is the rankest kind of irresponsibility. It tells people they don't have to exercise willpower or cultivate self-discipline. They can just take a pill.

And it's not just premature ejaculation. There's a booming multibillion-dollar pharmaceutical industry, which has pinned much of its hope for growth on convincing people that they need to take drugs.

Men are among the easiest marks for this fake medical machine, because the average American male will instantly *freak out* when confronted with the slightest hint that his penis may not compare favorably with the next guy's—whether in length, width, durability, shape, flexibility, flavor, temperature, texture, wattage, antilock brakes, bandwidth, battery life, megapixels, accessories and/or tensile strength.

The vast majority of these concerns are entirely psychological, but the vast array of drugs, pseudo-drugs and "herbal remedies" designed to treat these anxieties are quite real—Levitra, Cialis, dapoxetine, Enzyte, Pinnacle, Magna-RX, Naturomax, VPRX . . . the list is as long as the list of messages in your Bulk Mail folder, and then some.

The mountain of spam is only the tip of the iceberg. Medical diagnoses have become the latest way to hide from the everyday experience of life. It's a societal sickness, and it extends much further than the penis (no matter how large that penis might be).

Call it Inappropriate Syndrome Syndrome—the uncontrollable desire to transform any given problem into a disease by appending the word "disorder" or "syndrome." Everyone knows about premenstrual syndrome, attention deficit disorder, chronic fatigue syndrome, bipolar disorder, and post-traumatic stress syndrome. Make no mistake—some people do indeed have identifiable physical problems that cause these disorders. Those people—and only those people—should be receiving medical care, and there is no shame in receiving care for one of those conditions when it has been properly diagnosed.

Doctor please, some more of these
Outside the door, she took four more
What a drag it is getting old

But how many people have been properly diagnosed? How do you tell the difference? Increasingly, the answer to the latter question is "I just know." Thanks in large part to the pharmaceutical industry, consumers face an overwhelming cultural mandate to diagnose themselves.

The capacity to produce profitable drugs vastly outstrips the number of patients available to buy the drugs produced. There are two possible solutions to this imbalance: produce fewer drugs, or create new customers.

Pharmaceutical companies make more money by creating new customers than they do by selling fewer drugs. Economics is a cruel mistress.

"Somewhere between 24 and 30 million people have gone to their doctor to talk about a health problem they had never discussed before after seeing a prescription drug ad," Daniel L. Jaffe, executive vice president of the Association of National Advertisers, told the *New York Times* in June 2005.

In Jaffe's eyes, that statistic is a triumphant vindication of the free market. The American Medical Association took a more jaundiced view and promptly ordered a study to review the effects of such ads.

Drug advertisements offer two methods of self-diagnosis:

1. They show happy people living fulfilled lives and encourage viewers to ask: "Are you as happy as the people in this commercial? If the answer is 'no,' ask your doctor about (insert drug name here)."
2. They show unhappy people with problems. "Have you ever felt like this? If the answer is 'yes,' ask your doctor about (insert drug name here)."

Are you distracted at work? Surely it must be adult attention deficit disorder, and that means you can help yourself to an ample supply of the fastest-growing recreational drug of the twenty-first century, Ritalin.

Meditation and self-exploration are fine if you're looking for serenity, but who has the time? It only takes seconds to pop a twice-daily dose of Zoloft.

If you're frequently tired, you might have chronic fatigue syndrome. Sure, you could drink less coffee and cut back on your fourteen-hour workdays. But why bother when you can pop some modafinil?

And so it goes. Are you shy? No, you have "social anxiety disorder." Do you tap your foot when you sit down or go to bed? You have "restless legs syndrome." Feel rotten about having that abortion? Sounds like a case of "post-abortion syndrome." If you decided not to have that abortion after all, maybe you're currently inflicting "maternal deprivation syndrome" on your child with your lousy parenting.

Does your life suck for reasons beyond your control? That's "complicated grief," and it requires specialized psychiatric care. Are you a criminal? Sounds like a bad case of "antisocial personality disorder," which is similar to but not the same as "antisocial behavior syndrome."

Even pigs are getting into the act! Don't call that sickly piglet the runt of the litter! He's suffering from post-weaning multisystemic wasting syndrome!

Pandora has opened her box of diagnoses, and it shows. A recent magazine advertisement promoted Botox as a "treatment" for wrinkles! Wrinkles are not a disease!

Hair loss is not a disease! But you can "treat" it with any number of drugs—Rogaine, Propecia, dutasteride and countless other less reputable iterations, not to mention an ever-changing panoply of semisurgical procedures.

"So what's the harm?" you might ask. "Who cares if baldness is designated a disease? Who cares if people sell drugs to treat it?"

Here's the problem. Insurance companies waste thousands of man-hours investigating the latest made-up diseases in order to determine whether they should be covered. In addition to this flat-out, up-front waste of resources, the companies actually decide to cover these made-up diseases from time to time. Most companies cover Viagra, despite ubiquitous accounts of its recreational use. With a little coaxing, many insurers will even cover even such flagrantly non-medical treatments as Botox, Rogaine and cosmetic breast implants.

In the United States, health care is provided by a conglomeration of the worst aspects of fascism and communism known as "the insurance sector." Aside from the extremely wealthy, all Americans are hostage to insurance companies. As in fascism, participation is not optional. If you want health care in this country, you're getting it from an insurance company. You're paying an insurance premium for the privilege, and you have no choice in the matter. If you don't pay, you don't get health care.[1]

The actual process by which the insurance company funds your health care is strictly socialist. All the money paid in premiums goes into a gigantic pool, which the insurance company then redistributes according to need—in the form of payments to health care providers as reimbursement for their services.

I could wax on for hours about the desperate flaws that afflict the private-sector insurance model for providing health care, but the fake-medicine issue is particularly problematic. Every time an insurance company writes a check for premature ejaculation, it's paid for with your premiums. Every time an insurance company pays for Botox or Rogaine, every time it pays to treat complicated grief or adult ADD, it comes out of your premiums. And when that gigantic pool of money starts to run low, your premiums go up. Whether or not you have a problem with premature ejaculation, you're still paying for the drug.

Even if the drug never makes it to market, you're paying for the small army of bureaucrats and doctors who work forty-hour weeks reviewing every new medical diagnosis, trying to distinguish between real medical advances and marketing-derived effluvia. To offset this scrutiny, the pharmaceutical industry employs a similar army working toward the goal of convincing the first army to pay for the new drugs that treat the new disorders.

[1] If your employer pays for your health care, it's still coming out of the same pool of cash that would otherwise be reserved for paying your salary. Medicare and Medicaid are limited forms of insurance companies run by the federal government catering to special demographics.

We're not talking about trivial numbers here. The first edition of *The Merck Manual of Diagnosis and Therapy,* published in 1899, was 192 pages long. The seventeenth edition, published in 1999, is 2,833 pages long. The new edition is scheduled to debut in 2006, and it will certainly be larger still.

You're already paying for Viagra. Tomorrow, you could be paying for premature ejaculation, bad-hair days, boredom, lost keys, talking too much, bad taste, loss of faith in God, beer bellies, excessive Internet browsing, sexism, thoughtlessness, flat asses, not listening, sloppiness, stubbed toes, lack of talent, meanness, height, nipple size and hairy backs.

Ultimately, we only have ourselves to blame. Pharmaceutical companies push drugs on consumers because consumers are willing to buy them. Companies run television ads plugging prescription drugs because ads work, because 30 million people go out and ask their doctors for the pill *du jour*.

They just don't appreciate that you get tired
They're so hard to satisfy, you can tranquilize your mind
So go running for the shelter
Of a mother's little helper
And four help you through the night,
Help to minimize your plight

Forty years ago, the Rolling Stones warned us about where things were going. We didn't listen. The situation today is far worse than it was in 1965. Unless the trends change, the situation in 2045 will be worse still.

The manufacture of fake medicine is faux productivity—

instead of producing goods that drive economic growth, we produce goods that have no meaningful value.

We produce drugs to treat diseases that were only invented to sell drugs in the first place. Companies waste research money on nondiseases like premature ejaculation, then they waste more money inventing drugs to treat premature ejaculation. They spend money making the drugs, advertising the drugs and convincing insurance companies to pay for the drugs, and the insurance companies waste still more money on the drugs themselves.

That money is gone. It doesn't feed the economy, it only enriches stockholders. It doesn't help provide health care for the masses. It doesn't make the world a better place.

We're throwing that money away instead of using it to pay for quadruple bypasses, neonatal care for the underemployed, cancer research and universal health coverage.

And if you take more of those,
You will get an overdose
No more running for the shelter
Of a mother's little helper
They just helped you on your way,
Through your busy dying day

What a drag it is. . . .

FACTS

Minimum number of U.S. surgical patients sewn up each year with sponges, clamps, or other tools left inside them: 1,500
(*New England Journal of Medicine*)

Number of Americans who died in 2002 from infections they contracted while hospitalized for other ailments: 90,000
(Centers for Disease Control and Prevention)

Chance that an FDA scientist lacks confidence in the agency's ability to monitor the safety of current drugs: 2 in 3
(U.S. Food and Drug Administration)

Factor by which the number of U.S. girls under 19 who got breast implants in 2003 exceeded the number who did in 2002: 3
(American Society for Aesthetic Plastic Surgery)

Number of plastic surgeries undergone by the winner of last year's "Miss Artificial Beauty" pageant in China: 4
(Beijing Tianjiu Weiye Wenhua, Inc.)

Number undergone by the runner-up: 10
(Beijing Tianjiu Weiye Wenhua, Inc.)

What Will Become of Africa's AIDS Orphans?

from *The New York Times Magazine* (12/22/02)

Melissa Fay Greene

Four years ago, a fifth grader in my children's elementary school in Atlanta lost his father in a twin-engine private plane crash. The terrible news whipped through the community; hundreds attended the funeral. Even today, there is a wisp of tragedy about the tall, blond high-school freshman—fatherless, at so young an age. I find myself thinking about him when surveying the playground of one of the countless hole-in-the-wall orphanages of Addis Ababa, Ethiopia.

Behind corrugated iron walls off a dirt road, schoolgirls in donated clothing are throwing pebbles and waggling their long legs out behind them in hopscotch. Other girls sit on kitchen chairs in the shade of a cement wall, braiding and rebraiding one another's hair. They weave in plastic beads in arrangements so tight that the completed hairdo looks like an abacus. Boys lope back and forth with a half-deflated soccer ball.

Virtually all of these children have lost both parents, most to AIDS. Malaria, yellow fever and especially TB are fatal illnesses here, too. The children's grandparents have also died or are too poor and sick to care for the children; the same is true of their aunts and uncles, their neighbors and teachers. But no single one of these children has been isolated by tragedy: being orphaned is one of the common experiences of their generation. Ethiopia has one of the world's largest populations infected with H.I.V. and AIDS. The number of AIDS orphans in Ethiopia is estimated at a million, most of whom end up living on the streets.

But in a hierarchy among orphans, those here at Layla House are the most fortunate. They are H.I.V. negative and healthy, and they have landed in one of two excellent American adoption programs in this city, both generating high interest among prospective adoptive parents in the United States. But they have been plucked out of immeasurable tragedy.

"This is the most devastating pandemic to sweep the earth for many centuries," says Dr. Mark Rosenberg, executive director of the Atlanta-based Task Force for Child Survival and Development. He compares the moral imperative to stop the epidemic in Africa, Asia and South America to the era of the Holocaust and imagines that future generations will ask, "What did you do to help?"

When I visit one on one with some of the children in a cool cinder-block storeroom, I discover that each is more like the fatherless Atlanta boy than not. As a group, the children generate a carefree mood of ruckus and play, but their secret grief coexists with the brave frolicking. Being orphaned may be typical for their peer group, but it pierces each child in a uniquely tragic way. The boys and girls remember and long for their prior lives, their deceased families, their homes—whether middle-class house or rural hut—and their childhoods that once were normal.

Yemisrach is a big-boned, innocent-faced 15-or 16-year-old. "I live with my parents until age 9," she says. "We are two girls, two boys. First Mother died; then Father died of malaria. I become like a mother to the others."

Though they try to hold onto their memories, it is possible that the children don't have all of their facts straight. But no one is left to correct them, and the child becomes the family historian.

"My father drink too much, and he fall on the gate, and he get a stone on his head, and he went to the hospital and died," says sweet, worried-looking Yirgalem, whose forehead is too creased for his young age. "After that, he buried."

Robel is a rambunctious 8-year-old of the half-baked-schoolwork type. It is easy to picture him as a bike-riding, Nintendo-loving American boy. He has surmised that hospital treatment killed his mother. "I was born in Tigray," he says, speaking through a translator like most of the younger kids. "Then went with my parents to Sudan as refugees. My father would get food from the refugee camp and bring it to the house. Mother died in Sudan. She went to hospital for injection. First injection is good; second time, she is tired; third injection, she died. Then I hear people crying about father. They said, 'Your father has died.'

"My small sister, Gelila, is 4. When Gelila see something in my hand, she cry, so I give her. She does not remember our parents."

There is a terrible sameness to the stories. They all head down the same path: the mother's death, then the father's; or Father died, then Mother, then Small Sister, then funny Baby Brother. Alone, bringing out the words of the family's end, a child's eyes fill with tears; the chest fills with sobs. Bedtime is the worst, when all shenanigans die down. At night, ghosts and visions and bad dreams visit the children. Through the open windows, you can hear kids crying into their pillows.

• • •

The orphans are not confined to the cities. In small farming towns hundreds of miles outside of Addis Ababa, children rush cars, offering flip-flops, bars of soap, packages of tissue or tree branches heavy with nuts. Those with nothing to sell offer labor: they will wash your windshield or watch your car for you if you park it. Some of these children are, at very young ages, the sole wage earner for their families. Orphaned in the countryside, they have migrated to the villages and towns where they have become squatters, trying to feed themselves and their younger siblings in alley dwellings improvised from scrap lumber or cloth or plastic.

"Almost without exception, children orphaned by AIDS are marginalized, stigmatized, malnourished, uneducated and psychologically damaged," Carol Bellamy, executive director of Unicef, said last month in Namibia. "They are affected by actions over which they have no control and in which they had no part. They deal with the most trauma, face the most dangerous threats and have the least protections. And because of all this, they, too, are very likely to become H.I.V. positive." She warned that the growing numbers of AIDS orphans means that the world will see "an explosion in the number of child prostitutes, children living on the streets and child domestic workers."

Eight-year-old Mekdalawit, from Dire Dawa, living in Layla House, remembers the days of her parents' deaths: "My sister Biruktawit is a baby lying on the floor with her feet in the air—like this. Our older sister throw herself in front of the car and scream and yell that she wants to die if our father is dead. Then our mother becomes so ill that she cannot move from her bed. She cannot eat, and she has sores all over her body, and she loves for us to gently scratch her skin."

Mekdalawit and Biruktawit's eight older siblings tried to raise them, but they were obliged to leave home each day for school and for jobs. Worried that the youngest two would wander away from the family hut and be lost, the older children warned that monsters would catch and eat little girls if they didn't stay inside. Finally a few of the oldest brought the youngest two to the local authorities, who referred them to the Children, Youth and Family Affairs Department, known as the Children's Commission. It placed them in Layla House. The older sisters tearfully promised to visit, but their village is far from the capital.

Enat House in Addis Ababa, not far from Layla House, is run by a husband and wife, Gezahegn Wolde Yohannes and Atsedeweyen Abraham. The children who live here are all H.I.V. positive, the smallest victims of the continent's collision with H.I.V./AIDS: not only have they lost their mothers and fathers and siblings, but they themselves are sick. Some of them have begun to lose their hair; others are frighteningly thin; others have facial sores; and all but the babies and toddlers know precisely, in grim detail, what that means.

At Enat, the first clue that the health of another child has taken a downward turn is the child's refusal to enter into the games and exercises she enjoyed last week. A child sitting listlessly on the curb at this playground is an awful omen. The day I visit Enat (an Amharic word for "mother"), the directors and the teachers are mourning the death of a 6-year-old boy a few days earlier.

But on the dirt playground, shaded by eucalyptus trees, the little girls weave one another's hair, and the children are awaiting a visit from their beloved guitar-playing P.E. teacher. The homey sour smell of *injera*—the national bread, a spongy sourdough flat pancake—rises from an outdoor brick kitchen.

Later, in a sunny, freshly mopped dining hall, the children seat themselves at long tables for an art class. A glass vase of cut flowers sparkles with clean water on a tabletop. The children from rural areas never have seen scissors before, and their fingers wiggle with eagerness when the teacher begins handing out brightly colored plastic scissors. Yes, there are enough—Christ Lutheran Church of Forest Hills, Pennsylvania, sent plenty in their boxes of donations. Following instructions, the children generate a blizzard of paper scraps in their first attempts to form snowflakes. (They have never seen snowflakes either). Stocky little Bettye is a pint-size Ethel Merman with a husky belly laugh and a booming voice. She pokes her tongue out the corner of her mouth as she scissors, in classic kindergarten style. The children hold up their lopsided constructions for one another to see, and they hoot in surprise.

The teacher, a slim woman in a long brown dress and head scarf, murmurs words of praise and often bends to stroke a child on the cheek, a gesture of calming affection. Later, I watch a music class, which consists of much hands-on-hip swaying and jumping under the guidance of the guitar-playing young P.E. teacher. Bettye belts out the words of the songs and jerks her fat little tush around. Eyob is a handsome, endearing boy in baggy brown pants and loafers, who slightly stalls his hand claps and foot-stomps till the last moment of each beat; I think he is inventing swing. But Eyob's hair is coming out in tufts. So is Bettye's. And there are no older children at this house; there are no older H.I.V.-positive children at all.

"Our little ones think they are going to America like the children in adoption programs," Atsede says. She is a small, dignified woman with delicate features and fine hair, who stands ramrod straight and offers a mild smile that trembles between civility and grief; she has seen much death. "The older ones gradually understand: 'Because we have AIDS, we cannot go to America.'" In fact, though it is not explicitly U.S. policy to exclude H.I.V.-positive adopted children, and these children generally respond rapidly to the onset of medical treatment in America, the immigration paperwork is more complicated, and few families step forward for these youngsters.

So the Enat children are not in line for adoption; nor are they receiving medical treatment. "Medication to fight AIDS is not available," says Atsede's husband, Gezahegn, who has the dark, rumpled, bloodshot look of a man who has been up all night; he has wrestled AIDS for a dozen of these small lives already and has had every one of them pulled from his arms.

In America last year, thanks to vigorous treatment of infected pregnant women, only 200 H.I.V./AIDS-infected children were born, down from 2,000 in 1994. Most of those babies will live fairly normal lives and survive to adulthood. In Africa, without medications to treat complicating infections, 75 percent of H.I.V.-positive babies will be dead by the age of 2, says Dr. Mark Kline, director of the International Pediatric AIDS Initiative at the Baylor College of Medicine in Houston. Of the remaining 25 percent, he says, very few will reach age 11.

Until recently, Enat served as a holding center for children prior to testing. It was not always clear at first whether the children were infected or not. "We see nice kids, bright futures, then we must test them," Atsede says. "Some get the news that they are negative; then we can refer them to the Children's Commission for assignment to a foreign adoption program. Some will be adopted to America; others, to different countries. But other children test positive. When they first come, we often cannot guess. You'd think it would be the baby of a sibling group who will test positive, but then the results come back and sometimes it is the middle child, so the older child and the baby are transferred out."

Gezahegn's background was in business and government administration, not medicine; he was reluctant to enter this field. Now he finds it has swallowed his life. Nothing compares in importance with trying to sustain the lives of the ill children in his care. "We can fight pneumonia and small infections in the children, but that is all," he says. "We are running a hospice program. It is rather hard to see the children dying."

Still, these stricken children must be counted among the relatively blessed of their generation; the care they receive is the best available. "The children are happy here," Atsede says. "We celebrate holidays; we give them birthdays; we invite their living relatives to visit them. They know that the children at orphanages with adoption programs are learning English and other languages, so we teach them English here, too, so they don't feel left out. The hotels invite them to swing and climb on their playgrounds. We want them to enjoy life. We want them to see something of life."

Time for that is often short. "A child begins by losing weight," Gezahegn says. "Then she develops infections, stops eating, has diarrhea, pain in joints, pain in ears. It can take five months, three months, two months. A child does not talk about it, but she's kind of depressed. One day she is not playing on the playground; she just wants to sit and to be held."

It has become the life mission of this couple to do more than sit by the deathbeds of small children in pain. They are not participants in the debate among health-care professionals over whether treatment or prevention ought to be the public health priority in Africa, Asia and South America. Their question is simpler: how can they get hold of the triple cocktails that in America now have reduced deaths by AIDS by 76 percent since 1996?

By American standards, the cost doesn't sound extravagant. An average figure for pediatric triple-drug therapy in Africa is now $60 to $80 per child per month, and the price is dropping. But without serious commitment of financing from the industrialized world, even these modest costs are unreachable.

When Atsede sits down on a chair in the dirt yard under a shade tree for a rare break, the children skitter over to her and lay their heads upon her long cotton skirts or climb up into her arms and nuzzle their faces into her neck. She laughs as her face is dotted with kisses. "The children call me Abaye, Daddy, and her Emaye, Mommy," Gezahegn says. A little girl waits for him, eager to demonstrate for him a trick she has mastered at jump-rope. The music class waits for his attention to show that they have learned a song with synchronized dance steps. Children raise their hands and hop up and down to be chosen by Gezahegn to accompany him in the backfiring van on an errand to town. Until sickness comes, the faces under the bouncing braids of the little girls and the brimmed caps of the boys are round, happy and hopeful.

"Without therapy," Kline says, "as far as we know, all of the children will die."

Layla House, a shady compound with a paved common area, a baby house, dormitories for boys and for girls, a schoolroom and a kitchen and dining hall, is run by Adoption Advocates International, based in Port Angeles, Wash. A.F.A.A. House, on the outskirts of town, almost buried in flower gardens, is run by Americans for African Adoptions, based in Indianapolis and directed by Cheryl Carter-Shotts. These two are the only American agencies permitted by the Ethiopian government to arrange for adoption of healthy Ethiopian orphans to America. More than 100 children joined new families in the U.S. in 2001. At least a dozen other adoption agencies based in Addis Ababa represent Australia, Canada and seven nations of Western Europe and Scandinavia.

It is the first recourse of everyone ethically involved with intercountry adoption to place orphans with relatives, with friends or with families within their home countries; no one imagines or pretends that adoption is a solution to a generation of children orphaned by disease. It is one very small and modest option, a case of families in industrialized nations throwing lifelines to individual children even as their governments fail to commit the money to turn back the epidemic. "Consider the impact of *The Diary of Anne Frank* on the world," says Mark Rosenberg. "That was the journal of just one doomed child.

Though we are looking at the deaths of millions, the saving of even one life is not trivial."

In the dusty schoolroom at Layla House, students face forward on wood benches and chant lessons in high voices. It is a relief on this hot day to enter the cool, whitewashed room. The children's faces are soft and hopeful. Most are of elementary-school age, though a few perspiring teenagers tower over the rest with the same earnest, slightly anxious expressions. Their teacher, a young man who has never been to America though it is his fondest wish to go, writes American greetings on the chalkboard.

"How are you?" he taps out, while pronouncing the words.

"How are you?" the children repeat.

"I am fine," he dabs in chalk.

"I am fine," they call back in high voices.

"I am very well," he writes.

"I am very well," they sing. They roll their R's, giving a high-tone flourish to their "verys."

"I am doing nicely."

"I am doing nicely."

There is no preparation for bad news here, I notice. The working premise is that these children will be chosen by American families for adoption, and their airfare out of Ethiopia paid for by their waiting parents. From the vantage point of this ancient and poor country, this great opportunity would seem to leave no room for complaint and thus no need to prepare a vocabulary of grumbling.

"How are you this evening?"

"How are you this evening?"

"I am quite well, thank you."

"I am quite well, thank you."

With the next lesson, the teacher offers many ways to

express "I don't know." "I have no idea," the young man is calling over his shoulder. "I have no I-dea," sing the sweet voices, rising up near the end of each phrase. "I shouldn't think so." "I shouldn't think so." "I don't expect so." "I don't expect so." "Search me." "Search me." "I haven't a clue." "I haven't a clue." Through the square uncovered windows, sunlight and dust motes stream onto the pebbly floor. The kids, wearing T-shirts, cutoffs and flip-flops, begin to fidget in expectation of lunchtime.

The lessons in Americana do not cease at mealtime. At long wood tables, there are bowls of orange slices and carved-up bread. Though the children would welcome, at every meal, platters of injera used in lieu of silverware—they are being taught to use American forks and spoons and to maneuver foods like spaghetti and meatballs. "Please to pass the water," a boy booms. "Thank you very much." "Thank you very much," replies his friend, who has passed the pitcher. "How are you this evening?" "I am very well," shouts the roly-poly boy. "How are you this morning?" "I have no idea. Please how is your sister?" "I haven't a clue. Please to pass the meatball. Thank you very much." "Thank you very much."

Some of these kids once lived on the street, cried for food, tried to keep alive younger siblings and had few prospects of surviving to adulthood without their birth parents. They now enjoy fantasies that they will wear Walkmans and ride bicycles when they live in America. When asked by the adults in their lives, "What do you want to be when you grow up?" no one replies, "I didn't actually realize I was going to grow up," though some must think it. Instead, these boys and girls have learned to reply "doctor," "teacher," "scientist." "I want to drive a car," says a 6-year-old girl named Bethlehem; whether professionally or at her leisure, she doesn't specify. "I will be an actor!" cries a boy, "an actor like Jackie Chan." "I want to ride motorcycles!" shouts another boy. "When I grow up, I want to help the elderly people," says a merry dimpled 13-year-old girl, Mekdes, cognizant, like many of the young teens, that she is on the receiving end of charity and eager, herself, to be of service.

"I wasn't at all sure what the response of American families would be to our opening an Ethiopian adoption program," says Merrily Ripley, director of Adoption Advocates International. Her agency places children from Haiti, China and Thailand with American adoptive families and assists with a program focusing on children orphaned in Sierra Leone. She flies to Ethiopia nearly every other month and occasionally indulges the little girls who beg to fix her long, straight gray hair. On this day, she looks like a cross between someone's hippie grandmother and Bo Derek in *10*, with skinny beaded braids dangling over her shoulders. "Would we be able to find families for African children? Would we be able to manage a children's home half a world away? We never dreamed that Ethiopia would become our most popular program."

While a couple of the older children have arrived with psychological challenges based on early loss of mother or other relative, the majority began their lives in families as breast-fed, tickled, treasured children. They are like kids in any backyard or school playground in America. Though a round-roofed straw hut in Gondar, Ethiopia, may seem impossibly different from a suburban home outside Cleveland or San Francisco, it is not. Children who have known the love of parents are eager to enjoy it again, and their adjustment to American family life has been rapid.

No one grieves openly at Layla House except frightened newcomers. One day, it was 4-year-old Isak, an only child whose father died a year earlier and whose mother died just three months before. A kind neighbor walked Isak to the local authorities, who notified the Children's Commission, which placed him here. His head freshly shaved, Isak sat alone on a low curb at the far edge of the playground, mute with homesickness and embarrassment and misery. His round dark eyes looked too big for his bald head; his head looked too big for his body. Although he knew his mother was dead, he couldn't help looking up briefly at every adult, just in case, but the particle of hope in his eyes was nearly extinguished.

On his first night in the boys' dorm room, he shied back from the four sets of white metal bunk beds, but big boys were kind to him; Haptamu and Frew showed Isak that they slept within arm's reach. When he yelped in the night, one of the two sleepily murmured a word of comfort.

Within two weeks, Isak found his niche in the community of children. He made a long detour around the rough playground football game and shyly volunteered, instead, to partake in the traditional Ethiopian coffee ceremony arranged by little girls under the vines, with a wood plank for a table and used bottle caps as cups. His soft curly hair began to grow out; his haunted look softened; and his photograph was privately circulated by Adoption Advocates International to prospective adoptive families who had signed up with the agency.

Every child on the premises can recite which children have adoptive families waiting for them in America and which children are still hoping to be matched with a family. The assigned children have in their possession small photograph albums full of nearly unbelievable images: big grinning adults—white or African-American—standing on green lawns in front of pretty houses and happy children playing on swing sets, sitting astride ponies, wearing goggles and leaping off diving boards or appearing in hooded parkas and mittens pulling sleds up snowy hills. The orphans turn the plastic-covered pages of their photo albums slowly, trying to make sense of each image. These have to be fairy tales! Yet the owner of each album has been told it is his or her destiny to leap into these scenes.

"I think America has all things in her hands," says the boy who wants to be Jackie Chan. "Everyone is hoping to be chosen by American parents. When the children learn that they have parents, they tell from peoples to peoples their parents' names and their city."

Though still small, the number of Ethiopian children adopted by Americans has grown substantially in the last 10 years. "What families consistently tell us is how happy and well adjusted the children are, that they obviously had been well nurtured and that they are extremely intelligent," says Carter-Shotts of Americans for African Adoptions.

Some of the children from the countryside arrive in the United States with tribal markings or accidental scars from a cook fire or a goat's horn. Asrat, who is now 20 and was one of the early Ethiopian children to be adopted in this country, killed a lion when he was very young, using a stick from the fire in defense of his family compound. He proudly wore a ritual scar across one eyebrow, bestowed by his village of Welayta, which declared him a man. Within months after his referral to an adoption program, he was a fifth grader at a Seattle-area elementary school.

Samuel, a 7-year-old whose parents died of malaria, missed sleeping on his shelflike bed high under the roof of the family's round hut and listening to the rain scatter when it hit the corrugated metal. Shortly after he was adopted, he graciously asked his suburban mom if she would like him to butcher a cow for dinner.

Abebaw, 7, missed the doro wat—the chicken stew—of his homeland after he was adopted by an American family in South Korea. His mother, Anna, brought home chunks of cut-up chicken from the grocery.

"No, real chicken, you need," he protested.

"This *is* real chicken," she said.

"No, need real chicken. Ethiopia chicken."

"O.K., I give up. What is real chicken?"

"The kind you cut head off. Noisy one. Running around. Head off, but running. That Ethiopia chicken."

Yilkal, 10, was adopted by an African-American family in Katy, Texas. One-quarter of Adoption Advocates International's adoptive families for Ethiopian kids are African-American or Ethiopian-American. When Yilkal's mother, Naomi Talley, flew to Addis Ababa to meet him and take him home, her hosts all praised her beauty and said that her forebears must have come from Ethiopia. Once settled with his new father, mother, and younger sister into an upscale American house on a cul-de-sac, Yilkal revised his personal saga and told his new friends and teachers that the entire Talley family had just emigrated from Ethiopia. Naomi was startled when a local organization of African emigres left a welcome basket on the doorstep and an invitation to a picnic. "They'll know," she told her son, laughing. "I don't speak Amharic or any other African language."

"They won't know, Mama," he pleaded, looking at her adoringly.

Biruktawit and Mekdalawit, the little sisters with the eight older siblings, were referred by the Children's Commission to Adoption Advocates International and were adopted by Bob and Chris Little in Port Townsend, Washington. Chris, a petite blonde with a Peter Pan haircut, recently lingered at the doorway of the girls' bedroom and overheard Mekdalawit, now called Marta, loudly praying: "Thank you, God, for my mom. She's a good, good mom. She knows how to be a good mom. Even when I mad, she love me. Even when I sad, she love me. Even when I do bad thing, she love me. My mom, she so cute. My mom, she not ugly. But she ugly, I still love her. Even if she ugly, I love her. Even if she really ugly, I love her. And she love me, if she ugly. But she not; she cute. Thank you, thank you, God, for good and cute mom."

Meanwhile, the Children's Commission is referring orphans to both American-run orphanages in Addis, as well as to the city's other orphanages, foster homes and adoption programs. The referrals come to numbers far greater than can be housed by the existing institutions. Adoptive families are desperately sought, for each international program is like a finger in the dike, beyond which brims an inconceivably rising flood of orphaned, homeless, healthy children.

Last year, Helen, a shy and tiny 5-year-old with huge eyes and a high-pitched squeak of a voice, was handed a package on the orphanage playground telling her that she had been matched with an adoptive family in America. It was my husband and I who had prepared the presents while waiting for approval from the Ethiopian courts to bring Helen to America as our daughter. We have loved raising our children—four by birth and one by adoption; when we began to muse about adopting again, it seemed logical to think about Africa, described in newspapers as "a continent of orphans."

Hair ribbons, two pastel-colored plastic ponies with brushable hair, a photograph album, turquoise sunglasses and a pink T-shirt that said "Atlanta" spilled out of Helen's envelope that day, five months before I visited. An adoptive mother, at the orphanage to take home her child, delivered Helen's package and took pictures of the moment. So many kids shoved and grabbed to see Helen's photo album that it flew out of her grasp and traveled the length and breadth of the playground. Big boys called out approving comments to her. Though she couldn't get her book back, no one damaged it, and she contented herself with the ponies, allowing her best friend to brush one of them. Finally one of the big boys said, "Here, Helen," and gave the book back, and Helen tucked herself away on her lower bunk bed and examined the faces of white people who had labeled the pictures: "Your Big Sister," "Your Oldest Sister," "Your Brothers," "Our Dog," "Your Bedroom," "Your Father," "Your Mother." She looked at them with, and without, the turquoise sunglasses.

Helen's parents had lovingly reared their only child, taught her to read Amharic and English at age 4, planned for her future, and were separated from her by only illness and death. I learned of their devotion to her from friends of the family, who looked after Helen but were too old to adopt her. Before going to sleep on the night she received her package from America, Helen propped open her photo album on the bedside table to the page showing the new "Mommy and Daddy" arm in arm, laughing and dressed in fine clothes. She laid her head carefully on the pillow facing the picture and fell asleep looking at it. It became her bedtime ritual.

A few months later, I came to Ethiopia to meet Helen. She had been told I was planning to adopt her, though the completion of the process was still many months away. When I showed up at the orphanage for the first time, she was too shy and alarmed to look at me. I pulled bags of rocket balloons out of my purse—they blow up into long blimps, and when you release them, they zoom around and make embarrassing noises. The children began running wildly after them and screaming with laughter. I saw Helen watching us from across the playground, and for the first time in my presence, she laughed.

Although her hair was tightly, beautifully beaded and braided, she wore well-used boys' orphanage clothes. A driver I had hired, Selamneh, and I took her shopping at a children's store one evening, a boutique so small that most of its wares—toys and clothing—hung from hooks high up on the ceiling. Helen instantly took possession of the shop. She shrieked with happiness and quickly pointed out her desires: a pair of shiny red sandals, an electric guitar, a toy gun, a bicycle and a wedding dress. I said yes to the sandals, no to the rest, and pulled a different dress off the rack to show her. She turned her little nose up at it just like my children at home, who never appreciate my taste, and she selected her own dress, a complicated affair involving several layers and embroidered sheep.

She also bought pajamas, underwear, play clothes, and lacy socks with attached pink flowers. She opted to wear the socks to the apartment we stayed in during my visit. That night she scrubbed her new socks in the bathroom sink for half an hour, then hung them outside on the balcony to dry.

I opened a box of raisins one afternoon and handed her one. She examined it and ate it, and I ate one, too. Then I gave her the box of raisins to keep, and she zipped it into her new American backpack. A few nights later, she and I were dinner guests at the home of an Ethiopian family. Helen excused herself from dinner at one point, went to find her backpack, unzipped it, extracted the box of raisins, carefully opened it, and with great seriousness handed each person in the family one raisin before replacing the box. That's how they do it in America, she figured.

Last February, Merrily Ripley escorted Helen to the Atlanta airport, where my husband and I went to greet her and to take her home. She had memorized the photo album we had sent her and knew the names of the three older brothers, the two older sisters, and the dog. She was too shy to speak to anyone other than 9-year-old Lily, who was closest to her in age, to whom she whispered in Amharic. (Alas, Lily could not understand a word of it.) An Ethiopian friend in Atlanta visited every day to chat with Helen. "I feel happy," Helen told her in Amharic during that first week. And, "I forget the name of the tall brother." And, "I don't like cheese."

Seth, 17, was enormously tall to Helen, but on her third night in America, she snatched a sock off his foot and fled shrieking with it through the house. He gave chase. She ran past me at one point, her face flushed with excitement, threw me the sock to hide, and then ran up the stairs to escape. When Seth finally ambushed her and pried open her hands and searched her pockets, he discovered she didn't have the sock anymore and she cackled with laughter. The next morning, she tried his name aloud. "Tzetz!" she yelled, then dove under the kitchen table with stage fright.

She quickly adopted the American attitude that there is no problem technology cannot solve, including the fact that she didn't know how to swim. On repeated trips to the drugstore, she gathered essential items for weeks before the neighborhood pool opened, and on opening day, she emerged from the locker room encased in a foam life jacket, arm floaties and scuba-diving goggles, snorkle, and pink flippers. She flip-flopped to pool's edge and bravely dropped into the water. She wore so much equipment that she bobbed along the surface like a water bug, unable to submerge herself. Finally she pitched forward and dunked her head, so all that was visible was a tiny rear end moving across the pool like that of an upended duckling searching for fish underwater.

Another time, Helen showed up at my bedside in the middle of the night, saying, "I had a bad dream."

I opened the covers. "Come, lie here. Go back to sleep, and you'll have a good dream."

"How do you have a good dream?" she asked.

"Well, you think of a happy place, and then you'll dream about the happy place. When I was small, I used to imagine a little place in the forest where animals lived."

"Oh, O.K.!" she yelled. "I've got one! Guess!"

I so wanted to go back to sleep, but there seemed no way around it. "Is it the beach?"

"No!"

"The forest, with the little animals?"

"No!"

"Somewhere in Ethiopia?"

"No! . . . Can it be a store?"

"Helen!" I said, already knowing.

"It's Target!" she cried and snuggled down for a good sleep.

But it hasn't all been happiness. For at least an hour a day, for the first month after arrival, Helen was consumed by grief. We could see it coming on from a distance; we could see her trying to resist the approaching waves of sorrow. Finally they would overwhelm her, and she would begin to suck and suck and suck in air. Huge sobs and tears shook her, but she allowed us to try to comfort her. We would hold her, and she would wail with sadness.

Our Ethiopian friend translated for us that she was homesick for her friends at Layla House. Adoption Advocates International sponsors an annual reunion of Ethiopian kids adopted by American families. This summer, Helen was reunited with many of her pals from Addis, and I easily promised her that many more are coming to America and she will see them again.

But 8-year-old Eyob, the tap-dancing boy, was also her friend. They lived in the same orphanage for a while after losing their mothers, before blood tests separated them. "This is my friend," she says about Eyob's photo, laughing to remember how funny he is. But Eyob is H.I.V. positive and living at Enat, and Enat has no drugs. I can't promise my daughter that she will see Eyob again since he, like so many others, has been left to die.

One day not long ago, she collapsed in my arms to cry about her late mother. I held her as she writhed, wailing,

"Why she had to die?" A few moments later, she said, amid tears: "I know why she died. Because she was very sick and we didn't have the medicine."

"I know," I said. "It's true. I'm so sorry. I wish I had known you then. I wish I could have sent her the medicine."

"But we didn't have a phone," she cried, "and I couldn't call you."

Helen has made lots of friends in America and loves to chat, in fluent English, with all her new neighbors and classmates. I always hear her ask, near the start of every play date, "Do you have a mother?" If she is feeling shy, she will whisper to me, "Does she have a mother?" Most children and adults are surprised by the question—"Of course I have a mother!" they reply—but African friends are not surprised. Helen has a mother again now, too, as she is eager to tell, but she doesn't take it as a given about anyone.

FACTS

Number of new doctors sub-Saharan Africa would need for its per-capita number to match America's: 3,900,000
(Joint Learning Initiative/*Harper's* research)

Number of new doctors produced by sub-Saharan Africa's universities each year: 4,000
(World Health Organization)

BULLSHIT

with facts

True stories comfort, inform, connect, and instruct us; lies harm our culture, our society, and our civilization. The corporations and corrupt politicians who own and regulate the media lie to us to protect their power. Their control of the media at the start of the twenty-first century is so powerful that the truth is reduced to a whisper. Listen for it, and pass it on.

FACTS

Number of preteen "secret agents" in the Girls Intelligence Agency, a market research firm: 16,000
(Girls Intelligence Agency)

Amount a Nebraska man made this year by auctioning his forehead to advertisers: $37,375
(SnoreStop)

Number of American five-year-olds named Lexus: 353
(Cleveland Evans, Bellevue University)

The Media's Labor Day Revolution

from tompaine.com (9/6/05)

Russ Baker

The magnitude of the Hurricane Katrina disaster and the media's astonished—and astonishingly vigorous—response puts in perspective how hard it has generally become, in this country, to deliver the unadorned, unapologetic truth. Indeed, for at least as long as George Bush has been in office, the great unspoken challenge for mainstream journalists has been to do one's job while keeping one's job.

As the Bush organization has flipped one lever after

another of a vast and well-fueled propaganda machine, it has become ever more difficult for reporters to render useful, accurate information to the public without neutering it in the cop-out "on the one hand, on the other" format. Constant pressure from the White House is one challenge. Another is from corporate bosses who must produce untenable profit growth while maintaining friendly relations with the federal government.

One of the most tricky work environments surely must be the Fox News Network, Rupert Murdoch's vehicle for dispensing highly opinionated, fact-light "news" in the guise of helping provide Americans with "Fair and Balanced" journalism. And so it was with a sense of wonder that I viewed a clip of an exchange between two of Fox's stars, Shepard Smith and Geraldo Rivera, and hard-core propagandist talk show host Sean Hannity, who had morphed into the role of anchorman for a "Fox News Alert".

Smith, Fox's principal news anchor, and Rivera, its high-priced celebrity gunslinger, reported in from the scene of devastation in New Orleans. Smith and Rivera, both usually loyal to Fox's rigidly pro-administration line, yell, cry (Geraldo), and generally register disgust as Hannity seeks to gild the Bush administration's glacial response to the crisis. Here are a few choice excerpts:

> SMITH: They won't let them walk out of the . . . convention center . . . they've locked them in there. The government said, "You go here, and you'll get help," or, "You go in that Superdome and you'll get help."
>
> And they didn't get help. They got locked in there. And they watched people being killed around

> them. And they watched people starving. And they watched elderly people not get any medicine. . . .
>
> And they've set up a checkpoint. And anyone who walks up out of that city now is turned around. You are not allowed to go to Gretna, Louisiana, from New Orleans, Louisiana. Over there, there's hope. Over there, there's electricity. Over there, there is food and water. But you cannot go from there to there. The government will not allow you to do it. It's a fact.
>
> HANNITY: All right, Shep, I want to get some perspective here, because earlier today . . .
>
> SMITH: That is perspective! That is all the perspective you need!

Soon, Hannity switches to Geraldo, where he finds no relief:

> RIVERA (holding aloft a baby): Sean . . . I want everyone in the world to see, six days after Katrina swept through this city, five days after the levee collapsed, this baby—this baby—how old is this baby?
>
> UNIDENTIFIED FEMALE: Ten months old. . . .
>
> RIVERA: Look in the face of the baby. This is it. This is it. No sugar coating, no political spin, no Republicans or Democrats. People suffering.
>
> Let them go. Let them out of here. Let them go.

> Let them walk over this damn interstate, and let them out of here.
>
> HANNITY: All right. Thanks, Geraldo. Appreciate it. We appreciate—and from New Orleans tonight.

For once, Hannity was nearly speechless. His mandate—and preferences—were clear: Keep Fox's viewers, Bush's vaunted base, steady, until the administration spin machine could be shoved on top of the volatile events that threatened to expose the horrible truth about the priorities and competencies of this White House after an unprecedented, years-long free ride.

When Fox reporters are the most emphatically critical of the Bush administration, you know something is going on. Had Roger Ailes decided that it was simply impossible to ride out this storm with Bush? What of the defections of the *New York Times'* conservative columnist David Brooks and others in recent days? Perhaps they figure that this is simply too enormous a screw-up to defend, and hope that by joining the ranks of the indignant they may escape a sinking ship. Or, maybe, maybe, even they have finally had enough.

Another remarkable breakthrough came Sunday, on *Meet the Press*, Tim Russert freshened his typical beltway bonhomie mix with a "real" person, Jefferson Parish President (i.e., county manager) Aaron Broussard. His guest, who, by the way, is white, delivered a startlingly blunt indictment of the federal response to the death and destruction facing the largely poor, black population that had been unable to get out.

> BROUSSARD: [T]he aftermath of Hurricane Katrina

will go down as one of the worst abandonments of Americans on American soil ever in U.S. history. . . . Why did it happen? Who needs to be fired? And believe me, they need to be fired right away, because we still have weeks to go in this tragedy. We have months to go. We have years to go. And whoever is at the top of this totem pole, that totem pole needs to be chain-sawed off and we've got to start with some new leadership.

RUSSERT: Shouldn't the mayor of New Orleans and the governor of New Orleans bear some responsibility?

BROUSSARD: Sir, they were told like me, every single day, "The cavalry's coming," on a federal level, "The cavalry's coming, the cavalry's coming, the cavalry's coming." I have just begun to hear the hoofs of the cavalry. The cavalry's still not here yet, but I've begun to hear the hoofs, and we're almost a week out.

. . . We had Wal-Mart deliver three trucks of water, trailer trucks of water. FEMA turned them back. They said we didn't need them. This was a week ago. . . . We had 1,000 gallons of diesel fuel on a Coast Guard vessel docked in my parish. The Coast Guard said, "Come get the fuel right away." When we got there with our trucks, they got a word. "FEMA says don't give you the fuel." Yesterday—yesterday—FEMA comes in and cuts all of our emergency communication lines. They cut them without notice. . . .

. . . The guy who runs . . . emergency management

> . . . His mother was trapped in St. Bernard nursing home and every day she called him and said, "Are you coming, son? Is somebody coming?" And he said, "Yeah, Mama, somebody's coming to get you. Somebody's coming to get you on Tuesday. Somebody's coming to get you on Wednesday. Somebody's coming to get you on Thursday. Somebody's coming to get you on Friday." And she drowned Friday night. [Broussard was sobbing at this point]
>
> . . . Nobody's coming to get us. Nobody's coming to get us. The secretary has promised. Everybody's promised. They've had press conferences. I'm sick of the press conferences. For God sakes, shut up and send us somebody.
>
> RUSSERT: Just take a pause, Mr. [Broussard]. While you gather yourself in your very emotional times, I understand, let me go to Governor Haley Barbour of Mississippi.

And there we were, back in the bad old days. Russert had no tasteful way to note that Barbour had been GOP chairman in the mid-90s, a key strategist and fundraiser for the transformation of American government into a one-party state for the interests of the rich, and the dismantlement of the safety net, that, among other things, is supposed to protect all Americans from the most extreme ravages of natural disaster and daily life alike. Or to ask hard questions about Barbour's avid support for Bush's Iraqi war, and its unusual overseas deployment of National Guard units that properly should have been in place in the Gulf region to provide relief and order in case of emergency. It's hard to point this out when you work for NBC, a unit of General Electric, a huge defense contractor that has been one of the biggest beneficiaries of Bush administration priorities and policy.

Fixing journalism's deep structural deficiencies will take more than the Labor Day Revolt. Getting it right means more than expressing momentary indignation, however heartfelt, or reporting on the current crisis as if the important thing was how the disaster is affecting the administration's "approval" rating. Because it's not the administration's spin with which we need to concern ourselves. It is the media's long, long sleep in the face of mounting evidence that Bush and his team are not only ideologues seriously out of touch with the American public but grievously incompetent managers of the nation's commitments, resources and people.

As we take stock of the true costs of the failures surrounding Katrina, journalists should note their own role as collaborators. We, too, have been complicit in this.

FACTS

Number of full-time reporters for ESPN covering only Barry Bonds as of May 2005: 1
(ESPN, Inc.)

Number of U.S. newspapers at that time with a full-time reporter in Afghanistan: 2
(*Harper's* research)

Desperately Seeking Disclosure

from PR Watch (2Q 2005)

Dianne Farsetta

In some ways, Armstrong Williams got a bad rap. The conservative commentator, who was paid by the U.S. Department of Education to advertise and advocate for the controversial "No Child Left Behind" law, lost his syndicated newspaper column and was pilloried for not disclosing the payment.

Williams did betray the public trust, but he was a small fry—a subcontractor receiving a $240,000 piece of a $1 million deal between the Education Department and Ketchum, one of the world's largest public relations firms.

That deal, it turns out, was just the tip of the iceberg.

Ketchum is the number one recipient of recent U.S. government PR spending, with contracts totaling more than $100 million. Since 1997, nine PR firms have received at least $1 million in public funds in a single year. The Bush administration doubled federal PR spending over its first term, relative to the last term of the Clinton administration, to $250 million.

That's according to a January 2005 report by the House Committee on Government Reform, which examined federal procurement records going back eight years, looking for contracts with major PR firms. The Committee launched its investigation following two more "pundit payola" revelations in addition to Williams, and rulings by the Government Accountability Office, Congress' nonpartisan investigative arm, that fake television news segments (called video news releases or VNRs) produced for two government agencies were illegal "covert propaganda."

Yet there is little information about how these millions of dollars were—or are—spent. Despite evidence that public funds have been misused, the details of government contracts with PR firms remain hidden.

The ethics code of the Public Relations Society of America (PRSA), the largest PR trade organization, includes admonitions "to build trust with the public by revealing all information needed for responsible decision making," to "be honest and accurate," to "reveal the sponsors for causes and interests represented," and to "avoid deceptive practices." But, as readers of *PR Watch* know, ethics codes are often ignored.

When *PR Watch* asked the nine PR firms in the million-dollar league for information on their government work, responses ranged from cautious answers to deafening silence. None of the firms was willing to share any information not already publicly available—including contract agreements or "deliverables" like studies, brochures, and VNRs—to clarify what they did with taxpayers' money.

The million-dollar league PR firms are listed below, from the largest to the smallest recipient of federal funds since 1997, along with what PR Watch was able to uncover about their government work.

Ketchum

Ketchum has received a whopping $100.5 million in federal contracts. These include work for the Education Department; Internal Revenue Service; U.S. Army, to "reconnect the Army with the American people" and boost recruiting around its 225th birthday; and the Health and Human Services Department, to "change the face of Medicare," promote long-term health care planning, encourage preventative care, and present home care information. Large contract increases for Ketchum since 2003 mirror the Centers for Medicare and Medicaid Services' PR spending boost, suggesting that Ketchum's Medicare work may be more extensive than is currently known.

Apart from the Armstrong Williams scandal, the firm also produced a controversial VNR for the Education Department, promoting tutoring programs under "No Child Left Behind." The fake news segment featured then-Education Secretary Rod Paige and was narrated by PR flack Karen Ryan, who misrepresented herself as a reporter.

Ketchum representatives did not return repeated phone calls—making them among the least responsive firms contacted by *PR Watch*.

Fleishman-Hillard

The recipient of $77 million in federal funds, Fleishman-Hillard has worked for the Social Security Administration; Library of Congress; Environmental Protection Agency; and Defense Department, to introduce "managed care" to employees, due to "rising medical costs" and "decreasing resources." While Fleishman-Hillard also did not return phone calls, its application for PRSA's prestigious Silver Anvil Award noted that the main challenge of its Defense contract was "the anger and frustration of the retired military community who were now required to pay an annual fee for guaranteed access to health care they said was promised them by their recruiter as a free lifetime benefit."

The firm has also worked for the White House Office of

National Drug Control Policy (ONDCP), to "debunk the misconception that marijuana was harmless." For this contract, Fleishman-Hillard produced VNRs later ruled to be covert propaganda, because ONDCP "did not identify itself to the viewing audience as the producer and distributor of these prepackaged news stories."

In November 2004, Los Angeles' city controller accused Fleishman-Hillard of overbilling the city's Water and Power Department by $4.2 million. Several former employees said they were told to inflate the hours billed to the city. One described the firm's attitude as, "Get as much as you can because these accounts may dry up tomorrow." In April 2005, the firm settled with the city, agreeing to pay $4.5 million and waive $1.3 million in outstanding invoices.

Matthews Media Group

Matthews Media has received $67.9 million, most or all of which is for Health and Human Services Department contracts. The firm has worked for the National Cancer Institute, to analyze newspaper coverage of tobacco issues; and National Institutes of Health, to assist with "patient recruitment strategies."

Porter-Novelli

Porter-Novelli's government contracts total $59.3 million, also for Health and Human Services agencies. The firm has worked for the National Institutes of Health; National Institute of Mental Health; and Centers for Disease Control and Prevention, to carry out an "annual mail survey . . . that examines health-related attitudes and behaviors."

Equals Three Communications

Equals Three has won $23.8 million in federal contracts, including with the National Institutes of Health, on Colorectal Cancer Awareness Month; National Institute for Mental Health; and National Highway Traffic Safety Administration.

Vice-President of PR Kimberly Marr complained (a week after *PR Watch*'s first phone call) about "the extensive nature of your questions and the short timeline." She added, "Everything . . . is in the public domain."

What "public domain" she referred to is unclear, however, since searches of the Nexis news database, PR trade publications, and the Internet revealed little about Equals Three's federal work. Indeed, the firm's penchant for secrecy is so great that materials posted on its website are sized and cropped in such a way that it's difficult to determine who they were produced for.

Hill & Knowlton

Hill & Knowlton has collected $19.2 million in federal funds. Director of Business Development and Marketing Lily Loh refused to answer *PR Watch*'s questions, claiming they entailed "proprietary information that we cannot share due to client confidentiality," although some work is "available in the public record." Searches revealed just one contract with the General Services Administration, for work on the "Dedication of the Ronald Reagan Building and International Trade Center" in Washington, DC.

Hill & Knowlton's other government work could be well worth hiding. The firm is best known for pushing the first Gulf War on behalf of the Kuwaiti government; flacking for Indonesia during its brutal occupation of neighboring East Timor; helping organize the industry-funded Council for Tobacco Research, to downplay the dangers of smoking; and handling damage control for Wal-Mart in California.

Widmeyer Communications

Widmeyer has received $7.4 million in contracts from the Selective Service System; Federal Trade Commission; Health and Human Services Department, for its National Bullying Prevention Campaign; Education Department; National Institute for Literacy; Farm Service Agency; and Defense Department, for their Deployment Health Clinical Center.

Assistant Vice-President Scott Ward said that Widmeyer "never uses paid third-party spokespeople," and that the firm produces video footage, but not ready-to-air VNRs, for government clients.

Burson-Marsteller

Burson-Marsteller's federal contracts total $1.9 million, for work with agencies including the Census Bureau, on participation rates; Bureau of Engraving and Printing, on the $20 bill redesign; Treasury Department, on money laundering enforcement; and Postal Service, on "Managing Communication During the Anthrax Crisis."

The firm produces VNRs for government clients, according to global public affairs chief Richard Mintz. Mintz said the firm clearly labels its VNRs, but viewers don't see these labels. He added that Burson-Marsteller has not used paid spokespeople, "per se," but has signed contracts with third parties, such as senior and minority groups, to reach target populations.

Burson-Marsteller has a less than stellar track record in its corporate work, which includes directing "crisis communications" on mad cow disease for McDonald's and the National Cattlemen's Beef Association; running the front group "European Women for HPV Testing" for the U.S. biotechnology company Digene; creating the "National Smokers Alliance" for Philip Morris, to combat smoking restrictions; and infiltrating activist groups opposing the milk hormone BGH, for the companies developing the drug.

Ogilvy PR Worldwide

Ogilvy PR has received $1.6 million in federal funds, for work with ONDCP, on their National Youth Anti-Drug Media Campaign; and the National Heart, Lung, and Blood Institute (NHLBI), on the "Fashionable Red Alert" campaign, to raise awareness of heart disease among women. In April 2005, NHLBI renewed its contract with Ogilvy for another three years, at a cost of $4.9 million.

In February 2005, two former executives of the related marketing firm Ogilvy & Mather were found guilty of conspiracy and false claims, for inflating labor costs on the ONDCP account. According to the indictment, the executives "directed certain Ogilvy employees to revise time sheets and caused falsified time sheets to be submitted to the government."

In March 2005, the Homeland Security Department hired Ogilvy, "to provide real journalists for its biennial mock terrorist exercise." The director of the Project for Excellence in Journalism said the exercise "raises potential future conflicts even if the reporter doesn't now cover the governmental entity writing the check."

Oglivy is among the firms that did not respond to *PR Watch*'s repeated calls.

These PR firms' secrecy about publicly-funded campaigns indicates a serious lack of accountability. More alarming is the federal government's reluctance—even refusal, in many cases—to provide information on its contracts with PR firms. For example, documents on Ketchum's work for the Education Department obtained through Freedom of Information Act requests have every dollar amount redacted.

As the House Committee on Government Reform's report noted, "Not all government PR contracts are problematic," but they must be "authorized by Congress and conducted in a fashion that does not mislead the public." If, as Burson-Marsteller's Richard Mintz claims, the "public education campaigns" PR firms undertake for the U.S. government are "essential," why not release information about them? It's a question Americans must ask of their public officials, and one that PR firms must answer to combat their own image problem.

FACT

Minimum amount the Pentagon paid PR firm The Lincoln Group for services that included planting stories favorable to the U.S. occupation in Iraqi media: $20 million

(*Los Angeles Times*, 12/18/05)

FACTS

Average amount the Bush Administration has spent per year on contracts with PR firms: $62,500,000
(Committee on Government Reform, U.S. House of Representatives)

Average amount spent during the second term of the Clinton Administration: $32,000,000
(Committee on Government Reform)

Amount the Department of Homeland Security will spend this year directing research at U.S. universities: $45,000,000
(U.S. Department of Homeland Security)

Number of states where women seeking abortions are required to be told that abortion increases the risk of breast cancer: 3
(Planned Parenthood Federation of America)

Number of the eighty-nine experts convened in 2003 by the National Cancer Institute who found any evidence of such a link: 1
(National Cancer Institute)

What Are You Going to Do with That?

from *The New York Review of Books* (6/23/05)

Mark Danner

[The following is based on the commencement address given to the graduating students of the Department of English of the University of California at Berkeley in the Hearst Greek Theatre, May 15, 2005.]

When I was invited to give this speech, I was asked for a title. I dillied and dallied, begged for more time, and of course the deadline passed. The title I really wanted to suggest was the response that all of you have learned to expect when asked your major: What are you going to do with that? To be an English major is to live not only by questioning, but by being questioned. It is to live with a question mark placed squarely on your forehead. It is to live, at least some of the time, in a state of "existential dread." To be a humanist, that is, means not only to see clearly the surface of things and to see beyond those surfaces, but to place oneself in opposition, however subtle, an opposition that society seldom lets you forget: What are you going to do with *that*?

To the recent graduate, American society—in all its vulgar, grotesque power—reverberates with that question. It comes from friends, from relatives, and perhaps even from the odd parent here and there. For the son or daughter who becomes an English major puts a finger squarely on the great parental paradox: you raise your children to make their own decisions, you want your children to make their own decisions—and then one day, by heaven, they *make* their own decisions. And now parents are doomed to confront daily the condescending sympathy of your friends—*their* children, of course, are economics majors or engineering majors or pre-meds—and to confront your own dread about the futures of your children.

It's not easy to be an English major these days, or any student of the humanities. It requires a certain kind of determination, and a refusal—an annoying refusal, for some of our friends and families, and for a good many employers—to make decisions, or at least to make the kind of "practical decisions" that much of society demands of us. It represents a determination, that is, not only to do certain things—to read certain books and learn certain poems, to acquire or refine a certain cast of mind—but not to do other things: principally, not to decide, right now, quickly, how you will earn your living; which is to say, not to decide how you will justify your existence. For in the view of a large part of American society, the existential question is at the bottom an economic one: Who are you and what is your economic justification for being?

English majors, and other determined humanists, distinguish themselves not only by reading Shakespeare or Chaucer or Joyce or Woolf or Zora Neale Hurston but by refusing, in the face of overwhelming pressure, to answer that question. Whether they acknowledge it or not—whether they *know* it or not—and whatever they eventually decide to do with "that," they see developing the moral imagination as more important than securing economic self-justification.

Such an attitude has never been particularly popular in this country. It became downright suspect after September

11, 2001—and you of course are the Class of September 11, having arrived here only days before those attacks and the changed world they ushered in. Which means that, whether you know it or not, by declaring yourselves as questioners, as humanists, you already have gone some way in defining yourselves, for good or ill, as outsiders.

I must confess it: I, too, was an English major . . . for nineteen days. This was back in the Berkeley of the East, at Harvard College, and I was a refugee from philosophy—too much logic and math in that for me, too practical—and I tarried in English just long enough to sit in on one tutorial (on Keats's "To Autumn"), before I fled into my own major, one I conceived and designed myself, called, with even greater practical attention to the future, "Modern Literature and Aesthetics."

Which meant of course that almost exactly twenty-five years ago today I was sitting where you are now, hanging on by a very thin thread. Shortly thereafter I found myself lying on my back in a small apartment in Cambridge, Massachusetts, reading the *New York Times* and the *New York Review*—very thoroughly: essentially spending all day, every day, lying on my back, reading, living on graduation-present money and subsisting on deliveries of fried rice from the Hong Kong restaurant (which happened to be two doors away—though I felt I was unable to spare the time to leave the apartment, or the bed, to pick it up). The Chinese food deliveryman looked at me dispassionately and then, as one month stretched into two, a bit knowingly. If I knew then what I know now I would say I was depressed. At the time, however, I was under the impression that I was resting.

Eventually I became a writer, which is not a way to vanquish existential dread but a way to live with it and even to earn a modest living from it. Perhaps some of you will follow that path; but whatever you decide to "do with that," remember: whether you know it yet or not, you have doomed yourselves by learning how to read, learning how to question, learning how to doubt. And this is a most difficult time—the most difficult I remember—to have those skills. Once you have them, however, they are not easy to discard. Finding yourself forced to see the gulf between what you are told about the world, whether it's your government doing the telling, or your boss, or even your family or friends, and what you yourself can't help but understand about that world—this is not always a welcome kind of vision to have. It can be burdensome and awkward and it won't always make you happy.

I think I became a writer in part because I found that yawning difference between what I was told and what I could see to be inescapable. I started by writing about wars and massacres and violence. The State Department, as I learned from a foreign service officer in Haiti, has a technical term for the countries I mostly write about: the TFC beat. TFC—in official State Department parlance—stands for "Totally ######-up Countries." After two decades of this, of Salvador and Haiti and Bosnia and Iraq, my mother—who already had to cope with the anxiety of a son acquiring a very expensive education in "Modern Literature and Aesthetics"—still asks periodically: Can't you go someplace nice for a change?

When I was sitting where you are sitting now the issue was Central America and in particular the war in El Salvador. America, in the backwash of defeat in Vietnam, was trying to protect its allies to the south—to protect regimes under assault by leftist insurgencies—and it was doing so by supporting a government in El Salvador that was fighting the war by massacring its own people. I wrote about one of those events in my first book, The Massacre at El Mozote, which told of the murder of a thousand or so civilians by a new, elite battalion of the Salvadoran army—a battalion that the Americans had trained. A thousand innocent civilians dead in a few hours, by machete and by M-16.

Looking back at that story now—and at many of the other stories I have covered over the years, from Central America to Iraq—I see now that in part I was trying to find a kind of moral clarity: a place, if you will, where that gulf that I spoke about, between what we see and what is said, didn't exist. Where better to find that place than in the world where massacres and killings and torture happen, in the place, that is, where we find evil. What could be clearer than that kind of evil?

But I discovered it was not clear at all. Chat with a Salvadoran general about the massacre of a thousand people that he ordered and he will tell you that it was military necessity, that those people had put themselves in harm's way by supporting the guerrillas, and that "such things happen in war." Speak to the young conscript who wielded the machete and he will tell you that he hated what he had to do, that he has nightmares about it still, but that he was following orders and that if he had refused he would have been killed. Talk to the State Department official who helped deny that the massacre took place and he will tell you that there was no definitive proof and, in any case, that he did it to protect and promote the vital interests of the United States. None of them is lying. I found that if you search for evil, once you leave the corpses behind you will have great difficulty finding the needed grimacing face.

Let me give you another example. It's from 1994, during an unseasonably warm February day in a crowded market in the besieged city of Sarajevo. I was with a television crew—I was writing a documentary on the war in Bosnia for Peter Jennings at ABC News—but our schedule had slipped, as it always does, and we had not yet arrived at the crowded marketplace when a mortar shell landed. When we arrived with our cameras a few moments later, we found a dark swamp of blood and broken bodies and, staggering about in it, the bereaved, shrieking and wailing amid a sickening stench of cordite. Two men, standing in rubber boots knee-deep in a thick black lake, had already begun to toss body parts into the back of a truck. Slipping about on the wet pavement, I tried my best to count the bodies and the parts of them, but the job was impossible: fifty? sixty? When all the painstaking matching had been done, sixty-eight had died there.

As it happened, I had a lunch date with their killer the following day. The leader of the Serbs, surrounded in his mountain villa by a handful of good-looking bodyguards, had little interest in the numbers of dead. We were eating stew. "Did you check their ears?" he asked. I'm sorry? "They had ice in their ears." I paused at this and worked on my stew. He meant, I realized, that the bodies were corpses from the morgue that had been planted, that the entire scene had been trumped up by Bosnian intelligence agents. He was a psychiatrist, this man, and it seemed to me, after a few minutes of discussion, that he had gone far to convince himself of the truth of this claim. I was writing a profile of him and he of course did not want to talk about bodies or death. He preferred to speak of his vision for the nation.

For me, the problem in depicting this man was simple: the level of his crimes dwarfed the interest of his character. His motivations were paltry, in no way commensurate with the pain he had caused. It is often a problem with evil and that is why, in my experience, talking with mass murderers is invariably a disappointment. Great acts of evil so rarely call forth powerful character that the relation between the two seems nearly random. Put another way, that relation is not defined by melodrama, as popular fiction would have it. To understand this mass murderer, you need Dostoevsky, or Conrad.

Let me move closer to our own time, because you are the Class of September 11, and we do not lack for examples. Never in my experience has frank mendacity so dominated our public life. This has to do less with ideology itself, I think, than the fact that our country was attacked and that —from the Palmer Raids after World War I, to the internment of Japanese-Americans during World War II, to the McCarthyite witch-hunts during the Fifties—America tends to respond to such attacks, or the threat of them, in predictably paranoid ways. Notably, by "rounding up the usual suspects" and by dividing the world, dramatically and hysterically, into a good part and an evil part. September 11 was no exception to this: indeed, in its wake—coterminous with your time here—we have seen this American tendency in its purest form.

One welcome distinction between the times we live in

and those other periods I have mentioned is the relative frankness of our government officials—I should call it unprecedented frankness—in explaining how they conceive the relationship of power and truth. Our officials believe that power can determine truth, as an unnamed senior adviser to the President explained to a reporter last fall:

> We're an empire now, and when we act, we create our own reality. And while you're studying that reality—judiciously, as you will—we'll act again, creating other new realities, which you can study too, and that's how things will sort out.

The reporter, the adviser said, was a member of what he called "the reality-based community," destined to "judiciously study" the reality the administration was creating. Now it is important that we realize—and by "we" I mean all of us members of the "reality-based community"—that our leaders of the moment really do believe this, as anyone knows who has spent much time studying September 11 and the Iraq war and the various scandals that have sprung from those events—the "weapons of mass destruction" scandal and the Abu Ghraib scandal, to name only two.

What is interesting about both of those is that the heart of the scandal, the wrongdoing, is right out in front of us. Virtually nothing of great importance remains to be revealed. Ever since Watergate we've had a fairly established narrative of scandal. First you have revelation: the press, usually with the help of various leakers within the government, reveals the wrongdoing. Then you have investigation, when the government—the courts, or Congress, or, as with Watergate, both—constructs a painstaking narrative of what exactly happened: an official story, one that society—that the community—can agree on. Then you have expiation, when the judges hand down sentences, the evildoers are punished, and the society returns to a state of grace.

What distinguishes our time—the time of September 11—is the end of this narrative of scandal. With the scandals over weapons of mass destruction and Abu Ghraib, we are stuck at step one. We have had the revelation; we know about the wrongdoing. Just recently, in the Downing Street memo, we had an account of a high-level discussion in Britain, nearly eight months before the Iraq war, in which the head of British intelligence flatly tells the prime minister—the intelligence officer has just returned from Washington—that not only has the President of the United States decided that "military action was . . . inevitable" but that—in the words of the British intelligence chief—"the intelligence and facts were being fixed around the policy." This memo has been public for weeks.

So we have had the revelations; we know what happened. What we don't have is any clear admission of—or adjudication of—guilt, such as a serious congressional or judicial investigation would give us, or any punishment. Those high officials responsible are still in office. Indeed, not only have they received no punishment; many have been promoted. And we—you and I, members all of the reality-based community—we are left to see, to be forced to see. And this, for all of us, is a corrupting, a maddening, but also an inescapable burden.

Let me give you a last example. The example is in the form of a little play: a reality-based playlet that comes to us from the current center of American comedy. I mean the Pentagon press briefing room, where the real true-life comedies are performed. The time is a number of weeks ago. The dramatis personae are Secretary of Defense Donald Rumsfeld; Vice Chairman of the Joint Chiefs (and soon to be promoted) General Peter Pace of the Marine Corps; and of course, playing the Fool, a lowly and hapless reporter.

The reporter's question begins with an involved but perfectly well-sourced discussion of Abu Ghraib and the fact that all the reports suggest that something systematic—something ordered by higher-ups—was going on there. He mentions the Sanchez memo, recently released, in which the commanding general in Iraq at the time, Lieutenant General Ricardo Sanchez, approved twelve interrogation techniques that, as the reporter says, "far exceed limits established by the Army's own field manual." These include prolonged stress positions, sensory deprivation (or "hooding"), the use of dogs "to induce stress," and so on; the reporter also mentions extraordinary "rendition" (better known as kidnapping, in which people are snatched off the streets by U.S. intelligence agents and brought to third countries like Syria and Egypt to be tortured). Here's his question, and the officials' answer:

> Hapless Reporter: And I wonder if you would just respond to the suggestion that there is a systematic problem rather than the kinds of individual abuses we've heard of before.
>
> Secretary Rumsfeld: I don't believe there's been a single one of the investigations that have been conducted, which has got to be six, seven, eight, or nine—

> General Pace: Ten major reviews and 300 individual investigations of one kind or another.
>
> Secretary Rumsfeld: And have you seen one that characterized it as systematic or systemic?
>
> General Pace: No, sir.
>
> Rumsfeld: I haven't either.
>
> Hapless Reporter: What about—?
>
> Rumsfeld: Question?
>
> [*Laughter*]

And, as the other reporters laughed, Secretary Rumsfeld did indeed ignore the attempt to follow up, and went on to the next question.

But what did the hapless reporter want to say? All we have is his truncated attempt at a question: "What about?" We will never know, of course. Perhaps he wanted to read from the very first Abu Ghraib report, directed by US Army Major General Antonio Taguba, who wrote in his conclusion

> that between October and December 2003, at the Abu Ghraib Confinement Facility, numerous incidents of sadistic, blatant, and wanton criminal abuses were inflicted. . . . This *systemic* and illegal abuse was intentionally perpetrated. . . . [Emphasis added.]

Or perhaps this from the Red Cross report, which is the only contemporaneous account of what was going on at Abu Ghraib, recorded by witnesses at the time:

> These methods of physical and psychological coercion were used by the military intelligence in a *systematic* way to gain confessions and extract information or other forms of co-operation from persons who had been arrested in connection with suspected security offenses or deemed to have an 'intelligence value.' [Emphasis added.]

(I should note here, by the way, that the military itself estimated that between 85 and 90 percent of the prisoners at Abu Ghraib had "no intelligence value.")

Between that little dramatic exchange—

> Rumsfeld: And have you seen one that characterized it as systematic or systemic?
>
> General Pace: No, sir.
>
> Rumsfeld: I haven't either—

—and the truth, there is a vast gulf of lies. For these reports do use the words "systematic" and "systemic"—they are there, in black and white—and though the reports have great shortcomings, the truth is that they tell us basic facts about Abu Ghraib: first, that the torture and abuse was systematic; that it was ordered by higher-ups, and not carried out by "a few bad apples," as the administration has maintained; that responsibility for it can be traced—in documents that have been made public—to the very top ranks of the administration, to decisions made by officials in the Department of Justice and the Department of Defense and, ultimately, the White House. The significance of what we know about Abu Ghraib, and about what went on—and, most important, what is almost certainly still going on—not only in Iraq but at Guantánamo Bay, Cuba, and Bagram Air Base in Afghanistan, and other military and intelligence bases, some secret, some not, around the world—is clear: that after September 11, shortly after you all came to Berkeley, our government decided to change this country from a nation that officially does not torture to one, officially, that does.

What is interesting about this fact is not that it is hidden but that it is revealed. We know this—or rather those who are willing to read know it. Those who can see the gulf between what officials say and what the facts are. And we, as I have said, remain fairly few. Secretary Rumsfeld can say what he said at that nationally televised news conference because no one is willing to read the reports. We are divided, then, between those of us willing to listen, and believe, and those of us determined to read, and think, and find out. And you, English majors of the Class of 2005, you have taken the fateful first step in numbering yourselves, perhaps irredeemably, in the second category. You have taken a step along the road to being Empiricists of the Word.

Now we have come full circle—all the way back to the question: What are you going to do with *that*? I cannot answer that question. Indeed, I still have not answered it for myself. But I can show you what you can do with "that," by quoting a poem. It is by a friend of mine who died almost a year ago, after a full and glorious life, at the age of ninety-three. Czeslaw Milosz was a legend in Berkeley, of course, a Nobel Prize winner—and he saw as much injustice in his life as any man. He endured Nazism and Stalinism and then came to Berkeley to live and write for four decades in a beautiful house high on Grizzly Peak.

Let me read you one of his poems: it is a simple poem, a song, as he calls it, but in all its beauty and simplicity it bears closely on the subject of this talk.

A SONG ON THE END OF THE WORLD
On the day the world ends
A bee circles a clover,
A fisherman mends a glimmering net.
Happy porpoises jump in the sea,
By the rainspout young sparrows are playing
And the snake is gold-skinned as it should always be.

On the day the world ends
Women walk through the fields under their umbrellas,
A drunkard grows sleepy at the edge of a lawn,
Vegetable peddlers shout in
the street
And a yellow-sailed boat comes nearer the island,
The voice of a violin lasts in the air
And leads into a starry night.

And those who expected lightning and thunder
Are disappointed.
And those who expected signs and archangels' trumps
Do not believe it is happening now.

As long as the sun and the moon are above,
As long as the bumblebee visits a rose,
As long as rosy infants are born
No one believes it is happening now.

Only a white-haired old man, who would be a prophet
Yet is not a prophet, for he's much too busy,
Repeats while he binds his
tomatoes:
There will be no other end of the world,
There will be no other end of the world.

"There will be no other end of the world." I should add that there are two words at the end of the poem, a place and a date. Czeslaw wrote that poem in Warsaw in 1944. Can we think of a better place to put the end of the world? Perhaps Hiroshima 1945? Or Berlin 1945? Or even perhaps downtown New York in September 2001?

When Czeslaw Milosz wrote his poem in Warsaw, in 1944, there were those, as now, who saw the end of the world and those who did not. And now, as then, truth does matter. Integrity—much rarer than talent or brilliance—does matter. In that beautiful poem, written by a man—a poet, an artist—trying to survive at the end of the world, the white-haired old man binding his tomatoes is like yourselves. He may not have been a prophet but he could see. Members of the Class of September 11, whatever you decide "to do with that"—whether you are writers or professors or journalists, or nurses or lawyers or executives—I hope you will think of that man and his tomatoes, and keep your faith with him. I hope you will remember that man, and your own questioning spirit. Will you keep your place beside him?

FACTS

Number of times after prison-abuse photos aired in April that the president boasted of freeing Iraq of torture chambers: 13
(*Harper's* research)

Minimum number of miles that a private jet has been flown to take U.S. terror suspects to "rendition" abroad: 302,000
(Kalla Fakta, TV4, Stockholm)

Years since the Justice Department last released the number of U.S. terror suspects taken into "preventive detention": 3
(Human Rights Watch)

Estimated number of people who have been taken into such detention since then: 4,000
(David Cole, Georgetown University)

Minimum number of Al Qaeda suspects from overseas whom the United States has now "disappeared," by legal standards: 11
(Human Rights Watch)

Number of senators who voted in October 2005 for passage of anti-torture legislation opposed by the White House: 90
(*New York Times*, 12/15/05)

THE NEW GREED

with cartoons by Mr. Fish
and facts

America is once again becoming a nation of rich and poor—perhaps the worst thing that can happen to a democracy. It already is impossible for most American families to acquire the basic elements of a middle-class life: a home in a safe neighborhood with good schools, decent health care, and a secure retirement. Meanwhile, the rich get tax cuts and the fast-growing ranks of the poor go to the military or to jail—both government programs financed by the shrinking middle class.

The planet as a whole is likewise divided into rich and poor nations—and here again, the gap is widening. The results are starting to filter in: the chickens are coming home to roost.

It's going to get worse unless it gets better.

FACTS

Ratio in America of mobile homes to homes in gated communities: 1:1

(U.S. Census Bureau)

Percentage of jobs in America that pay poverty-level wages: 25

("Trickling Up" by Beth Shulman, TomPaine.com)

Estimated total federal assistance for which Wal-Mart employees were eligible last year: $2,500,000,000

(Democratic Staff of the Committee on Education and the Workforce)

Percent higher the minimum wage would be today if it were indexed to inflation: 36

("Trickling Up")

Number of Americans without health care: 45 million

("Trickling Up")

For Richer

from the *New York Times* (10/20/02)

Paul Krugman

I. The Disappearing Middle

When I was a teenager growing up on Long Island, one of my favorite excursions was a trip to see the great Gilded Age mansions of the North Shore. Those mansions weren't just pieces of architectural history. They were monuments to a bygone social era, one in which the rich could afford the armies of servants needed to maintain a house the size of a European palace. By the time I saw them, of course, that era was long past. Almost none of the Long Island mansions were still private residences. Those that hadn't been turned into museums were occupied by nursing homes or private schools.

For the America I grew up in—the America of the 1950s and 1960s—was a middle-class society, both in reality and in feel. The vast income and wealth inequalities of the Gilded Age had disappeared. Yes, of course, there was the poverty of the underclass—but the conventional wisdom of the time viewed that as a social rather than an economic problem. Yes, of course, some wealthy businessmen and heirs to large fortunes lived far better than the average American. But they weren't rich the way the robber barons who built the mansions had been rich, and there weren't that many of them. The days when plutocrats were a force to be reckoned with in American society, economically or politically, seemed long past.

Daily experience confirmed the sense of a fairly equal society. The economic disparities you were conscious of were quite muted. Highly educated professionals—middle managers, college teachers, even lawyers—often claimed that they earned less than unionized blue-collar workers. Those considered very well off lived in split-levels, had a housecleaner come in once a week and took summer vacations in Europe. But they sent their kids to public schools and drove themselves to work, just like everyone else.

But that was long ago. The middle-class America of my youth was another country.

We are now living in a new Gilded Age, as extravagant as the original. Mansions have made a comeback. Back in 1999 *The New York Times Magazine* profiled Thierry Despont, the "eminence of excess," an architect who specializes in designing houses for the superrich. His creations typically range from 20,000 to 60,000 square feet; houses at the upper end of his range are not much smaller than the White House. Needless to say, the armies of servants are back, too. So are the yachts. Still, even J. P. Morgan didn't have a Gulfstream.

As the story about Despont suggests, it's not fair to say that the fact of widening inequality in America has gone unreported. Yet glimpses of the lifestyles of the rich and tasteless don't necessarily add up in people's minds to a clear picture of the tectonic shifts that have taken place in the distribution of income and wealth in this country. My sense is that few people are aware of just how much the gap between the very rich and the rest has widened over a relatively short period of time. In fact, even bringing up the subject exposes you to charges of "class warfare," the "politics of envy" and so on. And very few people indeed are willing to talk about the profound effects—economic, social, and political—of that widening gap.

Yet you can't understand what's happening in America today without understanding the extent, causes, and consequences of the vast increase in inequality that has taken place over the last three decades, and in particular the astonishing concentration of income and wealth in just a few hands. To make sense of the current wave of corporate scandal, you need to understand how the man in the gray flannel suit has been replaced by the imperial C.E.O. The concentration of income at the top is a key reason that the United States, for all its economic achievements, has more poverty and lower life expectancy than any other major advanced nation. Above all, the growing concentration of wealth has reshaped our political system: it is at the root both of a general shift to the right and of an extreme polarization of our politics.

But before we get to all that, let's take a look at who gets what.

II. The New Gilded Age

The Securities and Exchange Commission hath no fury like a woman scorned. The messy divorce proceedings of Jack Welch, the legendary former C.E.O. of General Electric, have had one unintended benefit: they have given us a peek at the perks of the corporate elite, which are normally hidden from public view. For it turns out that when Welch retired, he was granted for life the use of a Manhattan apartment (including food, wine, and laundry), access to corporate jets, and a variety of other in-kind benefits, worth at least $2 million a year. The perks were revealing: they illustrated the extent to which corporate leaders now expect to be treated like ancien régime royalty. In monetary terms, however, the perks must have meant little to Welch. In 2000, his last full year running G.E., Welch was paid $123 million, mainly in stock and stock options.

Is it news that C.E.O.'s of large American corporations make a lot of money? Actually, it is. They were always well paid compared with the average worker, but there is simply no comparison between what executives got a generation ago and what they are paid today.

Over the past 30 years most people have seen only modest salary increases: the average annual salary in America, expressed in 1998 dollars (that is, adjusted for inflation), rose from $32,522 in 1970 to $35,864 in 1999. That's about a 10 percent increase over 29 years—progress, but not much. Over the same period, however, according to *Fortune* magazine, the average real annual compensation of the top 100 C.E.O.'s went from $1.3 million—39 times the pay of an average worker—to $37.5 million, more than 1,000 times the pay of ordinary workers.

The explosion in C.E.O. pay over the past 30 years is an amazing story in its own right, and an important one. But it is only the most spectacular indicator of a broader story, the reconcentration of income and wealth in the U.S. The rich have always been different from you and me, but they are far more different now than they were not long ago—indeed, they are as different now as they were when F. Scott Fitzgerald made his famous remark.

That's a controversial statement, though it shouldn't be. For at least the past 15 years it has been hard to deny the evidence for growing inequality in the United States. Census data clearly show a rising share of income going to the top 20 percent of families, and within that top 20 percent to the top 5 percent, with a declining share going to families in the middle. Nonetheless, denial of that evidence is a sizable, well-financed industry. Conservative think tanks have produced scores of studies that try to discredit the data, the methodology, and, not least, the motives of those who report the obvious. Studies that appear to refute claims of increasing inequality receive prominent endorsements on editorial pages and are eagerly cited by right-leaning government officials. Four years ago Alan Greenspan (why did anyone ever think that he was nonpartisan?) gave a keynote speech at the Federal Reserve's annual Jackson Hole conference that amounted to an attempt to deny that there has been any real increase in inequality in America.

The concerted effort to deny that inequality is increasing is itself a symptom of the growing influence of our emerging plutocracy (more on this later). So is the fierce defense of the backup position, that inequality doesn't matter—or maybe even that, to use Martha Stewart's signature phrase, it's a good thing. Meanwhile, politically motivated smoke screens aside, the reality of increasing inequality is not in doubt. In fact, the census data understate the case, because for technical reasons those data tend to undercount very high incomes—for example, it's unlikely that they reflect the explosion in C.E.O. compensation. And other evidence makes it clear not only that inequality is increasing but that the action gets bigger the closer you get to the top. That is, it's not simply that the top 20 percent of families have had bigger percentage gains than families near the middle: the top 5 percent have done better than the next 15, the top 1 percent better than the next 4, and so on up to Bill Gates.

Studies that try to do a better job of tracking high

incomes have found startling results. For example, a recent study by the nonpartisan Congressional Budget Office used income tax data and other sources to improve on the census estimates. The C.B.O. study found that between 1979 and 1997, the after-tax incomes of the top 1 percent of families rose 157 percent, compared with only a 10 percent gain for families near the middle of the income distribution. Even more startling results come from a new study by Thomas Piketty, at the French research institute Cepremap, and Emmanuel Saez, who is now at the University of California at Berkeley. Using income tax data, Piketty and Saez have produced estimates of the incomes of the well-to-do, the rich, and the very rich back to 1913.

The first point you learn from these new estimates is that the middle-class America of my youth is best thought of not as the normal state of our society, but as an interregnum between Gilded Ages. America before 1930 was a society in which a small number of very rich people controlled a large share of the nation's wealth. We became a middle-class society only after the concentration of income at the top dropped sharply during the New Deal, and especially during World War II. The economic historians Claudia Goldin and Robert Margo have dubbed the narrowing of income gaps during those years the Great Compression. Incomes then stayed fairly equally distributed until the 1970s: the rapid rise in incomes during the first postwar generation was very evenly spread across the population.

Since the 1970s, however, income gaps have been rapidly widening. Piketty and Saez confirm what I suspected: by most measures we are, in fact, back to the days of "The Great Gatsby." After 30 years in which the income shares of the top 10 percent of taxpayers, the top 1 percent and so on were far below their levels in the 1920s, all are very nearly back where they were.

And the big winners are the very, very rich. One ploy often used to play down growing inequality is to rely on rather coarse statistical breakdowns—dividing the population into five "quintiles," each containing 20 percent of families, or at most 10 "deciles." Indeed, Greenspan's speech at Jackson Hole relied mainly on decile data. From there it's a short step to denying that we're really talking about the rich at all. For example, a conservative commentator might concede, grudgingly, that there has been some increase in the share of national income going to the top 10 percent of taxpayers, but then point out that anyone with an income over $81,000 is in that top 10 percent. So we're just talking about shifts within the middle class, right?

Wrong: the top 10 percent contains a lot of people whom we would still consider middle class, but they weren't the big winners. Most of the gains in the share of the top 10 percent of taxpayers over the past 30 years were actually gains to the top 1 percent, rather than the next 9 percent. In 1998 the top 1 percent started at $230,000. In turn, 60 percent of the gains of that top 1 percent went to the top 0.1 percent, those with incomes of more than $790,000. And almost half of those gains went to a mere 13,000 taxpayers, the top 0.01 percent, who had an income of at least $3.6 million and an average income of $17 million.

A stickler for detail might point out that the Piketty-Saez estimates end in 1998 and that the C.B.O. numbers end a year earlier. Have the trends shown in the data reversed? Almost surely not. In fact, all indications are that the explosion of incomes at the top continued through 2000. Since then the plunge in stock prices must have put some crimp in high incomes—but census data show inequality continuing to increase in 2001, mainly because of the severe effects of the recession on the working poor and near poor. When the recession ends, we can be sure that we will find ourselves a society in which income inequality is even higher than it was in the late '90s.

So claims that we've entered a second Gilded Age aren't exaggerated. In America's middle-class era, the mansion-building, yacht-owning classes had pretty much disappeared. According to Piketty and Saez, in 1970 the top 0.01 percent of taxpayers had 0.7 percent of total income—that is, they earned "only" 70 times as much as the average, not enough to buy or maintain a mega-residence. But in 1998 the top 0.01 percent received more than 3 percent of all income. That meant that the 13,000 richest families in America had almost as much income as the 20 million poorest households; those 13,000 families had incomes 300 times that of average families.

And let me repeat: this transformation has happened very quickly, and it is still going on. You might think that 1987, the year Tom Wolfe published his novel *The Bonfire of the Vanities* and Oliver Stone released his movie *Wall Street,* marked the high tide of America's new money culture. But in 1987 the top 0.01 percent earned only about 40 percent of what they do today, and top executives less than a fifth as much. The America of *Wall Street* and *The Bonfire of the Vanities* was positively egalitarian compared with the country we live in today.

III. Undoing the New Deal

In the middle of the 1980s, as economists became aware that something important was happening to the distribution of income in America, they formulated three main hypotheses about its causes.

The "globalization" hypothesis tied America's changing income distribution to the growth of world trade, and especially the growing imports of manufactured goods from the third world. Its basic message was that blue-collar workers—the sort of people who in my youth often made as much money as college-educated middle managers—were losing ground in the face of competition from low-wage workers in Asia. A result was stagnation or decline in the wages of ordinary people, with a growing share of national income going to the highly educated.

A second hypothesis, "skill-biased technological change," situated the cause of growing inequality not in foreign trade but in domestic innovation. The torrid pace of progress in information technology, so the story went, had increased the demand for the highly skilled and educated. And so the income distribution increasingly favored brains rather than brawn.

Finally, the "superstar" hypothesis—named by the Chicago economist Sherwin Rosen—offered a variant on the technological story. It argued that modern technologies of communication often turn competition into a tournament in which the winner is richly rewarded, while the runners-up get far less. The classic example—which gives the theory its name—is the entertainment business. As Rosen pointed out, in bygone days there were hundreds of comedians making a modest living at live shows in the borscht belt and other places. Now they are mostly gone; what is left is a handful of superstar TV comedians.

The debates among these hypotheses—particularly the debate between those who attributed growing inequality to globalization and those who attributed it to technology—were many and bitter. I was a participant in those debates myself. But I won't dwell on them, because in the last few years there has been a growing sense among economists that none of these hypotheses work.

I don't mean to say that there was nothing to these stories. Yet as more evidence has accumulated, each of the hypotheses has seemed increasingly inadequate. Globalization can explain part of the relative decline in blue-collar wages, but it can't explain the 2,500 percent rise in C.E.O. incomes. Technology may explain why the salary premium associated with a college education has risen, but it's hard to match up with the huge increase in inequality among the college-educated, with little progress for many but gigantic gains at the top. The superstar theory works for Jay Leno, but not for the thousands of people who have become awesomely rich without going on TV.

The Great Compression—the substantial reduction in inequality during the New Deal and the Second World War—also seems hard to understand in terms of the usual theories. During World War II Franklin Roosevelt used government control over wages to compress wage gaps. But if the middle-class society that emerged from the war was an artificial creation, why did it persist for another 30 years?

Some—by no means all—economists trying to understand growing inequality have begun to take seriously a hypothesis that would have been considered irredeemably fuzzy-minded not long ago. This view stresses the role of social norms in setting limits to inequality. According to this view, the New Deal had a more profound impact on American society than even its most ardent admirers have suggested: it imposed norms of relative equality in pay that persisted for more than 30 years, creating the broadly middle-class society we came to take for granted. But those norms began to unravel in the 1970s and have done so at an accelerating pace.

Exhibit A for this view is the story of executive compensation. In the 1960s, America's great corporations behaved more like socialist republics than like cutthroat capitalist enterprises, and top executives behaved more like public-spirited bureaucrats than like captains of industry. I'm not exaggerating. Consider the description of executive behavior offered by John Kenneth Galbraith in his 1967 book, *The New Industrial State*: "Management does not go out ruthlessly to reward itself—a sound management is expected to exercise restraint." Managerial self-dealing was a thing of the past: "With the power of decision goes opportunity for making money. . . . Were everyone to seek to do so . . . the corporation would be a chaos of competitive avarice. But these are not the sort of thing that a good company man does; a remarkably effective code bans such behavior. Group decision-making insures, moreover, that almost everyone's actions and even thoughts are known to others. This acts to enforce the code and, more than incidentally, a high standard of personal honesty as well."

Thirty-five years on, a cover article in *Fortune* is titled "You Bought. They Sold." "All over corporate America," reads the blurb, "top execs were cashing in stocks even as their companies were tanking. Who was left holding the bag? You." As I said, we've become a different country.

Let's leave actual malfeasance on one side for a moment, and ask how the relatively modest salaries of top executives 30 years ago became the gigantic pay packages of today. There are two main stories, both of which emphasize changing norms rather than pure economics. The more optimistic story draws an analogy between the explosion of C.E.O. pay and the explosion of baseball salaries with the introduction of free agency. According to this story, highly paid C.E.O.'s really are worth it, because having the right man in that job makes a huge difference. The more pessimistic view—which I find more plausible—is that competition for talent is a minor factor. Yes, a great executive can make a big difference—but those huge pay packages have been going as often as not to executives whose performance is mediocre at best. The key reason executives are paid so much now is that they appoint the members of the corporate board that determines their compensation and control many of the perks that board members count on. So it's not the invisible hand of the market that leads to those monumental executive incomes; it's the invisible handshake in the boardroom.

But then why weren't executives paid lavishly 30 years ago? Again, it's a matter of corporate culture. For a generation after World War II, fear of outrage kept executive salaries in check. Now the outrage is gone. That is, the explosion of executive pay represents a social change rather than the purely economic forces of supply and demand. We should think of it not as a market trend like the rising value of waterfront property, but as something more like the sexual revolution of the 1960s—a relaxation of old strictures, a new permissiveness, but in this case the permissiveness is financial rather than sexual. Sure enough, John Kenneth Galbraith described the honest executive of 1967 as being one who "eschews the lovely, available and even naked woman by whom he is intimately surrounded." By the end of the 1990s, the executive motto might as well have been "If it feels good, do it."

How did this change in corporate culture happen? Economists and management theorists are only beginning to explore that question, but it's easy to suggest a few factors. One was the changing structure of financial markets. In his new book, *Searching for a Corporate Savior*, Rakesh Khurana of Harvard Business School suggests that during the 1980's and 1990's, "managerial capitalism"—the world of the man in the gray flannel suit—was replaced by "investor capitalism." Institutional investors weren't willing to let a C.E.O. choose his own successor from inside the corporation; they wanted heroic leaders, often outsiders, and were willing to pay immense sums to get them. The subtitle of Khurana's book, by the way, is *The Irrational Quest for Charismatic C.E.O.'s*.

But fashionable management theorists didn't think it was irrational. Since the 1980's there has been ever more emphasis on the importance of "leadership"—meaning personal, charismatic leadership. When Lee Iacocca of Chrysler became a business celebrity in the early 1980's, he was practically alone: Khurana reports that in 1980 only one issue of *Business Week* featured a C.E.O. on its cover. By 1999 the number was up to 19. And once it was considered normal, even necessary, for a C.E.O. to be famous, it also became easier to make him rich.

Economists also did their bit to legitimize previously unthinkable levels of executive pay. During the 1980s and 1990s a torrent of academic papers—popularized in business magazines and incorporated into consultants' recommendations—argued that Gordon Gekko was right: greed is good; greed works. In order to get the best performance out of executives, these papers argued, it was necessary to align their interests with those of stockholders. And the way to do that was with large grants of stock or stock options.

It's hard to escape the suspicion that these new intellectual justifications for soaring executive pay were as much effect as cause. I'm not suggesting that management theorists and economists were personally corrupt. It would have been a subtle, unconscious process: the ideas that were taken up by business schools, that led to nice speaking and consulting fees, tended to be the ones that ratified an existing trend, and thereby gave it legitimacy.

What economists like Piketty and Saez are now suggesting is that the story of executive compensation is representative of a broader story. Much more than economists and free-market advocates like to imagine, wages—particularly at the top—are determined by social norms. What happened during the 1930s and 1940s was that new norms of equality were established, largely through the political process. What happened in the 1980s and 1990s was that those norms unraveled, replaced by an ethos of "anything goes." And a result was an explosion of income at the top of the scale.

IV. The Price of Inequality

It was one of those revealing moments. Responding to an

e-mail message from a Canadian viewer, Robert Novak of *Crossfire* delivered a little speech: "Marg, like most Canadians, you're ill informed and wrong. The U.S. has the longest standard of living—longest life expectancy of any country in the world, including Canada. That's the truth."

But it was Novak who had his facts wrong. Canadians can expect to live about two years longer than Americans. In fact, life expectancy in the U.S. is well below that in Canada, Japan, and every major nation in Western Europe. On average, we can expect lives a bit shorter than those of Greeks, a bit longer than those of Portuguese. Male life expectancy is lower in the U.S. than it is in Costa Rica.

Still, you can understand why Novak assumed that we were No. 1. After all, we really are the richest major nation, with real G.D.P. per capita about 20 percent higher than Canada's. And it has been an article of faith in this country that a rising tide lifts all boats. Doesn't our high and rising national wealth translate into a high standard of living—including good medical care—for all Americans?

Well, no. Although America has higher per capita income than other advanced countries, it turns out that that's mainly because our rich are much richer. And here's a radical thought: if the rich get more, that leaves less for everyone else.

That statement—which is simply a matter of arithmetic—is guaranteed to bring accusations of "class warfare." If the accuser gets more specific, he'll probably offer two reasons that it's foolish to make a fuss over the high incomes of a few people at the top of the income distribution. First, he'll tell you that what the elite get may look like a lot of money, but it's still a small share of the total—

that is, when all is said and done the rich aren't getting that big a piece of the pie. Second, he'll tell you that trying to do anything to reduce incomes at the top will hurt, not help, people further down the distribution, because attempts to redistribute income damage incentives.

These arguments for lack of concern are plausible. And they were entirely correct, once upon a time—namely, back when we had a middle-class society. But there's a lot less truth to them now.

First, the share of the rich in total income is no longer trivial. These days 1 percent of families receive about 16 percent of total pretax income, and have about 14 percent of after-tax income. That share has roughly doubled over the past 30 years, and is now about as large as the share of the bottom 40 percent of the population. That's a big shift of income to the top; as a matter of pure arithmetic, it must mean that the incomes of less well off families grew considerably more slowly than average income. And they did. Adjusting for inflation, average family income—total income divided by the number of families—grew 28 percent from 1979 to 1997. But median family income—the income of a family in the middle of the distribution, a better indicator of how typical American families are doing—grew only 10 percent. And the incomes of the bottom fifth of families actually fell slightly.

Let me belabor this point for a bit. We pride ourselves, with considerable justification, on our record of economic growth. But over the last few decades it's remarkable how little of that growth has trickled down to ordinary families. Median family income has risen only about 0.5 percent per year—and as far as we can tell from somewhat unreliable data, just about all of that increase was due to wives working longer hours, with little or no gain in real wages. Furthermore, numbers about income don't reflect the growing riskiness of life for ordinary workers. In the days when General Motors was known in-house as Generous Motors, many workers felt that they had considerable job security—the company wouldn't fire them except in extremis. Many had contracts that guaranteed health insurance, even if they were laid off; they had pension benefits that did not depend on the stock market. Now mass firings from long-established companies are commonplace; losing your job means losing your insurance; and as millions of people have been learning, a 401(k) plan is no guarantee of a comfortable retirement.

Still, many people will say that while the U.S. economic system may generate a lot of inequality, it also generates much higher incomes than any alternative, so that everyone is better off. That was the moral *Business Week* tried to convey in its recent special issue with "25 Ideas for a Changing World." One of those ideas was "the rich get richer, and that's O.K." High incomes at the top, the conventional wisdom declares, are the result of a free-market system that provides huge incentives for performance. And the system delivers that performance, which means that wealth at the top doesn't come at the expense of the rest of us.

A skeptic might point out that the explosion in executive compensation seems at best loosely related to actual performance. Jack Welch was one of the 10 highest-paid executives in the United States in 2000, and you could argue that he earned it. But did Dennis Kozlowski of Tyco, or Gerald Levin of Time Warner, who were also in the top 10? A skeptic might also point out that even during the economic boom of the late 1990s, U.S. productivity growth was no better than it was during the great postwar expansion, which corresponds to the era when America was truly middle class and C.E.O.'s were modestly paid technocrats.

But can we produce any direct evidence about the effects of inequality? We can't rerun our own history and ask what would have happened if the social norms of middle-class America had continued to limit incomes at the top, and if government policy had leaned against rising inequality instead of reinforcing it, which is what actually happened. But we can compare ourselves with other advanced countries. And the results are somewhat surprising.

Many Americans assume that because we are the richest country in the world, with real G.D.P. per capita higher than that of other major advanced countries, Americans must be better off across the board—that it's not just our rich who are richer than their counterparts abroad, but that the typical American family is much better off than the typical family elsewhere, and that even our poor are well off by foreign standards.

But it's not true. Let me use the example of Sweden, that great conservative bête noire.

A few months ago the conservative cyberpundit Glenn Reynolds made a splash when he pointed out that Sweden's G.D.P. per capita is roughly comparable with that of Mississippi—see, those foolish believers in the welfare state have impoverished themselves! Presumably he assumed that this means that the typical Swede is as poor as the typical resident of Mississippi, and therefore much worse off than the typical American.

But life expectancy in Sweden is about three years higher than that of the U.S. Infant mortality is half the U.S. level, and less than a third the rate in Mississippi. Functional illiteracy is much less common than in the U.S.

How is this possible? One answer is that G.D.P. per capita is in some ways a misleading measure. Swedes take longer vacations than Americans, so they work fewer hours per year. That's a choice, not a failure of economic performance. Real G.D.P. per hour worked is 16 percent lower than in the United States, which makes Swedish productivity about the same as Canada's.

But the main point is that though Sweden may have lower average income than the United States, that's mainly because our rich are so much richer. The median Swedish family has a standard of living roughly comparable with that of the median U.S. family: wages are if anything higher in Sweden, and a higher tax burden is offset by public provision of health care and generally better public services. And as you move further down the income distribution, Swedish living standards are way ahead of those in the U.S. Swedish families with children that are at the 10th percentile—poorer than 90 percent of the population—have incomes 60 percent higher than their U.S. counterparts. And very few people in Sweden experience the deep poverty that is all too common in the United States. One measure: in 1994 only 6 percent of Swedes lived on less than $11 per day, compared with 14 percent in the U.S.

The moral of this comparison is that even if you think that America's high levels of inequality are the price of our high level of national income, it's not at all clear that this price is worth paying. The reason conservatives engage in bouts of Sweden-bashing is that they want to convince us that there is no tradeoff between economic efficiency and equity—that if you try to take from the rich and give to the poor, you actually make everyone worse off. But the comparison between the U.S. and other advanced countries doesn't support this conclusion at all. Yes, we are the richest major nation. But because so much of our national income is concentrated in relatively few hands, large numbers of Americans are worse off economically than their counterparts in other advanced countries.

And we might even offer a challenge from the other side: inequality in the United States has arguably reached levels where it is counterproductive. That is, you can make a case that our society would be richer if its richest members didn't get quite so much.

I could make this argument on historical grounds. The most impressive economic growth in U.S. history coincided with the middle-class interregnum, the post–World War II generation, when incomes were most evenly distributed. But let's focus on a specific case, the extraordinary pay packages of today's top executives. Are these good for the economy?

Until recently it was almost unchallenged conventional wisdom that, whatever else you might say, the new imperial C.E.O.'s had delivered results that dwarfed the expense of their compensation. But now that the stock bubble has burst, it has become increasingly clear that there was a price to those big pay packages, after all. In fact, the price paid by shareholders and society at large may have been many times larger than the amount actually paid to the executives.

It's easy to get boggled by the details of corporate scandal—insider loans, stock options, special-purpose entities, mark-to-market, round-tripping. But there's a simple reason that the details are so complicated. All of these schemes were designed to benefit corporate insiders—to inflate the pay of the C.E.O. and his inner circle. That is, they were all about the "chaos of competitive avarice" that, according to John Kenneth Galbraith, had been ruled out in the corporation of the 1960's. But while all restraint has vanished within the American corporation, the outside world—including stockholders—is still prudish, and open looting by executives is still not acceptable. So the looting has to be camouflaged, taking place through complicated schemes that can be rationalized to outsiders as clever corporate strategies.

Economists who study crime tell us that crime is inefficient—that is, the costs of crime to the economy are much larger than the amount stolen. Crime, and the fear of crime, divert resources away from productive uses: criminals spend their time stealing rather than producing, and potential victims spend time and money trying to protect their property. Also, the things people do to avoid becoming victims—like avoiding dangerous districts—have a cost even if they succeed in averting an actual crime.

The same holds true of corporate malfeasance, whether or not it actually involves breaking the law. Executives who devote their time to creating innovative ways to divert shareholder money into their own pockets probably aren't running the real business very well (think Enron, WorldCom, Tyco, Global Crossing, Adelphia . . .). Investments chosen because they create the illusion of profitability while insiders cash in their stock options are a waste of scarce resources. And if the supply of funds from lenders and shareholders dries up because of a lack of trust, the economy as a whole suffers. Just ask Indonesia.

The argument for a system in which some people get very rich has always been that the lure of wealth provides powerful incentives. But the question is, incentives to do what? As we learn more about what has actually been going on in corporate America, it's becoming less and less clear whether those incentives have actually made executives work on behalf of the rest of us.

V. Inequality and Politics

In September 2003 the Senate debated a proposed measure that would impose a one-time capital gains tax on Americans who renounce their citizenship in order to avoid paying U.S. taxes. Senator Phil Gramm was not pleased, declaring that the proposal was "right out of Nazi Germany." Pretty strong language, but no stronger than the metaphor Daniel Mitchell of the Heritage Foundation used, in an op-ed article in *The Washington Times,* to describe a bill designed to prevent corporations from rechartering abroad for tax purposes: Mitchell described this legislation as the "Dred Scott tax bill," referring to the infamous 1857 Supreme Court ruling that required free states to return escaped slaves.

Twenty years ago, would a prominent senator have likened those who want wealthy people to pay taxes to Nazis? Would a member of a think tank with close ties to the administration have drawn a parallel between corporate taxation and slavery? I don't think so. The remarks by Gramm and Mitchell, while stronger than usual, were indicators of two huge changes in American politics. One is the growing polarization of our politics—our politicians are less and less inclined to offer even the appearance of moderation. The other is the growing tendency of policy and policy makers to cater to the interests of the wealthy. And I mean the wealthy, not the merely well-off: only someone with a net worth of at least several million dollars is likely to find it worthwhile to become a tax exile.

You don't need a political scientist to tell you that modern American politics is bitterly polarized. But wasn't it always thus? No, it wasn't. From World War II until the 1970's—the same era during which income inequality was historically low—political partisanship was much more muted than it is today. That's not just a subjective assessment. My Princeton political science colleagues Nolan McCarty and Howard Rosenthal, together with Keith Poole at the University of Houston, have done a statistical analysis showing that the voting behavior of a congressman is much better predicted by his party affiliation today than it was 25 years ago. In fact, the division between the parties is sharper now than it has been since the 1920's.

What are the parties divided about? The answer is simple: economics. McCarty, Rosenthal, and Poole write that "voting in Congress is highly ideological—one-dimensional left/right, liberal versus conservative." It may sound simplistic to describe Democrats as the party that wants to tax the rich and help the poor, and Republicans as the party that wants to keep taxes and social spending as low as possible. And during the era of middle-class America that would indeed have been simplistic: politics wasn't defined by economic issues. But that was a different country; as McCarty, Rosenthal, and Poole put it, "If income and wealth are distributed in a fairly equitable way, little is to be gained for politicians to organize politics around nonexistent conflicts." Now the conflicts are real, and our politics is organized around them. In other words, the growing inequality of our incomes probably lies behind the growing divisiveness of our politics.

But the politics of rich and poor hasn't played out the way you might think. Since the incomes of America's wealthy have soared while ordinary families have seen at best small gains, you might have expected politicians to seek votes by proposing to soak the rich. In fact, however, the polarization of politics has occurred because the Republicans have moved to the right, not because the Democrats have moved to the left. And actual economic policy has moved steadily in favor of the wealthy. The major tax cuts of the past 25 years, the Reagan cuts in the 1980s and the recent Bush cuts, were both heavily tilted toward the very well off. (Despite obfuscations, it remains true that more than half the Bush tax cut will eventually go to the top 1 percent of families.) The major tax increase over that period, the increase in payroll taxes in the 1980s, fell most heavily on working-class families.

The most remarkable example of how politics has shifted in favor of the wealthy—an example that helps us understand why economic policy has reinforced, not countered, the movement toward greater inequality—is the drive to repeal the estate tax. The estate tax is, overwhelmingly, a tax on the wealthy. In 1999, only the top 2 percent of estates paid any tax at all, and half the estate tax was paid by only 3,300 estates, 0.16 percent of the total, with a minimum value of $5 million and an average value of $17 million. A quarter of the tax was paid by just 467 estates worth more than $20 million. Tales of family farms and businesses broken up to pay the estate tax are basically rural legends; hardly any real examples have been found, despite diligent searching.

You might have thought that a tax that falls on so few people yet yields a significant amount of revenue would be politically popular; you certainly wouldn't expect widespread opposition. Moreover, there has long been an argument that the estate tax promotes democratic values, precisely because it limits the ability of the wealthy to form dynasties. So why has there been a powerful political drive to repeal the estate tax, and why was such a repeal a centerpiece of the Bush tax cut?

There is an economic argument for repealing the estate tax, but it's hard to believe that many people take it seriously. More significant for members of Congress, surely, is the question of who would benefit from repeal: while those who will actually benefit from estate tax repeal are few in number, they have a lot of money and control even more (corporate C.E.O.'s can now count on leaving taxable estates behind). That is, they are the sort of people who command the attention of politicians in search of campaign funds.

But it's not just about campaign contributions: much of the general public has been convinced that the estate tax is a bad thing. If you try talking about the tax to a group of moderately prosperous retirees, you get some interesting reactions. They refer to it as the "death tax"; many of them believe that their estates will face punitive taxation, even though most of them will pay little or nothing; they are convinced that small businesses and family farms bear the brunt of the tax.

These misconceptions don't arise by accident. They

have, instead, been deliberately promoted. For example, a Heritage Foundation document titled "Time to Repeal Federal Death Taxes: The Nightmare of the American Dream" emphasizes stories that rarely, if ever, happen in real life: "Small-business owners, particularly minority owners, suffer anxious moments wondering whether the businesses they hope to hand down to their children will be destroyed by the death tax bill. . . . Women whose children are grown struggle to find ways to re-enter the work force without upsetting the family's estate tax avoidance plan." And who finances the Heritage Foundation? Why, foundations created by wealthy families, of course.

The point is that it is no accident that strongly conservative views, views that militate against taxes on the rich, have spread even as the rich get richer compared with the rest of us: in addition to directly buying influence, money can be used to shape public perceptions. The liberal group People for the American Way's report on how conservative foundations have deployed vast sums to support think tanks, friendly media, and other institutions that promote right-wing causes is titled "Buying a Movement."

Not to put too fine a point on it: as the rich get richer, they can buy a lot of things besides goods and services. Money buys political influence; used cleverly, it also buys intellectual influence. A result is that growing income disparities in the United States, far from leading to demands to soak the rich, have been accompanied by a growing movement to let them keep more of their earnings and to pass their wealth on to their children.

This obviously raises the possibility of a self-reinforcing process. As the gap between the rich and the rest of the population grows, economic policy increasingly caters to the interests of the elite, while public services for the population at large—above all, public education—are starved of resources. As policy increasingly favors the interests of the rich and neglects the interests of the general population, income disparities grow even wider.

VI. Plutocracy?

In 1924, the mansions of Long Island's North Shore were still in their full glory, as was the political power of the class that owned them. When Gov. Al Smith of New York proposed building a system of parks on Long Island, the mansion owners were bitterly opposed. One baron—Horace Havemeyer, the "sultan of sugar"—warned that North Shore towns would be "overrun with rabble from the city." "Rabble?" Smith said. "That's me you're talking about." In the end New Yorkers got their parks, but it was close: the interests of a few hundred wealthy families nearly prevailed over those of New York City's middle class.

America in the 1920s wasn't a feudal society. But it was a nation in which vast privilege—often inherited privilege—stood in contrast to vast misery. It was also a nation in which the government, more often than not, served the interests of the privileged and ignored the aspirations of ordinary people.

Those days are past—or are they? Income inequality in America has now returned to the levels of the 1920s. Inherited wealth doesn't yet play a big part in our society, but given time—and the repeal of the estate tax—we will grow ourselves a hereditary elite just as set apart from the concerns of ordinary Americans as old Horace Havemeyer. And the new elite, like the old, will have enormous political power.

Kevin Phillips concludes his book *Wealth and Democracy* with a grim warning: "Either democracy must be renewed, with politics brought back to life, or wealth is likely to cement a new and less democratic regime—plutocracy by some other name." It's a pretty extreme line, but we live in extreme times. Even if the forms of democracy remain, they may become meaningless. It's all too easy to see how we may become a country in which the big rewards are reserved for people with the right connections; in which ordinary people see little hope of advancement; in which political involvement seems pointless, because in the end the interests of the elite always get served.

Am I being too pessimistic? Even my liberal friends tell me not to worry, that our system has great resilience, that the center will hold. I hope they're right, but they may be looking in the rearview mirror. Our optimism about America, our belief that in the end our nation always finds its way, comes from the past—a past in which we were a middle-class society. But that was another country.

MR. FISH

FACTS

Average number of mandatory antiunion meetings held by U.S. employers during a union election: 11
(Kate Bronfenbrenner, Cornell University)

Percentage of employers that require at least one of these meetings to be one-on-one: 78
(Kate Bronfenbrenner)

Percentage of senior management positions in medium-sized Russian companies that are held by women: 42
(Grant Thornton International)

Percentage of senior management positions at equivalent U.S. companies that are: 20
(Grant Thornton International)

Factor by which the unemployment rate of African-American college graduates exceeds that of white graduates: 1.9
(Bureau of Labor Statistics/*Harper*'s research)

Average percentage of African-American men age 16 to 64 in New York City who were employed each month in 2004: 52
(Community Service Society of New York)

Percentage of the world's prison population incarcerated in the U.S. as of the year 2000: 25
(The Justice Policy Institute)

Percentage of the world's total population the U.S. represented: 5
(Justice Policy Institute)

Number of black American men between 20 and 40 in prison: 1 in 8
(Justice Now)

Gouging the Poor

from *The Progressive* (2/04)

Barbara Ehrenreich

There's been a lot of whining about health care recently: the shocking cost of insurance, the mounting reluctance of employers to share that cost, the challenge—should you be so lucky as to have insurance—of finding a doctor your insurance company will deign to reimburse, and so forth. But let's look at the glass half full for a change. Despite the growing misfit between health care costs and personal incomes, it is not yet illegal to be sick.

Not quite yet, anyway, though the trend is clear: Hospitals are increasingly resorting to brass knuckle tactics to collect overdue bills from indigent patients. Take the case of Martin Bushman, an intermittently insured mechanic with diabetes who, as reported in *The Wall Street Journal*, had run up a $579 debt to Carle Hospital in Champaign-Urbana. When he failed to appear for a court hearing on his debt rather than miss a day of work, he was arrested and hit with $2,500 bail. Arrests for missed court dates, which the hospitals whimsically refer to as "body attachments," are on the rise throughout the country. Again, on the half full side, we should be thankful that the bodies attached by hospitals cannot yet be used as sources of organs for transplants.

Mindful of their status as nonprofit charitable institutions, hospitals used to be relatively congenial creditors. My uninsured companion of several years would simply work out a payment arrangement—on the scale of about $25 a month for life—and go on consuming medical care without the least concern for his freedom. No longer, and it's not just the dodgier, second-rate hospitals that are relying on the police as collection agents. Yale-New Haven Hospital, for example, has obtained sixty-five arrest warrants for delinquent debtors in the last three years.

Of course, if you work for Yale-New Haven, it's not your body that gets "attached." On a recent visit to Yale hospital workers, I met Tawana Marks, a registrar at the hospital, who had the misfortune to also be admitted as a patient. Unsurprisingly, her hospital-supplied health insurance failed to cover her hospital-incurred bill, so Marks now has her paycheck garnished by her own employer—a condition of debt servitude reminiscent of early-twentieth-century company towns.

To compound the sufferings of the sick and sub-affluent, hospitals now routinely charge uninsured people several times more than the insured. The *Fort Lauderdale Sun-Sentinel* reports that one local hospital charged an uninsured patient

$29,000 for an appendectomy that would have cost an insured patient $6,783. According to the *Los Angeles Times*, in one, albeit for-profit, California hospital chain, the uninsured account for only 2 percent of its patients, but 35 percent of its profits. The explanation for such shameless gouging of the poor? Big insurance companies and HMOs are able to negotiate "discounts" for their members, leaving the uninsured to pay whatever fanciful amounts the hospital cares to charge, such as, in one reported case, $50 for the use of a hospital gown.

Back in 1961, psychiatrist Thomas Szasz noted the "medicalization" of behavior formerly classified as crime or sin, such as drug addiction or what was defined as sexual deviance. Rather than seeing this as a benign and potentially merciful trend, the crotchety Szasz complained about the growing concentration of power in the hands of a "therapeutic state." How quaint his concern sounds today, when instead of the medicalization of crime, we are faced with the criminalization of illness.

Because almost everyone, no matter how initially healthy and prosperous, is now in danger of falling into the clutches of the medical/penitentiary system. It could start with a condition—say, high blood pressure or diabetes—serious enough to be entered into your medical record. Next you lose your job, and with it your health insurance—or, as in the case of 1,000 or so freelance writers (including myself) once insured through the National Writers Union, the insurance company simply decides it no longer wants your business. You go to get new insurance, but no one wants you because you now have a "pre-existing condition." So when that condition flairs up or is joined by a new one, you enter the hospital as a "self-pay" patient, incur bills four times higher than an insured patient would, fall behind in paying them, and, given the hospitals' predatory collection tactics, wind up in jail.

Sociologists have long seen a connection between sickness and criminality, classifying both as forms of deviance. Certainly, the relevant vocabularies have been converging: Note the similarity between the phrases "pre-existing condition" and "prior conviction," as well as the use of the terms "record" and "case." A doctor once told me that, although he had detected a new and potentially life-threatening condition, he would refrain from prescribing anything to correct it, lest my record be marred by yet another pre-existing condition.

The day will come when we look back on such small acts of kindness with nostalgia. Even as I write this, some bright young MBA at Aetna or Prudential is no doubt coming to the conclusion that a great deal of money and valuable medical resources could be saved through the simple expedient of arresting people at the first sign of illness. Skip the intermediate stages of diagnostic testing, hospitalization, and attempted debt collection, and proceed directly to incarceration. The end result will be the same, unless you succeed in concealing that cough or unsightly swelling from the cop on his or her beat.

I'm prepared for this eventuality, having been raised by a mother who was in turn raised by her Christian Scientist grandparents, and had thus been trained to greet her children's symptoms with contempt and derision. I was conditioned, in other words, to conflate physical illness with moral failure. Should a rash or sore throat arrive, I stand ready, at some deep psychic level, to serve my time.

But for those of you who still imagine that illness and

pain should elicit kindly responses from one's fellow humans, I have one last half full observation: Our prisons do offer health care—grossly inadequate care to be sure—but at least it's free, even for child molesters, ax murderers, and those miscreants who have the gall to be both sick and uninsured.

FACTS*

Average total cost for an American 80-year-old to live out the rest of his or her days on a luxury cruise ship: $230,497

Average cost to live them out in an assisted-living facility: $228,075

* (Lee Lindquist, Northwestern University Feinberg School of Medicine)

TINO AND PHOEBE PLAYING DOCTOR.
MR. FISH

A Passage from India

from the *New York Times* (7/12/05)

Suketu Mehta

According to a confidential memorandum, I.B.M. is cutting 13,000 jobs in the United States and in Europe and creating 14,000 jobs in India. From 2000 to 2015, an estimated three million American jobs will have been outsourced; one in 10 technology jobs will leave these shores by the end of this year. Stories like these have aroused a primal fear in the Western public: that they might soon need to line up outside the Indian Embassy for work visas and their children will have to learn Hindi.

Just as my parents had to line up outside the American consulate in Bombay, and my sisters and I had to learn English. My father came to America in 1977 not for its political freedoms or its way of life, but for the hope of a better economic future for his children. My grandfathers on both sides left rural Gujarat in northwestern India to find work: one to Calcutta, which was even more remote in those days than New York is from Bombay now; and the other to Nairobi. Mobility, we have always known, is survival. Now I face the possibility that my children, when they grow up, will find their jobs outsourced to the very country their grandfather left to pursue economic opportunity.

The outsourcing debate seems to have mutated into a contest between the country of my birth and the country of my nationality. Of course I feel a loyalty to America: it gave my parents a new life and my sons were born here. I have a vested interest in seeing America prosper. But I am here because the country of my ancestors didn't understand the changing world; it couldn't change its technology and its philosophy and its notions of social mobility fast enough to fight off the European colonists, who won not so much with the might of advanced weaponry as with the clear logical philosophy of the Enlightenment. Their systems of thinking conquered our own. So, since independence, Indians have had to learn; we have had to slog for long hours in the classroom while the children of other countries went out to play.

When I moved to Queens, in New York City, at the age of 14, I found myself, for the first time in my life, considered good at math. In Bombay, math was my worst subject, and I regularly found my place near the bottom of the class rankings in that rigorous subject. But in my American school, so low were their standards that I was—to my parents' disbelief—near the top of the class. It was the same in English and, unexpectedly, in American history, for my school in Bombay included a detailed study of the American Revolution. My American school curriculum had, of course, almost nothing on the subcontinent's freedom struggle. I was mercilessly bullied during the 1979–80 hostage crisis, because my classmates couldn't tell the difference between Iran and India. If I were now to move with my family to India, my children—who go to one of the best private schools in New York—would have to take remedial math and science courses to get into a good school in Bombay.

Of course, India's no wonderland. It might soon have the world's biggest middle class, but it also has the world's largest underclass. A quarter of its one billion people live below the poverty line, 40 percent are illiterate, and the child malnutrition rate exceeds that of sub-Saharan Africa.

There's a huge difference between the backwater state of Bihar and the boomtown of Bangalore. Those Indians who went to the United States, though, have done remarkably well: Indians make up one of the richest ethnic groups in this country. During the technology boom of the late 1990's, Indians were responsible for 10 percent of all the start-ups in Silicon Valley. And in this year's national spelling bee, the top four contestants were of South Asian origin.

There is a perverse hypocrisy about the whole jobs debate, especially in Europe. The colonial powers invaded countries like India and China, pillaged them of their treasures and commodities, and made sure their industries weren't allowed to develop, so they would stay impoverished and unable to compete. Then the imperialists complained when the destitute people of the former colonies came to their shores to clean their toilets and dig their sewers; they complained when later generations came to earn high wages as doctors and engineers; and now they're complaining when their jobs are being lost to children of the empire who are working harder than they are. My grandfather was once confronted by an elderly Englishman in a London park who asked, "Why are you here?" My grandfather responded, "We are the creditors." We are here because you were there.

The rich countries can't have it both ways. They can't provide huge subsidies for their agricultural conglomerates and complain when Indians who can't make a living on their farms then go to the cities and study computers and take away their jobs. Why are Indians willing to write code for a tenth of what Americans make for the same work? It's not by choice; it's because they're still struggling to stand on their feet after 200 years of colonial rule. The day will soon come when Indian companies will find that it's cheaper to hire computer programmers in Sri Lanka, and then it's there that the Indian jobs will go.

Of course, it's heart-wrenching to see American programmers—many of whom are of Indian origin—lose their jobs and have to worry about how they'll pay the mortgage. But they are ill served by politicians who promise to bring their jobs back by the facile tactic of banning them from leaving. This strategy will ensure only that our schools stay terrible; it'll be an entire country run like the dairy industry, feasible only because of price controls and subsidies.

But we have a resource of incalculable worth right here to help us compete: the immigrants who've been given a new life in America. There are many more Indians in the United States than there are Americans in India. Indian-Americans will help America understand India, trade with it to our mutual benefit. Just as Arab-Americans can help us fight Al Qaeda, Indian-Americans can help us deal with the emerging economic superpower that is India. This is the return of the gift of citizenship.

And just in case, I'm making sure my children learn Hindi.

FACTS

Percentage of South African farmland owned by whites in 1994 and today, respectively: 87, 84
(International Crisis Group)

Ratio of the number of people in Haiti to the number of permanent full-time jobs there: 80:1
(Haiti Support Group)

Estimated average price of a female newborn in a Bulgarian infant-selling ring busted in 2004: $6,000
(State Police Headquarters)

Estimated average price of a male newborn: $18,000
(State Police Headquarters)

Chance that a resident of the former East Germany wants the Berlin Wall back: 1 in 8
(Forsa, Berlin)

Average number of East Germans who died each year trying to cross to West Germany: 18
(Mauermuseum Haus am Checkpoint Charlie, Berlin)

Average number of Mexicans who have died each year between 2000 and 2004 trying to cross to the United States: 407
(Embassy of Mexico)

Number of free-trade agreements between developing nations and developed nations in 1990 and today, respectively: 23, 109
(World Bank)

Projected change in world income over fifteen years if all developing nations were to enter such deals today: +$112,000,000,000
(World Bank)

Projected change, in this scenario, in the total income of developing nations: -$21,500,000,000
(World Bank)

Chance that a southern Sudanese woman will die in childbirth: 1 in 9
(United States Fund for UNICEF)

Chance that a southern Sudanese girl will complete primary school: 1 in 100
(United States Fund for UNICEF)

Projected lifespan in years of a Zimbabwean born in 1989 and one born in 2002, respectively: 60, 34
(UN Human Development Report Office)

Number of countries in which the average life expectancy was less than 40 in 2002: 6
(World Health Organization)

Number of African countries in which the average life expectancy has declined since 1978: 22
(World Health Organization)

Estimated percentage change since 1970 in sub-Saharan Africa's share of world trade: –57
(World Bank)

OUR DYING DEMOCRACY

Corruption in the Republic
BY JOSHUA HOLLAND–221

with cartoons by Mr. Fish
and facts

The sickly-sweet smell of failure hangs over Washington, where the Bush administration and its backers in both parties have had free rein for more than half a decade. Supported by Congress, the president and his cronies pander to the worst instincts of the crowd while slavishly implementing the agenda of their powerful backers and ignoring the problems of our democracy: the desperate condition of our schools and cities; the waste and exploitation of our natural resources; the failures of our prison system; the decay of our transportation infrastructure; the vulnerability of our population to terrorists and natural disasters brought on in part by the administration's own policies. Our policy makers are not merely incompetent, they are utterly corrupt—and so is the system of bribes and favors and lies that supports them.

Corruption in the Republic

from AlterNet (8/22/05)

by Joshua Holland

How could one not be appalled by the porcine politics that passes for American Democracy these days? Each bill that slithers its way through this Congress soaks us more brazenly than the last.

In an economy where wages barely outpace inflation, the influence industry is booming; the number of creepy-crawlies on K Street has more than doubled in five and a half short years under the Bush Administration.

We all have our favorite exhibit of pernicious looting posing as public policy. Mine is a local phenomenon: the mega-bucks tax-payer financed sports stadium swindle. It's a perennial favorite—some well-connected billionaire who makes the right contributions at City Hall and the Governor's mansion and is on the right cocktail circuit manages to convince a city full of hard-working Americans that they've got to buy him a new stadium. The pitch is always the same: the sweaty exertions of 'roid-raging pro athletes will bring prestige and prosperity and, most of all, jobs, jobs, jobs! As supporters of San Francisco's 3Com park pitched it: "Build the Stadium—Create the Jobs!"

It's basically an old-fashioned grift on an enormous scale. Almost a decade ago, economists Roger Noll and Andrew Zimbalist undertook a study sponsored by the Brookings Institution that's considered a public-policy classic. They found that stadiums cost cities tens of million dollars of dollars in subsidies per year. Contrary to supporters' claims, "Sports facilities attract neither tourists nor new industry":

> A new sports facility has an extremely small (perhaps even negative) effect on overall economic activity and employment. No recent facility appears to have earned anything approaching a reasonable return on investment. No recent facility has been self-financing in terms of its impact on net tax revenues. Regardless of whether the unit of analysis is a local neighborhood, a city, or an entire metropolitan area, the economic benefits of sports facilities are *de minimus.*

But despite the debunking of the economic rationale (in subsequent studies as well) we keep falling for it. And our cities' fat cats—the D.C. power-broker lawyer, the Cleveland shipping magnate, the computer direct-sales gazillionaire—get fatter and our happy local politicians sit in the owner's box and moon for the cameras; mom and dad complain about the $8 dollar beers and $5 dollar hotdogs and never think twice about the $184 dollar chunk of concrete that they paid for even if they never once go to the park.

There is no ideological stake in objecting to such outrages. Corporate socialism isn't conservatism, it just proves that there's no public participation keeping our "leaders" honest. The only way government builds stadium after stadium for a select circle of rich guys is if they're the ones doing the governing.

It's the same at every level, most visibly in D.C. Last month Molly Ivins wrote that we're "pigging out on pork," and Paul Krugman lamented that what passes for governance these days is little more than "machine politics at work, favors granted in return for favors received."

Ivins and Krugman look at a particularly corrupt administration but fail to see the ungovernable beast behind it, the hot blood of tax dollars coursing through its veins. The problem isn't that you can go to OpenSecrets.org and find out who owns your representative and how much they paid for him or her, it's that there has to be an OpenSecrets.org in the first place.

But while it's easy to gripe, it's harder for us to recognize the fact that the sorry state of affairs in government today is truly a monster of our own creation. I have seen Dr. Frankenstein and he is us.

We've built a country—the nation founded as a bold experiment in self-governance—into a glorious monument to apathy, a beacon of democratic neglect so far removed from the ideals we hold dear as to be completely unrecognizable.

It wasn't supposed to be this way. In a 1787 letter to Edward Carrington, a hero of the Revolution and member of the Continental Congress, Thomas Jefferson wrote of the role citizens played in keeping the government's nose to the grindstone: "If once they become inattentive to the public affairs, you and I, and Congress, and Assemblies, Judges, and Governors, shall all become wolves."

Jefferson and his fellow Framers understood that we'd lose control of our government the further distanced from its workings we became, and the less we believed in our capacity to govern ourselves.

We departed from their ideal following the Civil War. The 14th, 15th, and 16th Amendments shifted the balance of power from Boston, Albany, and Philadelphia to Washington, DC. The irony is that the price we paid for a central government that could guarantee us equal protection under the law also estranged us in perpetuity from that government and distanced us from its purse strings.

So we became oblivious to its workings. In the 2000 election cycle, before the upsurge in 2004 driven by the war in Iraq, gay marriage, and Swiftboaters, America ranked 131st in the world in voter participation—sandwiched between those bastions of Jeffersonian democracy, Chad and Botswana.

According to the most recent (1997) Household Survey of Adult Civic Participation, less than a third of American adults read a newspaper or news magazine "almost every day."

The natural consequence of this inattention is that many—perhaps most—Americans haven't a clue what their government is up to. Almost a third couldn't tell you what "job or political office" Al Gore held after he had spent five years in the vice-presidency, around a third didn't know which party held the majority in Congress and, *stunningly*, 49 percent of Americans surveyed didn't know "which party is more conservative at the national level."

Almost four in ten Americans find politics and government "too complicated to understand," and a similar number believed their families "had no say in what federal government does." They're right, of course, but it's nobody's fault but their own.

So who cares if politicians hand out hundreds of billions of dollars in corporate welfare to the boys down at the club while one in five American children lives in poverty? Nobody in America is paying attention anyway, even as the vultures continue to circle overhead. It is a mainstay of our political culture—and the greatest victory that powerful corporate interests have ever achieved—that we consider government as something apart from ourselves, and that we are powerless to change it.

And if you think the prescription is to elect more Democrats, as so many progressives do, the last week of business in the House should dissuade you of the perception. *Forty-one* Democratic members voted for President Bush's energy bill, about which the *Washington Post* carried the following headlines during the last week of July: "Energy Bill Raises Fears About Pollution, Fraud," "Energy Deal Has Tax Breaks for Companies," "Energy Tax Breaks Total $14.5 Billion" and "Bill Wouldn't Wean U.S. Off Oil Imports, Analysts Say."

Or consider the image of Representative Jim Moran, D-Virginia, who not only voted for the industry-authored Central American Free Trade Agreement, but also lobbied fellow Democrats to join him, receiving a "*standing ovation from lobbyists* and a word of thanks from the Speaker," as reported by *The Hill*.

It's true that Democrats needed six decades to achieve the kind of raw patronage system the Republicans have created in one, but they too got there eventually, thanks to our epic inattention.

So we find ourselves living in a perverse corporate welfare state, where military Keynesianism drives foreign policy and multinationals drain ever more of our public resources into their off-shore shelters.

But if our frustrations were ever to build to the point where we had had enough, we could bring down this sordid status quo in a minute simply by becoming engaged.

Just look at what the tenacious efforts of the fundamentalist Christian minority have achieved in the Republican Party. As Thomas Frank exposited so gracefully in *What's the Matter With Kansas?*, they staged a bloodless coup by taking over at the local level and forcing their agenda upwards. By running for precinct captain, school board member and dog-catcher, they *pushed* their party to toe the line they had drawn in the sand of American culture. Nothing is stopping us from following their model except for our intolerable somnolence.

So next time you're watching *Good Morning America* and the well-coiffed anchor talks about the latest pork-greased legislation slinking through Congress in the dead of night with the bemused "there they go again" half-smile of a parent discussing a recalcitrant child, and you feel that ire welling up within you, don't cast about for someone to blame. Peel your fat ass off the couch, go to your mirror, and stare the culprit right in the face.

FACTS

Funds earmarked in the transportation bill passed in 2005 for a documentary film "about infrastructure that demonstrates advancement in Alaska": $3 million
(*New York Times*, 10/7/05)

Funds earmarked in the bill for a bridge connecting Ketchikan, Alaska, with Gravina Island, population 50: $223 million
(*New York Times*, 10/7/05)

Reason, according to a White House official, why President Bush did not fly to San Antonio on 9/23/05 to help prepare for Hurricane Rita: "It was too sunny" for a good hurricane-themed photo op
(*New York Times*, 9/24/05)

Minimum number of Congress members Sun Myung Moon claims attended his March coronation as the "King of Peace": 20
(Interreligious and International Federation for World Peace)

Number of Congress members present at the June transfer of power from Coalition military forces to the Iraqi government: 0
(U.S. State Department)

Number of black U.S. senators during the entire 1800s, the entire 1900s, and today, respectively: 2, 2, 1
(U.S. Senate Historical Office)

Minimum amount Congressman Randy "Duke" Cunningham (R-CA) accepted in bribes from three defense contractors before resigning in November 2005: $2.4 million
(*New York Times*, 11/29/05)

Name of the 42-foot yacht loaned to Cunningham by defense contractor Mitchell Wade: The Duke-Stir
(*Newsday*, 11/28/05)

A functioning democracy is a society where the overwhelming majority of the population decides that it is not interested in the awesome task of self-governance, preferring instead that the job fall to a miniscule number of very greedy and ruthless-ly anti-democratic businessmen.

Mr. Fish

FACTS

Days a House committee postponed July hearings on antidepressants while its chair considered a pharmaceutical-lobbyist job: 50
(Congressman Jim Greenwood's Office)

Number of the five Republicans investigating Rep. Tom DeLay on ethics charges who have taken donations from his PAC: 4
(Federal Election Commission)

Minimum number of former senior government officials who have worked for a major U.S. defense contractor since 1997: 176
(Project on Government Oversight/*Harper's* research)

Chance that one of them was a member of Congress who became a registered lobbyist: 1 in 4
(Project on Government Oversight/*Harper's* research)

Estimated percentage of U.S. corporations that paid no federal taxes between 1996 and 2000: 61
(General Accounting Office)

Seconds it took a Maryland consultant in 2003 to pick a Diebold voting machine's lock and remove its memory card: 10
(Raba Technologies LLC)

Percentage of U.S. high school students who believe news stories should require "government approval" before publication: 36
(John S. and James L. Knight Foundation)

Percentage of Pentagon contracts since 1998 that have been awarded on a no-bid basis: 44
(Center for Public Integrity)

THE NEXT DEPRESSION

Countdown to a Meltdown
BY JAMES FALLOWS–233

with facts

The Great Depression taught us some valuable lessons, which we've since forgotten. The penalty may be another Great Depression.

Countdown to a Meltdown

from the *Atlantic Monthly* (7/05)

by James Fallows

JANUARY 20, 2016, MASTER STRATEGY MEMO
SUBJECT: THE COMING YEAR—AND BEYOND

Sir:

It is time to think carefully about the next year. Our position is uniquely promising—and uniquely difficult.

The promise lies in the fact that you are going to win the election. Nothing is guaranteed in politics, but based on everything we know, and barring an act of God or a disastrous error on our side, one year from today you will be sworn in as the forty-sixth president of the United States. And you will be the first president since before the Civil War to come from neither the Republican nor the Democratic Party. This is one aspect of your electoral advantage right now: having created our new party, you are already assured of its nomination, whereas the candidates from the two legacy parties are still carving themselves up in their primaries.

The difficulty, too, lies in the fact that you are going to win. The same circumstances that are bringing an end to 164 years of two-party rule have brought tremendous hardship to the country. This will be the first time since Franklin Roosevelt took office in 1933 that so much is demanded so quickly from a new administration. Our challenge is not just to win the election but to win in a way that gives us a chance to address economic failures that have been fifty years in the making.

That is the purpose of this memo: to provide the economic background for the larger themes in our campaign. Although economic changes will be items one through ten on your urgent "to do" list a year from now, this is not the place to talk about them in detail. There will be plenty of time for that later, with the policy guys. Instead I want to speak here not just as your campaign manager but on the basis of our friendship and shared efforts these past twenty years. Being completely honest about the country's problems might not be necessary during the campaign—sounding pessimistic in speeches would hurt us. But we ourselves need to be clear about the challenge we face. Unless we understand how we got here, we won't be able to find the way out once you are in office.

Politics is about stories—the personal story of how a leader was shaped, the national story of how America's long saga has led to today's dramas. Your personal story needs no work at all. Dwight Eisenhower was the last president to enter office with a worldwide image of competence, though obviously his achievements were military rather than technological. But we have work to do on the national story.

When it comes to the old parties, the story boils down to this: the Democrats can't win, and the Republicans can't govern. Okay, that's an overstatement; but the more nuanced version is nearly as discouraging.

The past fifty years have shown that the Democrats can't win the presidency except when everything goes their way. Only three Democrats have reached the White House since Lyndon Johnson decided to leave. In 1976 they ran a pious-sounding candidate against the political ghost of the disgraced Richard Nixon—and against his corporeal successor, Gerald Ford, the only unelected incumbent in American history. In 1992 they ran their most talented campaigner since FDR, and even Bill Clinton would have lost if Ross Perot had not stayed in the race and siphoned away votes from the Republicans. And in 2008 they were unexpectedly saved by the death of Fidel Castro. This drained some of the pro-Republican passion of South Florida's Cuban immigrants, and the disastrous governmental bungling of the "Cuba Libre" influx that followed gave the Democrats their first win in Florida since 1996—along with the election. But that Democratic administration could turn out to have been America's last. The Electoral College map drawn up after the 2010 census removed votes from all the familiar blue states except California, giving the Republicans a bigger head start from the Sunbelt states and the South.

As for the Republicans, fifty years have shown they can't govern without breaking the bank. Starting with Richard Nixon, every Republican president has left the dollar lower, the federal budget deficit higher, the American trade position weaker, and the U.S. manufacturing work force smaller than when he took office.

The story of the parties, then, is that the American people mistrust the Republicans' economic record, and don't trust the Democrats enough to let them try to do better. That is why—and it is the only reason why—they are giving us a chance. But we can move from electoral to *governmental* success only with a clear understanding of why so much has gone so wrong with the economy. Our internal polls show that nearly 90 percent of the public thinks the economy is "on the wrong track." Those readings should hold up, since that's roughly the percentage of Americans whose income has fallen in real terms in the past five years.

The story we will tell them begins fifteen years ago, and it has three chapters. For public use we'll refer to them by the names of the respective administrations. But for our own purposes it will be clearer to think of the chapter titles as "Cocking the Gun," "Pulling the Trigger," and "Bleeding."

1. Cocking the Gun

Everything changed in 2001. But it didn't all change on September 11.

Yes, the ramifications of 9/11 will be with us for decades, much as the aftereffects of Pearl Harbor explain the presence of thousands of U.S. troops in Asia seventy-five years later. Before 2001 about 12,000 American troops were stationed in the Middle East—most of them in Kuwait and Saudi Arabia. Since 2003 we have never had fewer than 100,000 troops in CENTCOM's theater, most of them on active anti-insurgency duty. The locale of the most intense fighting keeps changing—first Afghanistan and Iraq, then Pakistan and Egypt, now Saudi Arabia and the frontier between Turkey and the Republic of Kurdistan—but the commitment goes on.

Before there was 9/11, however, there was June 7, 2001. For our purposes modern economic history began that day.

On June 7 President George W. Bush celebrated his first big legislative victory. Only two weeks earlier his new administration had suffered a terrible political blow, when a Republican senator left the party and gave Democrats a one-vote majority in the Senate. But the administration was nevertheless able to persuade a dozen Democratic senators to vote its way and authorize a tax cut that would decrease federal tax revenues by some $1.35 trillion between then and 2010.

This was presented at the time as a way to avoid the "problem" of paying down the federal debt too fast. According to the administration's forecasts, the government was on the way to running up $5.6 trillion in surpluses over the coming decade. The entire federal debt accumulated between the nation's founding and 2001 totaled only about $3.2 trillion—and for technical reasons at most $2 trillion of that total could be paid off within the next decade. Therefore some $3.6 trillion in "unusable" surplus—or about $12,000 for every American—was likely to pile up in the Treasury. The administration proposed to give slightly less than half of that back through tax cuts, saving the rest for Social Security and other obligations.

Congress agreed, and it was this achievement that the president celebrated at the White House signing ceremony on June 7. "We recognize loud and clear the surplus is not the government's money," Bush said at the time. "The surplus is the people's money, and we ought to trust them with their own money."

If the president or anyone else at that ceremony had had perfect foresight, he would have seen that no surpluses of any sort would materialize, either for the government to hoard or for taxpayers to get back. (A year later the budget would show a deficit of $158 billion; a year after that $378 billion.) By the end of Bush's second term the federal debt, rather than having nearly disappeared, as he expected, had tripled. If those in the crowd had had that kind of foresight, they would have called their brokers the next day to unload all their stock holdings. A few hours after Bush signed the tax-cut bill, the Dow Jones industrial average closed at 11,090, a level it has never reached again.

In a way it doesn't matter what the national government intended, or why all forecasts proved so wrong. Through the rest of his presidency Bush contended that the reason was 9/11—that it had changed the budget as it changed everything else. It forced the government to spend more, for war and for homeland security, even as the economic dislocation it caused meant the government could collect less. Most people outside the administration considered this explanation misleading, or at least incomplete. For instance, as Bush began his second term the nonpartisan Congressional Budget Office said that the biggest reason for growing deficits was the tax cuts.

But here is what really mattered about that June day in 2001: from that point on the U.S. government had less money to work with than it had under the previous eight presidents. Through four decades and through administrations as diverse as Lyndon Johnson's and Ronald Reagan's, federal tax revenue had stayed within a fairly narrow band. The tax cuts of 2001 pushed it out of that safety zone, reducing it to its lowest level as a share of the economy in the modern era. And as we will see, these cuts—the first of three rounds—did so just when the country's commitments and obligations had begun to grow.

As late as 2008 the trend could have been altered, though the cuts of 2003 and 2005 had made things worse. But in the late summer of 2008 Senate Republicans once again demonstrated their mastery of the basic feints and dodges of politics. The tax cuts enacted during Bush's first term were in theory "temporary," and set to expire starting in 2010. But Congress didn't have to wait until 2010 to decide whether to make them permanent, so of course the Republican majority scheduled the vote at the most awkward moment possible for the Democrats: on the eve of a close presidential election. The Democratic senators understood their dilemma. Either they voted for the tax cuts and looked like hypocrites for all their past complaints, or they voted against them and invited an onslaught of "tax and spend" attack ads in the campaign. Enough Democrats made the "smart" choice. They held their seats in the election, and the party took back the presidency. But they also locked in the tax cuts, which was step one in cocking the gun.

From the Archives:
"The Coming Death Shortage" (May 2005)
Why the longevity boom will make us sorry to be alive. By Charles C. Mann

The explanation of steps two and three is much quicker: People kept living longer, and they kept saving less. Increased longevity is a tremendous human achievement but a fiscal challenge—as in any household where people outlive their savings. Late in 2003 Congress dramatically escalated the fiscal problem by adding prescription-drug coverage to Medicare, with barely any discussion of its long-term cost. David M. Walker, the government's comptroller general at the time, said that the action was part of "the most reckless fiscal year in the history of the Republic," because that vote and a few other changes added roughly $13 trillion to the government's long-term commitments.

FROM THE ARCHIVES:
"Spendthrift Nation" (January 2003)

It's a precarious situation: U.S. consumer spending is sustaining the economy—but we need to save more to prepare for the surge in retirements. Here's how to boost personal saving without undermining the economic recovery. By Michael Calabrese and Maya MacGuineas

The evaporation of personal savings was marveled at by all economists but explained by few. Americans saved about eight percent of their disposable income through the 1950s and 1960s, slightly more in the 1970s and 1980s, slightly less and then a lot less in the 1990s. At the beginning of this century they were saving, on average, just about nothing.

The possible reasons for this failure to save—credit-card debt? a false sense of wealth thanks to the real-estate bubble? stagnant real earnings for much of the population? —mattered less than the results. The country needed money to run its government, and Americans themselves weren't about to provide it. This is where the final, secret element of the gun-cocking process came into play: the unspoken deal with China.

The terms of the deal are obvious in retrospect. Even at the time, economists discussed the arrangement endlessly in their journals. The oddity was that so few politicians picked up on what they said. The heart of the matter, as we now know, was this simple equation: each time Congress raised benefits, reduced taxes, or encouraged more borrowing by consumers, it shifted part of the U.S. manufacturing base to China.

Of course this shift had something to do with "unfair"

trade, undereducated American workers, dirt-cheap Chinese sweatshops, and all the other things that American politicians chose to yammer about. But the "jobless recovery" of the early 2000s and the "jobless collapse" at the end of the decade could never have occurred without the strange intersection of American and Chinese (plus Japanese and Korean) plans. The Chinese government was determined to keep the value of its yuan as low as possible, thus making Chinese exports as attractive as possible, so that Chinese factories could expand as quickly as possible, to provide work for the tens of millions of people trooping every year to Shanghai or Guangzhou to enter the labor force. To this end, Chinese banks sent their extra dollars right back to the U.S. Treasury, in loans to cover the U.S. budget deficit; if they hadn't, normal market pressures would have driven up the yuan's value. This, in turn, would have made it harder for China to keep creating jobs and easier for America to retain them. But Americans would have had to tax themselves to cover the deficit.

FROM THE ARCHIVES:
"America's 'Suez Moment'" (January 2003)

The growing trade deficit threatens U.S. living standards and makes the country dangerously vulnerable to economic extortion. The way out is to make foreigners act more like us. By Sherle R. Schwenninger

This arrangement was called "Bretton Woods Two," after the regime that kept the world economy afloat for twenty-five years after World War II. The question economists debated was how long it could last. One group said it could go on indefinitely, because it gave each country's government what it really wanted (for China, booming exports and therefore a less dissatisfied population; for America, the ability to spend more while saving and taxing less). But by Bush's second term the warning signals were getting louder. "This is starting to resemble a pyramid scheme," the *Financial Times* warned early in 2005. The danger was that the system was fundamentally unstable. Almost overnight it could go from working well to collapsing. If any one of the Asian countries piling up dollars (and most were doing so) began to suspect that any other was about to unload them, all the countries would have an incentive to sell dollars as fast as possible, before they got stuck with worthless currency. Economists in the "soft landing" camp said that adjustments would be gradual, and that Chinese self-interest would prevent a panic. The "hard landing" camp—well, we know all too well what they were concerned about.

2. Pulling the Trigger

The 2008 election, like those in 2000 and 2004, could have gone either way. If Fidel Castro had died two years earlier, the second Bay of Pigs tragedy and related "regime change" difficulties might have been dim memories by Election Day. Or if he had died a year later, the Cuban-American bloc of Florida voters would have been as reliably Republican in 2008 as in the previous fifty years. Since the red state-blue state divide was otherwise the same as in 2000 and 2004, if the Republicans had held Florida they would presumably have held the White House as well—despite mounting unease about debt, deficits, job loss, and rising U.S. casualties in Pakistan.

But by dying when he did, at eighty-two, and becoming the "October surprise" of the 2008 campaign, Castro got revenge on the Republicans who had for years supported the Cuban trade embargo. Better yet, he got revenge on his original enemies, the Democrats, too. Castro couldn't have planned it, but his disappearance was the beginning —the first puff of wind, the trigger—of the catastrophe that followed.

Or perhaps we should call it the first domino to fall, because what then happened had a kind of geometric inevitability. The next domino was a thousand miles across the Caribbean, in Venezuela. Hugo Chavez, originally elected as a crusading left-winger, was by then well into his role as an outright military dictator. For years our diplomats had grumbled that Chavez was "Castro with oil," but after the real Castro's death the comparison had new meaning. A right-wing militia of disgruntled Venezuelans, emboldened by the news that Castro was gone, attempted a coup at the beginning of 2009, shortly after the U.S. elections. Chavez captured the ringleaders, worked them over, and then broadcast their possibly false "confession" that they had been sponsored by the CIA. That led to Chavez's "declaration of economic war" against the United States, which in practice meant temporarily closing the gigantic Amuay refinery, the source of one eighth of all the gasoline used on American roads— and reopening it two months later with a pledge to send no products to American ports.

From the Archives:
"The Fuel Subsidy We Need" (January 2003)
Oil dependence is still the Achilles' heel of the American

empire. It doesn't have to be—and if we don't want to lose economic ground to Europe, it can't be. By Ricardo Bayon

That was when the fourth—and worst—world oil shock started. For at least five years economists and oilmen alike had warned that there was no "give" in the world oil market. In the early 2000s China's consumption was growing five times as fast as America's—and America was no slouch. (The main difference was that China, like India, was importing oil mainly for its factories, whereas the United States was doing so mainly for its big cars.) Even a temporary disruption in the flow could cause major dislocations.

All the earlier oil shocks had meant short-term disruptions in supply (that's why they were "shocks"), but this time the long term was also in question. Geologists had argued about "peaking" predictions for years, but the concept was on everyone's lips by 2009.

The Democrats had spent George Bush's second term preparing for everything except what was about to hit them. Our forty-fourth president seemed actually to welcome being universally known as "the Preacher," a nickname like "Ike" or "Honest Abe." It was a sign of how much emphasis he'd put on earnestly talking about faith, family, and firearms to voters in the heartland, in his effort to help the Democrats close the "values gap." But he had no idea what to do (to be fair, the man he beat, "the Veep," would not have known either) when the spot price of oil rose by 40 percent in the week after the Chavez declaration—and then everything else went wrong.

Anyone who needed further proof that God is a Republican would have found it in 2009. When the price of oil went up, the run on the dollar began. "Fixed exchange rates with heavy intervention—in essence, Bretton Woods Two—have enormous capacity to create an illusory sense of stability that could be shattered very quickly," Lawrence Summers had warned in 2004. "That is the lesson of Britain in 1992, of Mexico in 1994, of emerging Asia in 1997, of Russia in 1998, and of Brazil in 1998." And of the United States in 2009. It didn't help that Hugo Chavez had struck his notorious then-secret deal with the Chinese: preferential future contracts for his oil, which China needed, in return for China's backing out of Bretton Woods Two, which Chavez wanted.

There had been hints of how the falling dominoes would look as early as January of 2005. In remarks made at the World Economic Forum in Davos, Switzerland, Fan Gang, the director of China's nongovernmental National Economic Research Institute, said that "the U.S. dollar is no longer seen as a stable currency." This caused a quick flurry in the foreign-exchange markets. It was to the real thing what the World Trade Center car bomb in 1993 was to 9/11.

When we read histories of the late 1920s, we practically want to scream, *Stop! Don't buy all that stock on credit! Get out of the market before it's too late!* When we read histories of the dot-com boom in the late 1990s, we have the same agonizing sense of not being able to save the victims from themselves: *Don't take out that home-equity loan to buy stocks at their peak! For God's sake, sell your Cisco shares when they hit 70, don't wait till they're back at 10!*

In retrospect, the ugly end is so obvious and inevitable. Why didn't people see it at the time? The same clearly applies to what happened in 2009. Economists had laid out the sequence of causes and effects in a "hard landing," and it worked just as they said it would.

Once the run on the dollar started, everything seemed to happen at once. Two days after the Venezuelan oil shock the dollar was down by 25 percent against the yen and the yuan. Two weeks later it was down by 50 percent. By the time trading "stabilized," one U.S. dollar bought only 2.5 Chinese yuan—not eight, as it had a year earlier.

As the dollar headed down, assets denominated in dollars suddenly looked like losers. Most Americans had no choice but to stay in the dollar economy (their houses were priced in dollars, as were their savings and their paychecks), but those who had a choice unloaded their dollar holdings fast. The people with choices were the very richest Americans, and foreigners of every sort. The two kinds of assets they least wanted to hold were shares in U.S.-based companies, since the plummeting dollar would wipe out any conceivable market gains, and dollar-based bonds, including U.S. Treasury debt. Thus we had twin, reinforcing panics: a sudden decline in share prices plus a sudden selloff of bonds and Treasury holdings. The T-note selloff forced interest rates up, which forced stock prices further down, and the race to the bottom was on.

Because interest rates had been so low for so long, much of the public had forgotten how nasty life could be when money all of a sudden got tight. Every part of the cycle seemed to make every other part worse.

Businesses scaled back their expansion or investment plans, since borrowed money was more expensive. That meant fewer jobs. Mortgage rates went up, so buyers who might have bid on a $400,000 house could now handle only $250,000. That pushed real-estate values down; over time the $400,000 house *became* a $250,000 house. Credit-card rates were more onerous, so consumers had to cut back their spending. Some did it voluntarily, others in compliance with the Garnishee Amendments to the Bankruptcy Act of 2008. Businesses of every sort had higher fixed costs: for energy, because of the oil-price spike; for imported components, because of the dollar's crash; for everything else, because of ripple effects from those changes and from higher interest rates. Those same businesses had lower revenues, because of the squeeze on their customer base. Early in Bush's second term economists had pointed out that the U.S. stock indexes were surprisingly weak considering how well U.S. corporations had been doing. The fear of just these developments was why.

Americans had lived through a similar self-intensifying cycle before—but not since the late 1970s, when many of today's adults were not even born. Back in those days the sequence of energy-price spike, dollar crash, interest-rate surge, business slowdown, and stock-market loss had overwhelmed poor Jimmy Carter—he of the promise to give America "a government as good as its people." This time it did the same to the Preacher, for all his talk about "a new Democratic Party rooted in the oldest values of a free and faithful country." When he went down, the future of his party almost certainly went with him.

The spate of mergers and acquisitions that started in 2010 was shocking at the time but looks inevitable in retrospect. When the CEOs of the three remaining U.S. airlines had their notorious midnight meeting at the DFW Hilton, they knew they were breaking two dozen antitrust laws and would be in financial and legal trouble if their nervy move failed. But it worked. When they announced the new and combined AmFly Corporation, regulators were in no position to call their bluff. At their joint press conference the CEOs said, Accept our more efficient structure or we'll all declare bankruptcy, and all at once. The efficiencies meant half as many flights (for "fuel conservation") as had been offered by the previously competing airlines, to 150 fewer cities, with a third as many jobs (all non-union). Democrats in Congress didn't like it, nor did most editorialists, but the administration didn't really have a choice. It could swallow the deal—or it could get ready to take over the routes, the planes, the payrolls, and the passenger complaints, not to mention the decades of litigation.

Toyota's acquisition of General Motors and Ford, in 2012, had a similar inevitability. Over the previous decade the two U.S. companies had lost money on every car they sold. Such profit as they made was on SUVs, trucks, and Hummer-style big rigs. In 2008, just before the oil shock, GM seemed to have struck gold with the Strykette—an adaptation of the Army's Stryker vehicle, so famous from Iraq and Pakistan, whose marketing campaign attracted professional women. Then the SUV market simply disappeared. With gasoline at $6 a gallon, the prime interest rate at 15 percent, and the stock and housing markets in the toilet, no one wanted what American car makers could sell. The weak dollar, and their weak stock prices, made the companies a bargain for Toyota.

For politicians every aspect of this cycle was a problem: the job losses, the gasoline lines, the bankruptcies, the hard-luck stories of lifetime savings vanishing as the stock market headed down. But nothing matched the nightmare of foreclosures.

For years regulators and financiers had worried about the "over-leveraging" of the American housing market. As housing prices soared in coastal cities, people behaved the way they had during the stock-market run-up of the 1920s: they paid higher and higher prices; they covered more and more of the purchase price with debt; more and more of that debt was on "floating rate" terms—and everything was fine as long as prices stayed high and interest rates stayed low.

When the market collapsed, Americans didn't behave the way economic theory said they should. They behaved the way their predecessors in the Depression had: they stayed in their houses, stopped paying their mortgages, and waited for the banks to take the next step. Through much of the Midwest this was a manageable problem: the housing market had gone less berserk to begin with, and, as in the Great Depression, there was a longer-term, more personal relationship between customers and financiers. But in the fastest-growing markets—Orlando, Las Vegas, the Carolina Research Triangle, northern Virginia—the banks simply could not wait. The deal brokered at the White House Security-in-Shelter Summit was ingenious: federal purchase of one million RVs and mobile homes, many of them built at idle auto or truck factories; subsidies for families who agreed to leave foreclosed homes without being evicted by marshals, such that they could buy RVs with no payments for five years; and the use of land at decommissioned military bases for the new RV villages. But it did not erase the blogcam live broadcasts of families being evicted, or the jokes about the "Preacher-villes" springing up at Camp Lejeune, the former Fort Ord, and the Philadelphia naval shipyard.

Here is how we know that a sitting president is going to lose: he is seriously challenged in his own party's primaries. So if the economic tailspin had left any doubts about the prospects for the Preacher and his party, they were removed by the clamor to run against him in the Democratic primaries of 2012. The party's biggest names were all there: the senators from New York, Illinois, and Florida; the new governors of California and Pennsylvania; the mayor of New York, when it looked as if the Olympic Games would still be held there that fall; and the actor who in his three most recent films had captured Americans' idea of how a president should look and sound, and who came closest to stealing the nomination from the incumbent.

He and the rest of them were probably lucky that their campaigns fell short—not that any politician ever believes that. The Democratic nomination in 2012 was obviously a poisoned chalice, but a politician can't help thinking that a poisoned chalice is better than no chalice at all. The barrier none of them could have overcome was the financial crisis of state and local government.

All that befell the federal budget during the collapse of 2009–2012 happened to state and local governments, too, but more so. They had to spend more—on welfare, Medicaid, jails, police officers—while taking in less. One by one their normal sources of funding dried up. Revenues from the multi-state lottery and the FreedomBall drawings rose a bit. Unfortunately, the surge of spending on casino gambling in forty-three states and on legalized prostitution in thirty-one didn't benefit state and local governments, because except in Nevada those activities were confined to Indian reservations, and had only an indirect stimulative effect.

And many governors and mayors faced a reality the president could avoid: they operated under constitutions and charters that forbade deficit spending. So they had no practical choice but to tighten the clamps at both ends, cutting budgets and raising taxes. The process had begun before the crash, as politicking in most state capitols was dominated by "intractable" budget disputes. When the downturn really hit, even governors who had never heard of John Maynard Keynes sensed that it was a bad idea to raise taxes on people who were being laid off and evicted. But they were obliged by law to balance their budgets. All mayors and governors knew that it would be dicey to renege on their basic commitments to education, public safety, public health, and public infrastructure. But even in hindsight it is hard to know what else they could have done. California did too much too fast in closing sixty-three of its 110 community colleges and imposing $9,500 annual "user fees" in place of the previous nominal fees. Its solution to the financing crisis on its high-end campuses was defter—especially the "Great Pacific Partnership" between the University of California and Tsinghua University, in Beijing. This was a win-win arrangement, in which the Chinese Ministry of Education took over the funding of the UC Berkeley physics, computer-science, and biology laboratories, plus the genomics laboratory at UC San Francisco, in exchange for a 51 percent share of all resulting patents.

State and local governments across the country did what they could. Fee-for-service became the norm—first for "enrichment" programs in the schools, then to underwrite teachers' salaries, then for emergency police calls, then for inclusion in routine police and fire patrols. First in Minnesota, soon after in Michigan, New York, and Pennsylvania, there were awkward moments when the governor, exercising his power as commander in chief of the state National Guard, ordered the Guard's medical units to serve in hospitals that had furloughed nurses and emergency-room doctors. The Democratic president decided not to force the question of who had ultimate control over these "citizen soldiers." This averted a showdown in the short term, but became one more attack point for the Republicans about weak and vacillating Democrats. Cities within 150 miles of the Mexican border opened police-service and trash-hauling contracts to companies based in Mexico. The state of Georgia, extending a practice it had begun in the early 2000s, said that it would hire no new public school teachers except under the "Partnership for Excellence" program, which brought in cut-rate teachers from India.

The chaos in public services spelled the end for the administration, and for the Democratic Party in the long run. The Democrats couldn't defend the unions. They couldn't defend pensioners. They couldn't even do much for their limousine liberals. The nation had never been more in the mood for firm leadership. When the "Desert Eagle" scored his astonishing coup in the Saudi Arabian desert just before Christmas of 2011, America knew who its next leader would be. For a four-star general to join his enlisted men in a nighttime HALO special-operations assault was against all established practice. The Eagle's determination to go ahead with the stunt revealed him to be essentially a MacArthuresque ham. But the element of surprise was total, and the unit surrounded, captured, and gagged Osama bin Laden before he was fully awake.

The general's news conference the next day had the largest live audience in history, breaking the record set a few months earlier by the coronation of England's King William V. The natural grace of this new American hero was like nothing the world had seen since Charles Lindbergh landed in Paris. His politics were indistinct, but if anything, that was a plus. He was strong on defense; urgent (without details) about "fighting smart against our economic enemies"; and broadly appealing on "values"—a devout Catholic who had brought the first openly gay commandos into a front-line combat unit. ("When we were under fire, I never asked who they loved, because I knew they loved our flag.") Political pros had always assumed that America's first black president would be a Republican and a soldier, and they were right. He just didn't turn out to be Colin Powell.

The only suspense in the election was how big the win would be. By Labor Day it was clear that the Democrats might lose even the District of Columbia, whose rich residents were resentful about their ravaged stock portfolios, and whose poor residents had been cut off from Medicaid, welfare, and schools. As the nation went, so went the District, and after fifty-seven presidential elections the United States had its first across-the-board electoral sweep.

3. Bleeding

The emergencies are over. As our current president might put it, it's a war of attrition now. His administration hasn't made anything worse—and we have to admit that early on his ease and confidence were like a balm. But he hasn't made anything better, either. If not fully tired of him, the public has grown as fatalistic about the Republicans' ability to make any real difference as it already was about the Democrats'. The two-party system had been in trouble for decades. It was rigid, polarizing, and unrepresentative. The parties were pawns of special interests. The one interest group they neglected was the vast center of the American electorate, which kept seeking split-the-difference policies. Eight years of failure from two administrations have finally blown apart the tired duopoly. The hopes of our nation are bleeding away along with our few remaining economic resources.

Here is the challenge:

- Our country no longer controls its economic fundamentals.
- Compared with the America of the past, it has become stagnant, classbound, and brutally unfair.
- Compared with the rest of the world, it is on the way down. We think we are a great power—and our military is still ahead of China's. Everyone else thinks that over the past twenty years we finally pushed our luck too far.

To deal with these problems once in office, we must point out basic truths in the campaign.

These truths involve the past sources of our growth: savings, investment, education, innovation. We've thrown away every one of these advantages. What we would do right now to have back the $1 trillion that Congress voted away in 2008 with the Freedom From Death Tax Act! A relatively small share of that money might have kept our aerospace programs competitive with Europe's—to say nothing of preparing us for advances in other forms of transportation. A little more might have made our road and highway system at least as good as China's. With what was left over, our companies might have been able to compete with Germany's in producing the superfast, quiet, efficient maglev trains that are now doing for travel what the jet plane did in the 1950s. Even if we couldn't afford to make the trains, with more money at least some of our states and regions might have been able to buy them, instead of just looking enviously at what China, India, and Iran have done.

Or we could have shored up our universities. True, the big change came as early as 2002, in the wake of 9/11, when tighter visa rules, whatever their effect on reducing terrorism, cut off the flow of foreign talent that American universities had channeled to American ends. In the summer of 2007 China applied the name "twenty Harvards" to its ambition, announced in the early 2000s, to build major research institutions that would attract international talent. It seemed preposterous (too much political control, too great a language barrier), but no one is laughing now. The Chinese mission to Mars, with astronauts from Pakistan, Germany, and Korea, indicates the scope of China's scientific ambition. And necessity has pushed China into the lead in computerized translation technology, so that foreign students can read Chinese characters. The Historic Campus of our best-known university, Harvard, is still prestigious worldwide. But its role is increasingly that of the theme park, like Oxford or Heidelberg, while the most ambitious students compete for fellowships at the Har-Bai and Har-Bei campuses in Mumbai and Beijing. These, of course, have become each other's main rivals—whether for scores on the World Ingenuity Test or in the annual meeting of the teams they sponsor at the Rose Bowl.

Or we could at last have begun to grapple with health-care costs. We've managed to create the worst of all worlds—what the Democrats call the "30-30 problem." Thirty percent of our entire economy goes for health and medical costs, but 30 percent of our citizens have no regular contact with the medical system. (Except, of course, during quarantines in avian-flu season.) For people who can afford them, the "tailored therapies" of the past decade represent the biggest breakthrough in medicine since antibiotics or anesthesia. The big killers—heart disease and cancers of the colon, lung, breast, and prostate—are now manageable chronic diseases at worst, and the big moral issues involve the question of whether Baby Boomers are living "too long." But the costs are astronomical, which raises questions of both efficiency and justice. Google's embedded diagnostic technology dramatizes our problem: based on nonstop biometric testing of the thirty-seven relevant enzymes and organ-output levels, it pipes into cell-phone implants instructions for which treatment, pill, or action to take next. The system is extremely popular—for the 10 million people who can afford it. NetJet flights to the Bahamas for organ replacement illustrate the point even more sharply, although here the breakthrough was less medical than diplomatic. The World Trade Organization, after the most contentious proceeding in its history, ruled that prohibiting commerce in human organs for transplant was an unjust trade barrier. The ruling may have caused the final, fatal split in the Republican Party (libertarians were jubilant, religious conservatives appalled), but it became the foundation of an important Caribbean industry after threats of violence dissuaded many transplant centers from operating within the United States. Meanwhile, despite the Strong America-Strong Americans Act of 2009, which tied income-tax rates to body-mass index and cigarette consumption, smoking, and eating junk food have become for our underemployed class what swilling vodka was for the dispossessed in Boris Yeltsin's Russia.

All these issues involve money, and we can't avoid talking about money in this campaign. But your ability to address an even harder issue will largely determine whether you can succeed in the job the voters are about to give you.

That problem is the sense of sunset, decline, hopelessness. America has been so resilient as a society because each American has imagined that the sky was the limit. Obviously it was not for everyone, or always. From the beginning we've had a class system, and a racial-caste system, and extended periods—the 1890s, the 1930s, the 1970s, the past few years—when many more people than usual were struggling merely to survive. But the myth of equal opportunity has been closer to reality here than in any other society, and the myth itself has mattered.

My father, in explaining why it was so painful for him to see a lifetime's savings melt away after the Venezuelan crisis, told me about a political speech he remembered from his own youth. It was by Daniel Patrick Moynihan, a Harvard professor who later became a politician. In the late 1960s, when American prosperity held despite bitter political turmoil, Moynihan told left-wing students why preserving that prosperity should be important even to them. We know Europe from its novels, Moynihan said: the old ones, by Austen and Dickens and Stendahl, and the more recent ones, too. We know it as a static society. Young people, seeking opportunity, have to wait for old people to die. A whole life's prospects depend on the size of an inheritance. People know their place. America, Moynihan said fifty years ago, must never become a place like that.

That is the place we have become. Half this country's households live on less than $50,000 a year. That sounds like a significant improvement from the $44,000 household median in 2003. But a year in private college now costs $83,000, a day in a hospital $1,350, a year in a nursing home $150,000—and a gallon of gasoline $9. Thus we start off knowing that for half our people there is no chance—none—of getting ahead of the game. And really, it's more like 80 percent of the public that is priced out of a chance for future opportunity. We have made a perfect circle—perfect in closing off options. There are fewer attractive jobs to be had, even though the ones at the top, for financiers or specialty doctors, are very attractive indeed. And those who don't start out with advantages in getting those jobs have less and less chance of moving up to them.

Jobs in the middle of the skill-and-income distribution have steadily vanished if any aspect of them can be done more efficiently in China, India, or Vietnam. The K-12 schools, the universities, the ambitious research projects that could help the next generation qualify for better jobs, have weakened or dried up. A dynamic economy is always losing jobs. The problem with ours is that we're no longer any good at creating new ones. America is a less attractive place for new business because it's a less attractive place, period.

In the past decade we've seen the telephone companies disappear. Programming, data, entertainment, conversation—they all go over the Internet now. Pharmaceuticals are no longer mass-produced but, rather, tailored to each patient's genetic makeup. The big airlines are all gone now, and much of publishing, too. The *new* industries are the ones we want. When their founders are deciding where to locate, though, they'll see us as a country with a big market—and with an undereducated work force, a run-down infrastructure, and a shaky currency. They'll see England as it lost its empire. They'll see Russia without the oil reserves, Brezhnev's Soviet Union without the repression. They'll see the America that Daniel Patrick Moynihan feared.

This story is now yours to tell, and later I'll turn to notes for the stump speech. But remember that the reality of the story reaches backward, and that is why I have concentrated on the missed opportunities, the spendthrift recklessness, the warnings America heard but tuned out. To tell it that way in public would of course only make things worse, and we can't afford the recriminations or the further waste of time. The only chance for a new beginning is to make people believe there actually is a chance.

FACTS

Projected year by which U.S. Treasury bonds will sink to junk status, based on fiscal policy as of June 2005: 2026
(Standard & Poor's)

Chances of a U.S. "currency crisis" within five years, according to former Federal Reserve chief Paul Volcker: 3 in 4
(Office of Paul Volcker)

OUR PATHETIC LIVES

with cartoons by Mr. Fish
and facts

What's the connection between our celebrity obsession, Christian fundamentalism, bestiality, ubiquitous violence, materialism, and low teacher salaries? They're all symptoms of narcissism. We form loveless and artificial ties to famous people like hollow man Tom Cruise. We tell lies about Jesus Christ to justify our anger and confusion rather than confront their causes. We buy Hummers to make ourselves feel powerful. We underpay teachers because the truth frightens us.

The Great Tom Cruise Backlash

from SFGate.com (7/6/05)

Mark Morford

Let it begin now. Let it start with a wry askance glance and evolve into full-fledged annoyance and then move into raging hell-bent OK that's quite enough now please stop before we slap you silly.

Note to Tom Cruise: You are maxing out. Wearing out the welcome. Becoming less the tolerable and moderately talented and mildly likable megastar and more like an itchy boil on the deranged ferret of popular culture, requiring lancing.

The signs are all in place. The crazy ranting, the jumping on couches, the crazed grins, the enormous piles of money, the incessant photos of you sucking the face off your new and bewildered and child-like fiancee, the weird diatribes about psychiatry and mental health, the relatively common knowledge that you are super-seriously involved at the highest levels with one of the creepier money-hungry pseudo-religions in the nation.

Also: the assigning of a "handler" from said cult to tag along with your new bewildered young fiancee everywhere she goes to "keep her on the path" and make sure she doesn't, I don't know what. Talk about the nightmares? Break down in a heap and confess that it's all a staged setup? Reveal your true lizard identity?

Yes, Tom Cruise is getting weirder, more annoying than ever. Or maybe he was already deeply weird and we just didn't know it because he was famously tight-lipped in interviews and was never much of a deep thinker and wasn't all that articulate and no one really paid much attention because, well, who really cares?

But now, oh, Tom is opening up. Tom is speaking extemporaneously on talk shows and in interviews about life and love and Scientology, free of the careful grooming and aggressive protection of his former publicist, and while he's still not all that interesting, he is indeed letting his true colors beam right through and those colors are sort of a strange reddish brown with lots of unbecoming blue polka dots and weird slashes of hot pink all overarched by a vague hint of a rainbow flag waving just overhead.

There are rumors, and they are all juicy and fun. Rumors that Cruise "interviewed" numerous young actresses to play the part of his fiancee so as to crank the Scientology awareness quotient and downplay the gay rumors. Rumors of Katie Holmes being essentially trained by the "church" to forgo her former self. Rumors that Holmes essentially vanished for sixteen days just before emerging with Cruise on her arm and a hundred million more dollars in her future and a new, decidedly odd Scientology gleam/haze over her eyes.

Aren't rumors fun? Totally silly? But somehow, in the age of Bush and bogus wars and massive, commonplace deceptions, weirdly believable?

Also: Rumors persist that Tom's Scientology-rich pseudo-love somehow convinced Katie that she must immediately dump her longtime, beloved manager and agent to switch to his. And she is rumored to be disassociating with old friends and not communicating with her close family (cult behaviors, all)—and did we mention the part about how the Scientologists have allegedly assigned her a handler/new best friend to tag along wherever she goes and answer questions for her and coach her on how to behave and speak when asked about their "religion"?

Hell, not even Mel Gibson has a beady-eyed priest from the Holy Family uber-Catholic sect following him around everywhere he goes, answering, in hissing Latin, questions from *Vanity Fair* reporters and spraying everyone with fake stage blood and sitting next to Mel in all the big studio meetings and screaming "Jesus wants twenty percent off the back end, plus international DVD rights!" while twitching madly.

But then again, Mel's an old hand at being a slightly creepy religious nuthead. And now, apparently, so is Tom. After all, he's been deep into Scientology for upward of 20 years, and is rumored to have progressed to the level of an OT6 (Operating Thetan 6), which is a super-secret high level of the church with super-secret knowledge of the alien story (called "The incident") and ESP, and they all get super-secret decoder rings with access to all the best alien-bred hallucinogens in the L. Ron Hubbard Bone Room, where high-ranking devotees gather to drink bunny blood and watch old Travolta movies and discuss what the hell to do about Kirstie Alley.

But Katie Holmes, she's not like them. She's just a kid. She needs lots of creepy brainwashi . . . er, gentle religious coaching into the super-secret ways of the "church" of Scientology, with their incredibly vicious army of lawyers who attack anyone who says anything at all negative about their cult . . . er, religion.

(Note to Scientology: first signs that you are not a true religion: You cannot take a joke. You have an army of attack lawyers. You are so unstable as a religion you are unable to handle satire. You think the Kabballah is suing everyone who trashes Madonna? They'd be broke in a week. Just a thought.)

One thing the weird TomKat relationship is not, we can be reasonably sure, is a publicity stunt designed to lure more fans to *War of the Worlds* and *Batman Begins*. Reason: Tom Cruise does not need the money. As Edward Jay Epstein points out in his excellent *Slate* piece, Tommy raked in well over $120 million on the first two *Mission: Impossible* movies *alone,* and stands to make easily that much from *War of the Worlds* and the forthcoming *M:I-3* and he is quickly accumulating more power and money than God or than the giddy accountants over at the bizarre Scientology compound outside Hemet, Calif., ever wet-dreamed.

Should we be worried? Should anyone care? Should it at all matter beyond buying yourself a Free Katie T-shirt and shaking your head and laughing it all off as just more pop culture chyme and then going to rent the surprisingly decent *Minority Report*? Of course it doesn't. Getting deeply involved in the lives of annoying, semiarticulate celebs is like getting all wrapped up in what Paris Hilton feeds her Chihuahua. It just has no bearing.

But then again, we have a warning. Remember, won't you, the savage impact Mel Gibson had, coming out of the blue and slapping the culture with his ultraviolent, blood-drenched vision of a very miserable Jesus being pulverized into raw veal and calling it spiritual enlightenment. Kooky-rich celebs with pseudo-religious agendas can be dangerous indeed, if for no other reason than they annoy the living hell out of you when you're trying to meditate.

It just feels like Tom is gearing up for something,

doesn't it? Like it's no more Tom Cruise the cute kid from *Risky Business* or the hot gay stud from *Top Gun* or the chick-flick dreamboat from *Jerry McGuire*, but now it will be Tom Cruise, the bizarre Hollywood power player, the unstoppable, outspoken cult-head with a gleaming, glazed-eyed "wife," proselytizing like a ferret and working hard to convert the masses.

It feels like this is all some sort of bizarre precursor to, say, 2015, when Cruise's powerful production company suddenly whips out *The Passion of the Hubbard*, depicting the cheesy sci-fi hack writer and Scientology founder as the new Jesus, dancing with 75-million-year-old aliens and battling the evil overlord Xenu while busting "engrams" like water balloons and calling on the people of Earth to join him in the bunker so we may all join hands and look to the skies for the next big comet to pass by so we may leap from this Earthly plane and join the UFOs on their journey and . . . oh wait, sorry, wrong sect.

So anyway. Thanks, Tom, for all the decent movies, aggro performances, that mega-intense, frat-boy-on-'roids stare. But please, before you get any weirder, would you maybe consider exiting calmly? Is it too late to ask? If we all buy a copy of Hubbard's silly little *Dianetics* and send it to Brooke Shields, will you go away and leave us alone? Damn. I didn't think so.

FACTS

Days after Brad Pitt and Jennifer Aniston separated in January that an *Us Weekly* executive called the story "our tsunami": 4
(*New York Post*, 1/12/05)

Name of the quasi-divinity promoted by pro-anorexia Web sites such as Salvation Through Starvation and Nothing's Gonna Stop Me: Ana
(NewsoftheWeird.com)

I Hate *The Passion of the Christ*

from Darn-Tootin.com (9/17/04)

by Ron Rummel-Hudson

Well, thanks to the magic of Netflix, I finally got to watch *The Passion of the Christ* last night. I'd toyed with seeing it in the theater but I decided to wait until it came out on DVD, as my living room is almost certain to be free of zealots on most evenings. I wanted to have the option of hating it without having to fear a smiting from moviegoers around me.

In retrospect, that was an excellent idea, because I am exercising my option to hate the film. What's surprising to me is how much. I may actually hate this film more than any other movie I have ever seen in my entire life.

And yes, that includes *Simon Birch*. Take a moment to let that sink in. I'll wait.

Done? Okay, great. Let me start off with the good things about *The Passion*. John Debney's haunting score is beautiful. Also, the cinematography is great; it's a lovely film, right up until the beatings begin.

And that's about where the positive ends for me. Because those beatings start almost immediately, and don't stop until the end.

I guess I'll get right to the point. When *The Passion* first came out, I saw a lot of arguments on both sides of the fence regarding whether or not it was an anti-Semitic film. Having already written about Jewish overreactions to the idea of films about Hitler, I found myself wondering if this was a similar situation. Now that I've seen the film, I am left wondering how any sane person could ever make the argument that *The Passion of the Christ* is anything *but* rabidly anti-Semitic.

In Mel Gibson's telling of the story, it is obvious from the first few minutes of the film who the villains are going to be. Caiphas and the high priests are depicted as sinister, snarling, swarthy Jews with bad teeth and pimped-out clothes. They are straight out of central casting of those 1930s German anti-Jewish propaganda films, so much so that I find it pretty hard to believe that there are people out there who honestly think there's a case to be made that Gibson's portrayal of Jews in this film is even remotely decent or fair.

In *The Passion*, Jews are clearly responsible for the death of Christ, no doubt about it. Although the execution and most of the beatings are administered by the lower-class Roman soldiers (most of whom behave like stereotypical Italian movie goombas), Pilate is portrayed as a good-hearted man who sympathizes with Jesus and tries to resist the barbarity of the Jews before eventually being forced to give in to the demands of the mob.

As one of the few non-Jews in the story, Pilate has a lot of white man's guilt to carry, and he does so admirably. It's almost too bad that the real-life Pilate was such a historically verifiable bastard who was so corrupt and cruel to the Jews in Judea that he was eventually recalled by the equally horrible Roman emperor Tiberius to explain his actions. His crimes included crucifying thousands of Jews and slaughtering a huge crowd of Samaritans. Pilate being portrayed so compassionately is a shockingly egregious and offensive twisting of history.

It is worth pointing out that the suffering of Christ on the Cross may have been demanded by those wicked Jews, but it was a Roman execution device and was handed out to thousands of Jews in Judea under Roman control, usually for political reasons. It is ridiculous to suggest that the Romans were simply innocent puppets of the Jews. Ridiculous, and as offensive as Holocaust deniers. For most of the world, the fall of Rome centuries later was met with a resounding "good riddance." Thanks for the plumbing, but go away.

The Gospels themselves are a problem. Mel Gibson may be interpreting them irresponsibly, but unfortunately he may also be doing so fairly accurately. The four Gospels from which the Passion story is drawn do place the blame for Christ's trial and execution directly at the feet of Jewish leaders rather than the Romans, who, despite centuries of ironfisted rule of their eastern provinces were all of a sudden supposedly so compassionate towards Jesus (whose Kingdom of God presented a very real threat to Caesarean rule of the known world) and were powerless to resist the bloodlust of the Jewish mob. It's ridiculous but not surprising; the Gospels were written between fifty and seventy-five years after the death of Christ, in a Roman world that was still hundreds of years away from embracing Christianity. It's not surprising that the writers of the original accounts of the story chose to deemphasize Roman guilt and play the blame squarely at the feet of the very Jewish leadership whom they were attempting to change in the first century AD.

Mel Gibson appears to take the ugliest parts of the Gospel that have been problematic for Christians all along (and were repudiated by Vatican II, which Gibson's ultra-traditional Catholic sect does not recognize) and embrace them wholeheartedly. His Caiphas and Jewish priests not only demand Christ's crucifixion, but then escort him happily to his death on the eve of Passover, in blatant defiance of Jewish law. The Jews are specifically indicted by the Good Thief, who, after the dying Christ says "Father, forgive them, for they know not what they are doing," tells Caiphas that "He prays for you." Caiphas says (from Matthew) "his blood be upon us and our children" (Gibson later chose to leave the line unsubtitled because of the controversy), validating the centuries-old canonical "blood guilt" justification for pogroms against Jews. The Jews are specifically blamed by Christ himself, who offers Pilate consolation by telling him that "It is he who has delivered me to you who has the greater sin."

The film provides almost no context for the teachings of Christ. For non-Christian viewers, it is basically a soulless snuff film. For Christians, it provides a lot of pure conjecture and gratuitous violence and gore to tap into a visceral emotional well without spending more than a few brief flashback moments on the actual message of Christ, as well as lots of reasons to blindly hate Jews. The film goes far beyond the content of the Gospels to emphasize Roman virtue and Jewish barbarism, and does so with the subtlety of, well, a Mel Gibson movie.

The film is at its most hypocritical when it quotes Jesus preaching about rejecting hatred and loving one's enemies, all the while stirring as much hate for the enemies of Christ (whoever *they* might be, right? Oy vey . . .) at every conceivable moment. Matthew's earthquake at the moment of Christ's death is there, but the Roman soldier who declares Christ's divinity at that moment in the Gospel doesn't say a word in the film. Christ may have believed that the hearts of evil men should be changed, not fought, but Mel's not too concerned with such subtleties.

(There are also two moments of unintentional comedy. One takes place when a young girl wipes the face of the bleeding Jesus with a cloth, and when you see her standing there with it later, why, it's now the Shroud of Turin, by golly! The other takes place near the end, when a crow lands on the cross of the Bad Thief, and suddenly he is being attacked by a silly-looking bird puppet. Bock bock!)

There are other strange touches in the film, such as a somewhat cool Satan who wanders through from time to time (and whom the notoriously misogynist Mel Gibson cast as a woman, for some reason), but mostly it is simply a shockingly violent and depressing film from beginning to end. The movie celebrates Christ not as a figure of love or compassion so much as a survivor who, Rocky-like, takes as much suffering as the Jews and the Romans can give him and always stands back up for more. He is Christ by way of Chumbawamba, who gets knocked down but gets back up again. Mel's Jesus isn't about preaching hope and love and compassion, but rather taking a beating and coming back for more. It's less of "Forgive them, they know not what they do" and more of "Is that the best you can do?"

One might ask the same of Mel Gibson and the people who hold this film up as an inspiration and a message of hope. (Some people took their kids to see this. No joke. I'd let Schuyler watch *Kill Bill* before I'd let her sit through this.) Unless you enjoy gore and violence and hate Jews and have no use for Christ's actual message of peace and compassion and forgiveness, I can't imagine how this film doesn't offend you.

Particularly if you are a Christian.

JESUS TEACHING THE VIRTUES OF LOVE, HOMOPHOBIA, THE 2nd AMENDMENT, THE DEATH PENALTY, DISDAIN FOR MEXICANS, UNILATERALISM, ENGLISH-ONLY LEGISLATION, TEARING DOWN THE WALL BETWEEN CHURCH AND STATE, CENSORSHIP, WAR IN SPACE, A SHITTY HEALTHCARE SYSTEM, AND PATRIOTISM AMPED FANATICALLY INTO AN UGLY PREJUDICE TO CHILDREN.

MR. FISH

The New Sex Ed

from *Rolling Stone* (9/18/03)

Ken Kegan

It's 9:50 P.M. on a warm Saturday night. An unmarked van enters Isla Vista, a Santa Barbara suburb packed with tanned skateboarders and cyclists. Seconds from the beach and the University of California at Santa Barbara, Isla Vista is one of America's hardest-partying neighborhoods; around 20,000 students are crammed into its high-rise towers, residence halls, and frat houses. Inside the vehicle are two Sony PD150 digital-video cameras, two cameramen, a bullhorn, a black Man-o-War Jumbo Jack sex toy, two pink dildos, pacifiers, bottles, diapers, and, most notably, five wisecracking, business-savvy porn stars. This crew has been assembled by Shane's World, a porn company from Van Nuys, California, that specializes in reality TV with a twist. Tonight they will be filming College Invasion, the first in a new video series. Asked about this evening's action, a cameraman who calls himself Andy Treehorn says, "You'll see some students humiliate themselves for the promise of oral sex. That's always crazy."

The van pulls up at a seven-bedroom former frat house located two blocks from the university. Three security guards monitor an overflow crowd of beer-swilling students. Starting with an initial top-secret guest list of 400 people. the party planner for Shane's World, known as Justin Cider, has carefully whittled the crowd down to 150 photogenic students, giving guests the closely guarded address only minutes before the party. Provided they don't pass out or get bounced for fighting, a select few will get to star in tonight's "gonzo porn" documentary.

The van door slides open, and out bounds Calli Cox, perky blond porn star and publicist for Shane's World. She grabs the megaphone and yells, "The party has arrived!" The crowd roars, and the video cameras light Calli's way as she and her co-stars strut into the barren living room—no furniture, just a keg of beer, black tarps covering the walls and a sea of dirty-dancing drunks. When asked what he expects tonight, Ben, a twenty-one-year-old chemistry major, says, "A little fucking lesbian action, a little double-sided dildo." He doesn't plan on participating himself, though. "It's like a pretty painting," he says. "You don't want to blow it by touching it."

Calli is quickly surrounded by a screaming crowd of drunks. She whips out her bullhorn and asks for volunteers to strip down to their underwear. This is the modus operandi for Shane's World: Loosen up the crowd with silly party games, humble a few guys, then use them as performers. Three come forward. Calli instructs them to strap on diapers and suck on the baby bottles and pacifiers. After a few seconds of highly subjective adjudication, she decides that Hagen, a twenty-one-year-old UC8B film major, makes the best baby of the bunch. His prize: a blow job. Hagen looks anxious, saying, "No, no, no. I'm not going to get a blow job on camera." Calli takes him up to a bedroom and whispers how great it will feel. Hagen's friends mock him, chanting, "Don't be a bitch! Don't be a bitch!" But Hagen lets them down with "My mother would kill me."

So Calli gives up, grabs the second-place baby, twenty-one-year-old Matt, and they enter a filthy, sweltering, windowless bathroom. Shane's World's co-owner, who goes by the name Brian Grant, follows with his video camera, along with Matt's best friend, who locks the door behind them. Calli takes off her shirt. Kisses Matt. Then kneels at his feet.

When she's finished with Matt, Calli bounces down to the living room for the breast-sucking competition. The rules: Calli and her petite brunet colleague, Taylor Rain, will bare their chests. Then a row of guys will take turns sucking their breasts. Best breastman wins a tag-team blow job. The security guards clear a circle around Calli and Taylor. Trevor, 18, a business student, wins the skills test, but he's too drunk to get it up. He passes his prize on to another contestant, his buddy Danny, 18. Eyes wide, Danny gladly whips it out. The porn stars gather around Danny's midsection. Female students push to the front to get a better view. The crowd is roaring. Guys are high-fiving Danny. A kitchen table crashes under the weight of cheering spectators.

The action moves to an upstairs bedroom. Fifteen students watch Dez, a twenty-six-year-old Viagra-popping porn stud, as he rides Taylor doggy-style. As Taylor writhes and moans, Dez grins at the thirty students on the balcony outside. Their faces are mashed against the French windows, and behind them, forty more faces are straining to see over their shoulders. Three attractive female students cheer Dez on, smack his butt, and hand him a beer. After twenty minutes of sweaty pounding, Dez gives up to drink beer with the students.

On the far end of the balcony, two dozen kids are also drinking beer but hiding from the video cameras. "Someday, your kid may be cruising the Internet and find you naked on a fucking porno tape," says one of the students, Ray Anthony, 24. "Because video is forever." Somebody tells Ray Anthony to lighten up, but he shakes his head and adds. "I want to be somebody someday. Because once you're dubbed a porn star, you're sociologically barred forever."

Shane's World was the brainchild of Shannon Hewitt, better known as Shane, a now-retired porn star who appeared in nearly 100 films—many of them directed by her one-time boyfriend, Adam Glasser, who is better known as the reality-porn pioneer Seymore Butts. When Shane and Glasser broke up in 1995, she launched her own production company and started shooting her own unscripted porn documentaries. After 1999's *Shane's World, Vol. 18: The Roller Coaster of Love,* Shane quit porn to start a family with her husband, Bobby Hewitt. drummer for the metal band Orgy.

In the wake of leaving Shane's World, Shane was involved in a nasty trademark battle with two former employees: her personal assistant, a freckled redhead who goes by the name Jennie Grant, and Jennie's partner, cameraman Brian Grant. (Even though these two make a large amount of money exploiting college students, many of whom are inebriated when the cameras are rolling, they are afraid to put their real names on their work.) When the dust settled, Jennie and Brian owned the company and agreed to license the Shane's World name.

After the Grants took over, they moved Shane's World into a lucrative new venue: college campuses. They started with *Shane's World, Vol. 22: Scavenger Hunt,* secretly filmed at "two very popular Southern California universities." With the success of that film, Brian realized that university campuses were a reality-porn gold mine, offering a deep pool of cheap and horny talent.

When asked what she thinks about Jennie and Brian's new campus-porn flicks. Shane, who now has two young children, says, "It's just wrong. College kids are there to do something with their lives. Whatever they do on that video will always be around. Their families are always going to know, and wherever they go and work, it's only a matter of time until those people find out, too."

Two summers ago, on a sunny morning in Tempe, Arizona, twenty-two-year-old Brian Buck was doing laundry in his crowded Arizona State University frat house. Suddenly, a stretch Hummer pulled up outside. A cameraman and three Shane's World porn stars jumped out: Calli Cox, blond bombshell Bobbie, and a token stud who called himself Tony Pounds. Dressed in a tight cutoff shirt and short-shorts, Calli explained to Buck and his Sigma Nu housemates that they were filming a sex scavenger hunt. Two teams of porn stars were racing around the campus, asking students to help them complete a sexual "to do" list. "We're doing crazy stuff right now," Calli said. As if that weren't enough, she added, "We're going to be naked, too." Buck and some of his frat brothers leapt at the opportunity. Calli persuaded them to strip naked and put on diapers. She then asked the students to stick a dildo inside her. So they did, and videotaped themselves waving to the camera. Next on the list: a dorm shower scene. Moist and nude, Calli called from the shower, "Who wants to make out with me?" Buck volunteered. He kissed Calli and Bobbie while his buddies chanted, "Buck, Buck,

Buck!" Minutes later, Calli gave Buck a hand job in the hallway. Then he followed the porn stars out to the Hummer, stripped again, and videotaped his buddies getting stroked off.

At the time, Brian Buck was executive vice president of the Arizona State University student body. But when *Shane's World, Vol. 29: Frat Row Scavenger Hunt 3* was released, the new ASU president, Michael Crow, blew a gasket. Concerned the incident would revive ASU's image as a party school, Crow slammed the students' behavior in a statement to the press and demanded a full investigation into the fraternity-porn video. Within hours, reporters were peeking through Buck's bedroom window and phoning his parents in Portland, Oregon, for their reactions. Then the story broke on CNN. "That's how my grandparents found out," Buck says. They were watching TV with friends at their yacht club when CNN aired his three-way shower kiss. "There was so much anxiety that I was throwing up for the next two days," he said. "I couldn't eat." Though the students' eyes were blacked out in the video, ASU quickly singled out Buck for sacrificial slaughter—partly because of his position in ASU student government, and partly because he was the only guy in the video whose name was chanted over and over by his buddies. Still, Buck refused to resign his vice-presidency. He told the *Arizona Republic*, "I'm not apologizing for anything I did. It's not like this is Harvard." ASU kicked Buck out of his Sigma Nu frat house, barred him from living on ASU property, prohibited him from university employment and put him on permanent probation. They also made him write four apology letters, do 100 hours of community service, and write a twenty-page paper. Its somber title: "Reflections on Integrity." After weeks of stress, legal hell, and physical threats from students and strangers, Buck caved in and resigned his vice-presidency. "I will always be discriminated against and thought of in a poor light," says Buck.

The Shane's World office is in an industrial park on the outskirts of Los Angeles. It's stuffed with toys, a heavyweight punching bag, and stacks of promo T-shirts, ski hats, and DVDs. Video lights are aimed at a neatly made bed. Friendly but worried about bad press and angry parents, Jennie and Brian are both clean-cut and college educated. They claim their campus parties are providing a fun and healthy service for the youth of today. "Everybody wants to see movies that they can relate to," says Jennie. "Our movies fill a certain niche. The college guys that are in our movies aren't in regular adult movies. Guys in the business are beefier, have really large penises, and are really buff. Most guys don't look like that." Brian adds, "I think college students like our sense of humor. We're just like them. We're the MTV of porn."

For Jennie and Brian, the Arizona shoot was a revelation. "This is about the most fun we could ever have," says Jennie. "Nobody else is really making adult movies that are geared towards the college audience. This was awesome."

Taking another run at its huge success, Shane's World flew to Bloomington, Indiana, in October. "We picked Indiana University because the *Princeton Review* ranked it as the number-one party school in the nation," Calli says. With four female stars (Calli, Mallory, Belladonna, Evalyn) and two obligatory studs (Tex and Mr. Marcus), it didn't take long for sparks to fly and flies to unzip. After the girls were kicked out of the campus radio station, WIUS, for performing cunnilingus on Evalyn while on the air, the performers drifted around the leafy campus. Evalyn picked up Alexander, a freshman, who escorted her and the film crew back to his dorm.

Inside Alexander's room, Evalyn prophetically told the camera, "I definitely think we're going to do some damage at this school." She quickly blew the freshman before the resident manager chased the porn crew out and called the campus police.

Undeterred, Shane's World dropped in on five parties that week. At the Roach Motel, an off-campus shack, Calli and Company fellated four Hoosiers lying side by side. The porn team then visited the apartment of Nicole, a freshman. There, Evalyn squeezed into a closet with Nicole and her roommate Jamie, where Jamie sucked Evalyn's breast for the camera. After that, Nicole locked porn star Tex in a bedroom and, posing for photographs, she grabbed Tex's penis while Jamie licked it. At another party, hosted by sophomore Josh Baxter, Belladonna and Mr. Marcus filmed an anal scene on Baxter's bed while Baxter kissed Calli and told viewers, "I'm going to be a rock star soon. And this is going to be on VHI Behind the Fucking Music. I'm going to regret this. . . . I'm sorry, Mom and Dad, I'm just trying to get my name out there."

Six weeks later, *Shane's World, Vol. 32: Campus Invasion* was released. And that's when Bill O'Reilly stepped in, reporting the "dorm porn" story on his Fox News Channel show, *The O'Reilly Factor*. In the course of four shows, O'Reilly accused the IU administration of knowing about the porn tapings in advance but doing nothing to stop them. IU Chancellor Sharon Brehm refused to appear on the show to defend the school, so O'Reilly interrogated Baxter, Shane's World spokeswoman Calli Cox, plus an IU associate professor who, out of 124 invited IU officials and instructors, was the only one who agreed to appear. O'Reilly huffed that "the administrators should be fired immediately" because of their seemingly "laissez-faire" promotion of porn. Then he played a scene from *Campus Invasion*.

According to a friend, that's how the parents of one of the girls who partied with Tex found out their daughter was now an amateur adult-film actress. The girl's mother phoned her in tears. The girl's father made her sit and watch the entire tape with him, including hard-core scenes that don't contain his daughter. Psychologists call this aversion therapy. When asked if this tactic successfully controlled her urge to touch porn stars, neither the girl nor her parents were willing to comment.

In an IU news release, Brehm slammed Shane's World, stating, "These were deplorable actions by a company intent on exploiting the university and our students. These are sexual predators whose behavior violates all basic principles of common decency." Calli responded for Shane's World by saying, "One student told us he films his own adult movies in his dorm room all the time. These things happen on your campus whether we are involved or not." Adds Brian, "It's a fucked-up situation. Students should have the right to have a private life. I feel bad that they've gotten in trouble. That is not what we're about. The schools made it worse for themselves by making it such a big deal. They're the ones who got the press involved."

Local police refused to press charges, so IU conducted its own investigation and chose to discipline two students, one of them, Alexander, the freshman who let Shane's World enter his dorm. Alexander avoided expulsion but refused to reveal the terms of his discipline. When pressed, however, he expressed remorse about his moment in the porn spotlight, describing it as "a mistake that should never have happened, and it did, and I'm sorry that it did."

Out in Arizona, Brian Buck is low on cash. His mom and dad are no longer paying his tuition, so Buck demanded money from Shane's World. They offered him $500 for his troubles. According to Calli, he refused the offer and wanted them to pay for his three years of law school. Shane's World told him to go pound sand. "He got greedy," says Calli. Buck graduates from IU in May with a business degree. "There was a lot of things I wanted to do in my life that I may not be able to do now," says Buck. "I wanted to go to law school and maybe be in politics. But what community would want me to represent them now? For years I will have problems, all because of a two-minute mistake." Asked if he has any advice for the California students fresh on the reel, Buck says, "I wish I could warn those kids about what this is going to do to their life. I wish I could have my anonymity back." He adds, "Without showing any ethics, Shane's World has done severe damage to my life and many others' for their own gain."

In December, concerned about the punished students, Calli Cox announced that the company planned to use a portion of its Indiana profits to establish a Shane's World Scholarship Fund. "It just makes sense to do this, because we market toward the college crowd," she said. To qualify for the porn scholarship "students must be eighteen and enjoy porn."

In January, Campus Invasion won Best Gonzo Film at the Adult Video News Awards in Los Angeles. Although porn sales figures are notoriously inflated, Jennie says Frat Raw Scavenger Hunt 3 sold three times as much as their other titles, and Campus Invasion sold five times the normal amount. "Whether we got paid a dollar or a gazillion dollars," she says, "it would still be an awesome job to have."

For the company's next project, Jennie says Shane's World is always looking for invitations from college students: "If we get an invitation, we'll be there in a New York minute." Brian says students at one campus have just invited Shane's World to visit their college town. Their inspiration? The Indiana video. "It's all set up . . . and they say their parties will kick [Indiana's] ass," Brian says. "They even said they'd go in and take AIDS tests. They want to fuck the porn stars. This is something that every college guy dreams about. So why not make that happen for them?"

Danny has an epic hangover. It's the Sunday morning after Shane's World invaded Isla Vista. He squints an eye open, hugs his pillow, and says, "Whoa, dude, I feel like shit. But I'm on top of the world. It's a win-win situation." Asked how he'll feel when he sees himself in a porn video, Danny laughs and says, "I'll just claim it wasn't me. 'I didn't inhale.'" When told about the Arizona and Indiana students who got in trouble, Danny says, "Dude, [my school] isn't going to give a fuck."

Trevor stumbles in. "I'm buying it the first day," he says. "I'm going to show it to everyone. I really hope the fifty contest is in there, just so I can say I was in a porn. Just good times. Memories." But he's still upset that he passed on the blow job: "I regret it. And I will regret it for the rest of my life! It was two porn stars on their knees. I mean, just one is good enough, but two!"

Matt, who received a blow job last night, is a bit panicked but grins and says, "I was like, 'Dude, I will kick myself in the face every day if I don't do this.' That was the meanest, wickedest blow job I ever got in my life. Probably will ever get. I totally felt like I was watching a porno. I was looking down at my dick, and I was like, 'That is not my dick.'"

Unlike Brian Buck and his dashed political dreams, Danny has no desire for public office. But he wouldn't mind a career in porn. ("If he contacts us, we certainly would give him a chance," says Brian. "What he did at the party was very unusual and very difficult. To come while getting head from two girls in a crowded room with people shouting and high-fiving is very difficult, even for professionals.") Jokingly, Danny says, "I think I'm going to be the next big thing."

Brian Buck: Casualty of Porn

Brian Buck may have the name and physique of a porn star, but the Arizona State student has paid a hefty price for his brief foray into Shane's World. When footage surfaced of Buck cavorting with two Shane's World pros, the twenty-two-year-old was expelled from his fraternity, barred from ASU housing and employment, placed on permanent probation and was forced to write a twenty-page essay, complete 100 hours of community service, and resign his post as student-body vice president. Worse yet, his parents have refused to pay his tuition, and he was offered a measly $500 from Shane's World for his troubles. "For years I'll have problems," says Buck, "because of a two-minute mistake."

FACT

Minimum hours of videotape showing horse-on-human sex that police seized in July 2005 from a Washington-state farm: 100

(*Seattle Times*, 7/16/05)

The Love Song of J. Alfred Roker

J. M. Berger

Let us go then, you and I,
When the storm front is spread out against the sky
Like a viewer etherised upon a table;
Let us go, through certain slightly slippery streets,
the meteorological retreats,
of restless nights in the Storm Trak Center's halls,
trying to estimate accumulated snowfalls.
Streets with gusting winds like a tedious argument
of a late February snow event,
To lead you to an overwhelming question . . .
Do not ask, "How many inches is it?"
Let us go and make our visit.

In the room the women come and go
Talking of light, intermittent snow.

The yellow fog event that rubs its back upon the
windowpanes,
Licked its tongue into the barometric pressure of
the evening,
Slipped by the terrace, made a sudden leap,
And seeing that it was the coldest October night
since 1975,
Curled once about the house, and fell asleep.

And indeed there will be time
For the yellow haze that slides along the street,
raising the pollen index outside the windowpanes;

There will be time, there will be time
To prepare a winter storm warning to meet the
winter that you meet;
There will be time for wintry mixes late,
And time for all the weak storm-system winds
that lift and drop some hail upon your plate.
Time for you and time for me,
And time yet for a hundred forecast versions,
And for a hundred wet warm-air inversions,
Before the taking of donuts and Fresca.

In the room the women come and go
Talking of light, intermittent snow.

And indeed there will be time
To wonder, "Humid air?" and, "Humid air?"
Time to return the teleprompter's stare,
With a bald spot in the middle of my hair—
(Producers say: "How his hair is growing thin!")
My necktie from Men's Wearhouse, but asserted by
a Rotary pin—
Do I dare
Disturb the 3-D weather graphic?
In a minute there is time
To draw squiggly lines and asterisks and point out
jammed-up traffic.

For I have shown them all already, shown
them all:
Have forecast snow for mornings, afternoons,
I have measured out precip with coffee spoons;
I know Chopper Seven's rotors dying with a dying fall

Beneath the jazzy weather music of a farther room.
So how should I presume?

And I have known the highs already, known them all—
High-pressure centers that fix temps in a formulated phase,
And when I am formulated, with scattered clouds and drizzle,
When I am pinned and wriggling for photo ops at malls,
Then how should I begin
To explain the Doppler radar's mysterious ways?
And how should I presume?

I should have been a mass of Arctic air
Scuttling across the jet streams of silent seas.

And the rush hour traffic, please drive carefully!
Backed up along Route 95 it lingers,
Leave work early . . . watch for black ice . . . it malingers.
Stretched along the turnpike, with freezing rain and sleet.
Should I, after donuts and coffee cakes and ices,
Have the strength to force the suburbs to their crisis?

Would it have been worthwhile
To have bitten off the overnight with a smile,
To have squeezed the extended outlook into a ball
To roll it toward some overwhelming question,

To say: "The ozone index can be felt within your
head,
I am come to chart the rainfall, chart rainfall"—
If one, flipping channels on the TV by her bed,
Should say: "It is not cold at all.
I should not have bundled up, at all."

It is impossible to say just what I mean!
But as if a magic weather map threw my nerves in
patterns on the screen,
Would it have been worthwhile
If one, checking the windchill outside the hall
And opening the window, should say:
"It is not cold at all,
This is not the forecast at all."

No! I am not Willard Scott, nor was meant to be;
Am a local weatherman, one that will do
To tease the 11 o'clock news, announce a school
closing or two,
Laugh with the anchorman; no doubt, an easy
tool,
Deferential, glad to be of use,
Subjected when the weather is bad to much abuse;
Full of high sentence, but as a forecaster, a bit
obtuse;
At times, indeed, almost ridiculous—
Almost, at times, the Fool.

It grows cold . . . It grows cold . . .
I shall advise my viewers to bundle up and wear
their trousers rolled.

Shall I chart the Gulf Stream's winds?
Do I dare to eat a peach?
I shall wear white flannel trousers, and send
viewers to the beach.
Sent my resume to the Weather Channel, tried to
reach—

I do not think that they will call for me.

We have lingered on warm, humid air blowing in
from the sea,
With satellite photos of landscapes green and
brown,
Till producers' voices wake us, and we drown.

FACTS*

Number of states, provinces, or territories of the United States, Canada, and Mexico that lack a McDonald's: 1

Population per square mile of that territory, the Nunavut region of Canada: 0.03

* (McDonald's)

I Love Professional Wrestling

J. M. Berger

I love pro wrestling.

Please don't hate me.

I wish I could have typed the first sentence without feeling compelled to add the second.

Pro wrestling has a reputation for being racist, anally obsessed, sexist, classless, juvenile, homophobic, and otherwise appalling on any given day.

Unfortunately, this reputation is well deserved.

I blame Vince McMahon.

Vince's World Wrestling Entertainment has been the undisputed public face of pro wrestling for the last four years. There are other products out there, but you generally have to go to a gymnasium, a foreign country, or Florida to find them.

Some of us are willing to go to such lengths, but most are not. And really, why would they? Their view of pro wrestling is based on the product presented by WWE, and that product—as already noted—is usually appalling.

Once upon a time, there were many small regional wrestling promotions. Big stars might travel from territory to territory, but the "bookers"—essentially the guys who write the scripts*—were based in a specific region, where they had families and lives outside of wrestling.

Over the second half of the twentieth century, this territorial system evolved into a few dominant promotions with national television clearances, which eventually became one dominant promotion—the World Wrestling Federation.**

* Yes, it's fake.

** WWF became WWE after a devastating loss to the World Wildlife Fund in a lawsuit over the international trademark rights to the initials WWF.

With the regional system largely in disarray, independent wrestling promotions became smaller and less influential.

Today, WWE has rivals, but it doesn't have any competition. There are a handful of promotions with a national reach and some top-level athletes, but none of them are easy to find. You have to see them live, buy DVDs or pay-per-views, download matches and shows over the Internet, or cruise obscure cable channels late at night.

WWE has the top-rated show on cable, in addition to airing on a national broadcast network. All the other promotions put together reach only a fraction of WWE's audience. If you decided one day that you were interested in checking out some wrestling, the odds are overwhelming that you would start with one of WWE's programs.

Unfortunately, when you click on the television, you probably won't make it through half an hour of programming before you see something that inspires the average American to click the TV back off and go wash your eyes out with soap. WWE's social awareness has barely advanced since the days when pro wrestling was epitomized by the fey antics of Gorgeous George mincing around the ring in coiffed curls and satin robes.

Vince McMahon, the founder and absolute dictator of WWE, would like you to believe that wrestling is good, clean family entertainment.

"There is no murder, no rape, no robbery. We're extremely aggressive. We're like rock 'n' roll. We're a little bit naughty," Vince told a newspaper recently, a claim which he has repeated in interview after interview. Amazingly, no one has responded to this statement by calling him a liar to his face. His own show indicts him.

Murder: There is no murder on WWE . . . but not for lack of trying. One of WWE's most prominent wrestlers is Kane, who poured gasoline on an announcer and set him on fire (the announcer survived) and set his storyline brother, the Undertaker, on fire in a casket (he either survived or was raised from the dead). The Undertaker was recently involved in a storyline (known as an "angle") that involved his manager being drowned in a cement mixer (the manager survived). The Undertaker was also recently the victim of attempted strangulation/decapitation with piano wire (more on this below). Granted, all these victims survived their ordeals, as opposed to Al Wilson, father of female wrestler Torrie Wilson, who died of a heart attack while copulating with Torrie's rival, Dawn Marie. This may or may not technically qualify as murder.

Rape: A former Olympic wrestling gold medalist called a married black woman a "gutter slut" and repeatedly attempted to sexually assault her. The same athlete in a recent interview mouthed the McMahon party line: "There's no rape, no murder and no robbery (on WWE), which you see on every other show on TV." The aforementioned Kane coerced female superstar Lita into marriage and forced her to engage in sexual intercourse, resulting in a pregnancy which miscarried after she was attacked by another wrestler. Then she turned on him, inexplicably making him into a "babyface"—in wrestling parlance, the "good guy" you're supposed to root for.

> Robbery: In 2004, Eddie Guerrero became WWE champion. His slogan and theme song proudly declared "I lie, I cheat, I steal." He lived up to his slogan by stealing various vehicles, gold medals, and a host of lesser bits of personal property. In vignettes, he and his nephew robbed random strangers on the street for laughs. Eddie is hardly the only culprit.* Grand theft auto is a routine occurrence on WWE programming, to the point that it lacks dramatic impact when it does happen. Championship belts should come installed with LoJack, because if it isn't nailed down, you're likely to see it around the waist of a rival.

In addition to the above infractions, you don't have to look far to find examples of atrocious and disturbing behavior. Since the days of Gorgeous George, gay-bashing has been an integral part of wrestling. Effeminate gay stereotypes were long paraded around the ring as "heels"—the bad guys you're supposed to boo—and beaten soundly by babyfaces.

In recent times, "gay" characters have become babyfaces—not because WWE writes them that way, but because the crowds cheer them in spite of how the scripts are written. Not content to let the gay guys become stars, WWE inevitably trashes the characters once this starts to happen.

Perhaps the most egregious example was the sad case of Billy and Chuck, two wrestlers who had a long run as tag team champions and who were also depicted as "special

* Please don't hold any of this nonsense this against Eddie. He is a giant among wrestlers and he made these segments incredibly entertaining.

friends." As per usual, the gay routine was designed to be just slightly ambiguous—in other words, lots of hugs, lots of symbolic phallicism, lots of crude double entendres, but no mouth-kissing. Finally, Billy and Chuck "came out" and announced they would hold a "commitment ceremony" in the middle of the ring.

Crowd reactions were somewhat mixed, but the mainstream media took notice. Several articles portrayed the characters as groundbreaking, and gay advocacy groups gave their blessing to the commitment ceremony, which WWE billed as a major event. Thanks to the mainstream media coverage, many people tuned in to wrestling for the first time ever—or revisited wrestling for the first time in a long time.

These viewers were rewarded with a scene that could only happen in the WWE. The commitment ceremony was interrupted by the Godfather—a wrestler whose character is that of a 1970s blaxploitation pimp—accompanied by his "Ho Train." This prompted Billy and Chuck to reveal that the whole thing had been a publicity stunt to get ratings and that they were actually straight.

Not only did a million or so new viewers simultaneously change the channel at that moment, but most of them did so with the exact same thought: "I should have known better than to watch wrestling."

The list of such incidents goes on . . . and on . . . and on. . . . Racist clichés not heard since Reconstruction still have a home on WWE television. Women are openly treated as property under the pretext of "contracts" for their "services" as a manager. There are numerous wrestling routines that are inordinately concerned with the male buttocks—whether thrusting them, slapping them, clenching them, primping them, gyrating them, violating them with a foreign object, placing them on top of someone's face, or hurling them through the air to land with high impact on another human being.

Readers will be forgiven if, by this point, they have forgotten the sentiment with which this essay opened. So let me repeat it.

I love pro wrestling.

By now, you are probably wondering why.

Let me tell you.

When I was a kid, I loved comic books (like many other wrestling fans). I loved the tales of righteous, muscular men in colorful tights who stepped out into the world to reverse injustices and kick some ass. Later, I found the same satisfaction in well-crafted Westerns like *Shane* and well-crafted action movies like *Die Hard*.

I know absolutely that men and women are equally strong and carry the same potential for heroism. As it happens, I was born male, and I respond strongly to male archetypes in storytelling. For me, there is a simple, primal appeal in the story of a strong male figure stepping up to do "what must be done."

Wrestling—when it's done right—invokes the same archetypes as Westerns and comic books. All three genres vividly invoke a clear battle between right and wrong. All three genres tell stories that, in the end, come down to a hero and a villain locked in a solitary struggle for victory.

The difference between wrestling and a Western has to do with suspension of disbelief. In a Western (or any kind of movie), viewers immerse themselves in an alternate world. The format of a movie allows for great artistry and diversity, but it also creates a disconnect between the action and the viewer's individual personality. Allowing for the occasional exception, we watch movies silently and respectfully—from a distance.

Wrestling is different. It's participatory. We cheer and boo, even when sitting at home. The audience is part of the show, and the best wrestlers respond to audience reactions by adjusting their performance.

The suspension of disbelief is different as well. In a Western, viewers must assimilate the internal logic and rules of an entirely different world—an existence foreign to our daily lives. Wrestling is presented as a sporting event, something familiar to us all. It's not outside of personal experience; it's part of personal experience. To complete the spell, all you have to do is forget—for only a moment—that the outcome of the match is predetermined. And then something extraordinary happens.

When you get caught up in that golden moment, when you forget all the backstage producers and scriptwriters, a wrestling match blooms like some prickly tundra flower. The violence takes on *immediacy*, and you respond with *adrenaline*. Within that supercharged span of time, the best wrestlers unfold a story with tremendous power.

In a real fight, of course, the goal is to end the fight as efficiently as possible (in your favor). In general, real fights tend to be simple, quick, and brutal. A wrestling match is different. In wrestling, the performers are not really fighting. Instead, they're acting out a physical story.

In the best wrestling matches, the story is much more than a prolonged act of violence. That story includes violence, of course. More important, it includes the *threat* of violence, the specter of harm surging to the surface again and again, only to be evaded or endured.

This story surely portrays acts of physical strength and

athleticism. But it also incorporates acts of mental and emotional strength—such as perseverance, courage, fear, stamina, relief, suffering, experience, imagination, doubt, pride, and intelligence.

Reversals of fortune and narrow escapes. Suspense and momentum. Surprises and inevitabilities. And towering above it all, heroic figures, larger than life, who attain triumph or taste failure, but never live life in half measure.

There is something of splendor in professional wrestling, a sliver of greatness, an entirely unique grandeur that rises out of the format.

That special something is squandered when Vince McMahon and his WWE roll out the latest atrocity on any given week, whether it's racism, sexism, homophobia, or just plain bad taste. And it doesn't have to be this way.

The comic books I read as a child have grown up and evolved to reflect changing times and an increasingly adult audience. When I was a kid, Batman commonly battled costumed villains who barked like seals while perched atop giant typewriters and the like. Today, Batman battles mobsters, gangs, and serial killers, all realistically depicted. Batman struggles with himself as well, and the stories depict the toll that violence exacts on his life and the lives of those around him.

The simplistic twenty-eight-page morality tales of my youth have been replaced by graphic novels and multipart story arcs. The characters are subtle, shaded. Heroes are still heroes, but they struggle with the challenges they face—external challenges, like villains, and internal challenges that arise from their psyches. They face and fight discrimination. They have become modern.

Westerns have undergone a similar transformation,

thanks in large part to the efforts of Clint Eastwood. *Unforgiven* depicted a protagonist who turned the clichés of yesteryear on their heads—an antihero who might be his own worst enemy. The movie delivered a terrifyingly cathartic and violent climax—yet it also managed to carry a message. The movie was powerful but not preachy, thoughtful but never dull—the Western evolved for a modern audience.

Wrestling—as represented by WWE—has adapted its superficial format with flashy graphics and expensive production values, but it hasn't evolved its storytelling. Instead, WWE continues to rely on stereotypes that alienate modern viewers and disrupt the suspension of disbelief. WWE continues to rely on racism, misogyny, and homophobia to drive two-dimensional storylines that encourage fans to indulge their darkest instincts.

Longtime fans have a pat response when faced with complaints about the too-often offensive content served up by WWE: "It's just wrestling." It doesn't bother them; they have been desensitized. But new fans are not so jaded, and they have no motivation to stick around.

These storylines do not draw in new viewers—in fact, they alienate a vast swathe of people who might otherwise find wrestling entertaining. They don't sell tickets, and they don't sell pay-per-views. And the customers who are most likely to be offended are also the customers with the most money to spend on pay-per-views, live-show tickets, and merchandise—urban professionals, suburban parents, and the A-list celebrities who helped drive wrestling's biggest boom during the 1980s and 1990s.

Wrestling won't grow until things change. It's the twenty-first century, but wrestling heels still hurl slurs and steel chairs at black babyfaces and gay heels—and they're rewarded for this behavior when they are booked in the main event.

When a heel wrestler sexually threatens a woman, there is no social stigma in the context of the show. Even *baby-faces* call Arabs "sand people" and "ragheads" and disparage Puerto Ricans as "nappy-haired" or "Buckwheat."

It doesn't take an Oscar-winning screenwriter to lift these stories out of the gutter, it just takes common sense. Many forms of literature and entertainment feature racist villains. But those villains are ostracized by their peers; they are depicted in the context of modern society—where racism is not tolerated.

In the final analysis, lack of context is at the heart of wrestling's problem.

WWE runs an entertainment machine like no other. It runs live shows in a different city every night, usually at least four shows a week, every week of the year. WWE produces six hours of original television each and every week, including holidays, as well as producing a four-hour pay-per-view every month.

The people who produce and write WWE wrestling are a traveling band of workaholics. Virtually all their time is spent on the road—producing wrestling, promoting wrestling, and hanging out afterward with their fellow employees. The wrestlers themselves train, perform, and travel year-round. The writers and road agents are on call twenty-four hours a day. They are expected to drop everything when Vince McMahon picks up the phone.

For all these reasons and more, the hermetically sealed world of WWE has become badly out of sync with the real world. They don't understand what real people want, what they think and feel, how they act.

I don't know if anything can crack open that seal.

Although WWE is a public company, the majority of its shares are controlled by the McMahon family.

The McMahons have very little contact with the world outside wrestling. They are insanely wealthy and they don't have to answer to anyone. When attendance and ratings are down, the McMahons still make money (even when the wrestlers performing in the ring do not).

As long as the McMahons keep making money, they have no motivation to change their product or catch up with the times. Unless someone with deep, deep pockets succeeds in the risky proposition of competing with WWE on a national level, the odds are pretty good that the McMahons will keep on making money.

It's a shame. Because I think there are a lot of people like me out there.

People who grew up with wrestling and want to share it with their own children.

People who are afraid to take their kids to a live show because it might feature simulated rape on any given day.

People who want to introduce wrestling to their friends.

People who find themselves apologizing to their friends for what's happening on the TV screen ten minutes into the show.

People who want to cheer for a hero.

Without holding back.

FACTS

Amount that makers of the video game *JFK Reloaded* will pay the player who best replicates the murder of Kennedy: $100,000
(Traffic Management)

Percentage of songs on Billboard's Top 20 list during 2004 whose lyrics mention at least one brand name: 40
(Agenda Inc.)

Percentage that mention weaponry: 50
(Agenda Inc.)

Price a haunted-house supplier charges for a male figure "being tortured like never before," flesh-ripping sounds included: $2,295
(Halloween Productions, Inc.)

HILLARY CLINTON ASKING CONGRESS TO LAUNCH A 90 MILLION DOLLAR STUDY OF HOW CHILDREN ARE AFFECTED BY THE GRATUITOUS SEX AND VIOLENCE IN VIDEO GAMES.

MR. FISH ASKING HILLARY CLINTON TO SPEND 50 CENTS OF HER OWN FUCKING MONEY TO CALL HER FUCKING HUSBAND AND TO ASK HIM WHAT EFFECT MONICA LEWINSKY AND WACO AND SUDAN AND KOSOVO AND SERBIA AND IRAQ AND BELGRADE HAD ON ALL OF US AND OUR ABILITY TO FIND HER FUCKING CONCERN CREDIBLE.

Top Ten Reasons Not to Buy a Hummer

from CodePink4Peace.org

On the streets of Iraq, Hummers are the transportation of choice of the U.S. military. They are in every city and town, guarding gas stations and government buildings, and usually they carry U.S. soldiers who are holding machine guns.

Now Hummers are on the streets of the United States, too. Just as the Bush administration plays on Americans' fears of terrorism and tries to make us believe that the Iraq war made the world safer, so do Hummer ad campaigns play on people's fears by using images of apocalypse and destruction. They also try to make Americans believe that we are safer in large, gas-guzzling vehicles like the Hummer, despite clear evidence that Hummers are a danger both to their passengers and other drivers.

Hummers are horribly destructive to the environment. With an Environmental Protection Agency rating of two out of ten, because of the Hummer's average gas mileage of nine miles per gallon, it is not difficult to see how Hummers hurt the environment through their astronomical consumption of fossil fuels. Oil consumption is a major contributor to pollution and global warming. Hummers literally threaten the very air our children breathe.

Additionally, the Hummer is fueling this country's dependence on oil, which ends up pushing the U.S. into conflicts around the world, most recently Iraq.

To top it all off, small business owners who purchase Hummers receive a $100,000 tax break under Bush's new

Economic Stimulus Plan. This same plan only grants a tax break of $4,000 for the Toyota Prius hybrid. Hummers cost upwards of $55,000, which means that yet again wealthier individuals (the only people able to afford a $55,000 car) receive disproportionately more in tax breaks.

Top Ten Reasons Not to Buy a Hummer

Hummers may look cool on the outside. They might even appear to be a symbol of patriotism and solidarity with our troops in Iraq. But don't let appearances fool you. Peer beneath the surface and you'll find a host of reasons why the Hummer . . . is a bummer.

1. The Gas Mileage Alone Will Kill You

The Hummer has the worst gas mileage of any civilian vehicle. Although the number is tightly guarded (vehicles that weigh over 8,400 lbs, the weight of the smaller and lighter model of Hummer, the H2, are exempt from revealing their gas mileage to consumers) it hovers somewhere around 9 mpg. The Environmental Protection Agency gave a 2 out of 10 rating for the H2. In fact, the Hummer's gas mileage is less than half the mileage of the Model T Ford, the first car ever mass-produced. As our country's gas prices continue to soar and our economy continues to sink, ask yourself, can you honestly afford the astronomical cost of driving a Hummer?

2. The Hummer Receives More Complaints Than Any Other Car

Hummers are full of bugs. According to the 2003 J. D. Power and Associates Automotive Survey, Hummers received more complaints than any other line of cars both foreign and domestic—225 reported problems per 100 new vehicles compared to an industry average of 133. Complaints ranged from wind noise to poor performance to . . . you got it: poor gas mileage.

3. Oil Addiction Leads to War

The global addiction to oil is leading to resource wars throughout the world, and the US is the #1 addict. According to a recent World Bank study, countries that export oil are 40 times more likely to be engaged in war than non-exporting countries. Would so many American soldiers and countless Iraqis have died if our country was not addicted to fossil fuels? The EPA reported that an improvement of just 3 mpg overall would save 1 million barrels of oil per day. Considering that the United States imports 740,000 barrels of oil per day from Iraq, a modest improvement in fuel economy would free the country from its dependence on this unstable state. And if we all drove hybrid cars, which get over 50 miles per gallon, we could prevent all future wars for oil.

4. They Are Killers on the Road

According to a study by the National Highway Safety Traffic Administration, if you are in an accident with an SUV, you are 3.4 times more likely to be killed than if you had been hit by another car. Simply put, on the road, mass wins. The 8,400 pound H2 and 10,000+ H1 weigh significantly more than the average SUV, and are thus some of the most dangerous killers on the road. Their height, weight, and the stiffness of their frames put drivers of smaller cars at great risk for fatalities. Tough luck for the other guy (or woman or child), you might say, but at least

I'll be protected, right? Wrong! Hummers are not safe for their own drivers, either. The higher mass of SUVs and Hummers make them more difficult to stop. This lack of maneuverability increases the numbers of fatal accidents.

5. Soldiers Are Dying in Them

Although the Army does not keep a breakdown of Humvee casualties, almost every week the media reports incidents of soldiers being wounded or killed in their Humvees. Some officers estimate that upwards of 60% of the casualties suffered by their troops occurred in Humvees. Beyond the unavoidable dangers of war, there are two primary causes of the high number of Humvee casualties: faulty armor and terrible maneuverability. Most Humvees being used in active duty in Iraq were originally built with no armor whatsoever, as they were not meant for frontline combat. The newer armored models are not expected to arrive in Iraq until 2005. The weak or non-existent armor of the Humvees allows roadside bombs to rip through the vehicles. This leads to countless deaths and amputees. Beyond the lack of armor a significant percentage of Humvee casualties is due to accidents such as tipping over, resulting from the Humvee's poor maneuverability.

6. The Tax Break Is Unfair . . . and Unpatriotic

Hummer dealers are snagging new customers by telling them they can get a tax write-off of up to $100,000 as a business expense. How can that be? This tax break was originally designed for farmers and their trucks, but the legislation defines the vehicle by weight, not use, creating a loophole big enough to drive a Hummer through. Many people are furious about this loophole and are pushing for Congress to change the law. With our nation facing a $500 billion deficit, is it fair for Hummer owners to rip off the US government and their fellow taxpayers? Is it patriotic? Hardly.

7. People Won't Like You

Hummer drivers have become a target for angry pedestrians, cyclists, and other drivers who don't like seeing super-sized gas guzzlers lumbering down their roads or parked in over-sized spaces on our city streets. Hummer drivers get yelled at, flipped off, cut off; their vehicles get plastered with anti-Hummer bumper stickers. The website FUH2.com, for example, features pictures sent in from around the world of people flipping off Hummers. As anti-Hummer campaigns continue to pick up speed and disseminate information, the public sentiment against Hummers and their owners will only increase. Do you want this anger focused on you and your vehicle?

8. Mother Earth Won't Like You, Either

Beyond compromising the safety and well-being of yourself, your passengers, and other drivers, by driving a Hummer you are endangering the health of the planet itself. Hummers, with their absurd weight, are exempt from meeting Any emission standards. In other words, Hummers and other extremely large SUVs, such as the Ford Excursion, are allowed to pollute as much as they want without any government interference. Not only does the Hummer emit over 3 times more carbon dioxide than an average car, hastening global warming, but it gives off substantially more smog-producing pollutants and dangerous particulates as well. These are issues affecting all of us today, especially children. In fact, rates of asthma among our nation's children have increased to the point of constituting an epidemic. Furthermore, the EPA released a devastating report on 4/15/04 that indicates nearly one in five counties nationwide are breathing unhealthy air, affecting an estimatetd 159 million Americans. Is your Hummer really worth the very air you breathe?

9. Will You Really Survive a Falling Asteroid?

A recent ad campaign for the Hummer says: "When the asteroid hits and civilization crumbles, you'll be ready." Makes you sound pretty safe, no? But if the military Humvees can't even protect soldiers in Iraq against roadside bombs, how well do you think the unarmored civilian version will fare against the apocalypse?

10. There Are MUCH Better Deals

The H2 starts at $50,000, the H1 at $100,000! They are super-expensive, not very comfortable and big gas guzzlers. Stack that up against a Toyota or Honda hybrids, which cost under $25,000 and get 50 miles a gallon. If you really need a bigger car, in 2005 you can buy a hybrid SUV that will get significantly improved mileage. So why not save $25,000, be kinder to the planet, and join the "cool crowd"? What are you doing wasting your time with the Hummers? Go on over to your nearest Toyota or Honda dealer. You'll be glad you did.

FACTS*

Amount spent by school districts in Denton and Round Rock, Texas, respectively, for new high school football stadiums: $20 million and $27 million

Amount Denton spent on its stadium's three-story scoreboard: $900,000

* (NewsoftheWeird.com)

THE END OF THE WORLD

with facts

At a certain point in our continuing saga of self-destruction there will be nowhere left to hide—not the Antarctic, not the Sahara Desert, not even the womb of an American mother-to-be. This just in: We've reached that point.

It's Not Just Eskimos in Bikinis

from MotherJones.com (6/6/05)

Chip Ward

When we hear the term "global warming," we usually imagine collapsing Antarctic ice shelves, melting Alaskan glaciers, or perhaps starving polar bears wandering bewildered across an ice-free, alien landscape. Warnings about climate change tend to focus on the Earth's polar regions, in part because they are warming twice as fast as the rest of the planet and the dramatic changes underway there can be easily captured and conveyed. We may not be able to see the 80% decline in the Antarctic krill population —the tiny, shrimp-like creatures that are a critical food source for whales, seals, and sea birds—but we can easily see satellite photos of state-sized chunks of ice shields separating from the continent. We can grasp the enormity of planetary glacial melting simply by comparing photos of glaciers taken just a decade apart. But as long as we're talking about ice in distant climes, global warming seems like something that's happening elsewhere and to somebody else—or some other set of creatures.

So when you hear about global warming, the odds are good that you never think of the yellow-bellied marmot. Probably, you've never even heard of the critters, but the big rodents, common not to the distant Arctic but to Rocky Mountain meadows, have been acting like so many canaries lately—coal-mine canaries, that is. They may be the first among many species in the Lower 48 to die off, thanks to close-to-home global warming effects that we hear little about. They are dying of confusion.

As a term, global warming is so benign-sounding—we all like "warmth," after all—that it masks what's actually going on. Yes, temperatures overall are rising, low-lying islands are disappearing under the sea, and epic wildfires are becoming more routine. But some places like Europe could get much colder in a globally "warmed" world, if warm ocean currents shift away from them; while across the planet, however counterintuitive this might seem, floods are likely to be as commonplace as drought. "Climate disruption" is probably a more accurate description of what we are experiencing than mere "warming." Although the radical break in climate patterns now underway will lead to rising oceans and expanding deserts, the most insidious changes may be more subtle—and as unnoticed as the disappearance of the marmots may be.

The intricate and precisely timed collaborations of plants, animals, birds, and insects, fine-tuned over endless thousands of years of evolution, is inevitably short-circuited when the weather goes wacky over periods of time that are the geological equivalent of a wink. When environmental events and biological events that once fit together lose their synchronicity, the consequence can be extinction. Even the Pentagon realizes that, if dependable local weather patterns become erratic, chaos can ensue as, for instance, crops begin to fail. Some of the less adaptable wild creatures, great and small, who share our American backyards are already coping with the kind of eco-havoc we can as yet only imagine for ourselves. For them, a more accurate description of what is happening might be Eco-Topsy-Turvy or, perhaps, Climate Helter-Skelter.

Take that marmot, for example. The yellow-bellied marmot's hibernation habits are guided by ancient circadian rhythms that are cued by seasonal changes in light and temperature. Like their cousin Punxsutawney Phil, the marmots awake from winter hibernation in their underground burrows and surface when they sense that the earth is warming. In recent years, conservationists have been reporting that marmots are emerging from their holes a month sooner than expected. But if the ground warms before deep snowpack melts, which is now often the case, the emerging marmots cannot get to their food and they starve.

For the Purple Larkspur, which shares the marmot's meadow, the problem is the opposite. When spring temperatures grow warmer ever earlier, snow cover melts earlier as well and the larkspur, one of the first plants to bloom in American alpine meadows, puts out vulnerable buds weeks too soon—for even if the snow cover has mostly melted, frost remains a serious threat in early spring and a single cold night will wipe out those tender buds. No buds, no seeds. No seeds, eventually no larkspurs. No larkspurs, no nectar for queen bumblebees which produce worker bees for hives and no larkspur blossoms for hummingbirds. When pollinators like bees and hummingbirds disappear from a landscape that depends on them to carry out its annual renewal, a cascade of ill-effects ripples through the ecosystem.

Changes in snow patterns also present wolves with an unusual challenge. The re-introduced wolf, that symbol of our determination to restore the health of ecosystems that long suffered their loss, uses snow as an ally in chasing down and eating elk. The elk are weakened by starvation in winter and cannot as easily escape the nimble wolves through dense snowpack or across sheets of slippery ice.

In Yellowstone this past winter, snow and ice were sparse and the elk generally got away from the wolves. It wasn't just wolves that went hungry. Other animals and birds, including endangered Grizzly bears, depend on sharing carcasses the wolves leave behind to make it through the winter, so they also fared poorly.

When there is less snowpack to melt and rivers are thin, endangered and diminished stocks of salmon have less habitat and less mobility. In addition, salmon spawning cycles are adapted to the rhythms of local stream-flows as they have been experienced over tens of thousands of years. Adult salmon return from the ocean to the mouths of rivers to begin their spawning runs upstream just as those rivers are peaking and conditions for swimming are optimal. Or should be. When warmer spring temperatures thaw snowpack too soon, rivers peak earlier and the mature salmon arrive too late to make the journey up shallow rivers depleted by drought (and by what we draw off to keep exotic lawn grasses and golf greens vibrant). No journey, no spawning, and soon enough, no salmon. As conservation biologists have shown us, salmon are the glue that holds the food-webs and nutrient cycles of Northwest ecosystems together. Goodbye evolution, hello helter-skelter.

A report co-written by University of Texas biologist Camille Parmesan and University of Colorado ecologist Hector Galbraith for the Pew Center for Global Climate recently assessed 40 scientific studies linking climate change with observed ecological changes. A growing body of evidence, they found, shows that sudden climate change is not just about Eskimos in bikinis. Significant changes are underway even in temperate regions. The geographic ranges of many plant and animal species are either contracting altogether or shifting northward, causing species like the Red Fox to compete with the Arctic Fox for food and territory. Flowering patterns, breeding behaviors, and the timing of migrations are all undergoing change. The distribution of plants, insects, animals, and even soil bacteria is shifting rapidly in response to recent alterations in weather patterns. The question is: Can plants and creatures adapt fast enough to survive such rapid changes? Can evolution run on "fast-forward"?

If trying to evolve at warp speed while Mother Nature is having hot flashes isn't enough, birds and animals in the Lower 48 are also struggling to adapt to such changes within habitats that have been drastically reduced, fragmented, and often contaminated by human development over the past century. First, wildlife was thrown off the mother-ship; now the lifeboats, the isolated remnant habitats left to them, are being battered by fickle weather. No doubt the extinction wave already underway, thanks to man-made assaults on wild habitat, will only accelerate as climate disruption kicks in, swamping those last remaining wild refuges.

On land, the powerful impact of habitat degradation and loss makes it hard for conservation scientists to sort out which wildlife behavioral changes are due to ongoing stress and which may be the result of sudden climate change. All this is made even more complex by the fact that species adapting to climate change face man-made limitations and barriers as they try to compensate by moving northward or to higher ground. Their potential escape routes are regularly blocked by roads, fences, buildings, and human activity.

On the sea, however, where man-made barriers are fewer, changes have been tracked and measured that are clearly linked to climate change. In the coastal waters of Monterey Bay where the ranges of northern and southern Pacific fish overlap, for example, scientists have tracked changing species distribution. Northern species are heading further north while southern species have greatly increased their dominance in the bay. Typically, Humboldt squid, which until recently ranged from Southern California to South America, have now been spotted as far north as Alaska. Ocean studies confirm that species are responding as best they can to the changes in their historical habitats and food webs. In the ocean, as on land, when species overlap and invade one another's territories, ecological relationships between interdependent species are broken and chaos can follow. Again, it becomes a helter-skelter world.

Soil itself—the ground we walk on—is also a habitat that is shaped by climate regimes and patterns. Berkeley professor John Harte's research shows that, across the West, sagebrush is replacing mountain meadows because of warmer temperatures at higher altitudes. Mountain meadows are lush with diverse grasses and wildflowers. The litter from wildflowers—the leaves, flowers, and stems that fall into the soil each autumn—is easy for microorganisms to digest. Sage litter is thinner and less diverse. It makes poor soil. Warming will also result in accelerated evaporation from soils. Microorganism and insect pests that can survive the winter in drier, warmer soils will flourish and do more damage to crops and trees. The bark beetle, for instance, thrives in drought and is devastating Western forests, while generating more dead timber to fuel future catastrophic fires.

Humans are not exempt. If ecosystem relationships become disconnected and ecological processes break down, we will eventually suffer as well. Adaptability and the inclination to take over neighboring yards when ours are used up or fall apart can keep us from consequences for only so long. Although we live in a culture that encourages and enables us to think, feel, and act as if we were above and beyond nature (or, perhaps, beside it—nature being what we visit by car on weekends), we are, in fact, embedded in the natural/physical world. Like it or not, the fluids that sustain our lives come from watersheds. Our food is a synthesis of soil, sunlight, and rain. We depend on the biological diversity, ecological processes, and powerful global currents of wind and water that are the operating systems of all life on Earth. Signs that these operating systems are faltering should be a wake-up call for us to begin real planning to kick our fossil-fuel addiction, while creating laws, policies, and projects that aim at ecological preservation and restoration.

But we don't act and doubt reigns supreme. The cynical Bushites say they want to make a culture that values life while they sow whatever doubt they can about the reality of global climate disruption. Worse yet, they are intent on obstructing the rest of the world from taking collaborative steps to reduce human influence on the planetary climate that is the very basis of all life, including that of fetuses and persistently vegetative legislators.

Because the patterns we are trying to understand are so vast in scale, so long in scope, and fluctuate chaotically over time, it is hard to tease out trends from the variations that are possible. Could the dramatic climate changes we are experiencing just be another spike in a long, spiky record of the earth's climate? Maybe significant numbers of us can continue to believe this a while longer; but as the scientific evidence mounts and man-made influences seem ever more likely to be the culprits, the fear that we could cross a kind of climate tipping-point with catastrophic consequences for life on Earth will become more palpable. Yes, there are unknowns in the global climate prediction game, but does Russian Roulette make more sense if you can show that there is only one bullet in the chamber instead of two?

If inaction risks drought, flood, monster storms, pestilence, epidemics, extinctions, ecological dysfunction, refugees, war, and more squalor (as even the Pentagon suspects may be the case), not to mention all that potential underwater real estate in Manhattan, Miami, and New Orleans, then we would be prudent and wise to take precautionary actions now. That we continue to ignore the signs all around us is not just a political failure, though it certainly is that. It is undoubtedly also a failure of empathy and awareness. I suspect we will not find the political will to stop the damage we are doing until we begin to see ourselves within the picture frame and realize that it is in our self-evident self-interest to act boldly and soon.

So, get in the picture. Put on those Ray-Bans and stand in the purple mountain meadow next to that yellow-bellied marmot—the one blinking in the snow-reflected sun. Face the camera. Say "cheese!" Now that's a shot you can show your grandchildren when they ask you, "What's a marmot?"—or "What's a meadow?"

FACTS

The five hottest years, in order, since record-keeping began in 1861: 1998, 2002, 2003, 2001, 1997
(*National Geographic News*, 12/6/04)

Expected rank of 2005 on the list of hottest years, as of October: 1
(*Washington Post*, 10/12/05)

Difference between the average size of the arctic ice cap between 1979 and 2000 and its size in the summer of 2005: 500,000 square miles
(*Washington Post*, 10/12/05)

Approximate percentage by which the Arctic ice cap has shrunk in the last half-century: 50
(*New York Times*, 10/19/05)

Number of glaciers in Glacier National Park when the park was founded in 1910: 150
(*National Geographic News*, 12/6/04)

Number today: fewer than 30
(*National Geographic News*, 12/6/04)

Year by which scientists expect the snows of Kilimanjaro to disappear: 2020
(*National Geographic News*, 12/6/04)

Number of people worldwide who live within three feet of sea level: 100 million
(*National Geographic News*, 12/6/04)

Height in feet the sea is expected to rise by 2100 due to global warming: 2
(*New York Times*, 9/27/05)

Number of species that a recent study estimated would become extinct due to global warming by 2050: 1 million
(*New York Times*, 9/27/05)

Factor by which the annual number of Sahara dust storms has increased in the last 50 years: 10
(Andrew Goudie, Oxford, England)

Rank of 2004's desert-locust plague in northern Africa among the world's worst in 15 years: 1
(UN Food and Agriculture Program)

Number of countries susceptible to such a plague: 65
(UN Food and Agriculture Program)

Profits of Doom

from MotherJones.com (4/18/05)

Dave Gilson

If you want to hear some tough talk about global warming, talk to an insurer. Take this recent statement by Richard Jones, the vice president for engineering of the Hartford Insurance Company. "Climate change is real," said Jones. "To me, proving that earth's climate is changing from human actions—namely global warming—is like statistically 'proving' the pavement exists after you have jumped out a 30-story building. After each floor, your analysis would say, 'so far, so good,' and then, at the pavement, all uncertainty is removed." Jones's alarm over the impending climate catastrophe is not uncommon, even in an industry known for its buttoned-down, by-the-book image. As the cost of droughts, floods, wind storms, and other weather events linked to climate change multiply, insurers have taken a remarkably active role in speaking out about global warming.

For nearly 15 years, some of the world's largest insurance companies have been on the forefront of effort to confront man-made climate change. They've been watching the warning signs for years: as early as 1973, the German company Munich Re identified climate change as a potential problem. By the 1990s, other European insurers such as the Zurich-based insurance giant Swiss Reinsurance were publicly discussing how the science of global warming was borne out not only by the world's changing weather patterns but also by their own corporate ledgers. In November 1990, the general manager for Swiss

Re made the case for taking climate change seriously in the trade publication *Business Insurance*. Noting the recent rise in natural catastrophes, he warned, "if the feared climate change is confirmed, it will obviously stretch the insurance industry to is limits." In other words, if global warming ran its predicted course, it could bankrupt the world's insurers.

At first glance, such concerns may seem counterintuitive. After all, *Business Insurance* is not the kind of publication where you'd expect to find a call to arms on global warming. "People typically assume that big industry will come down on other side of the issue, i.e. saying that doing anything to prevent climate change would be bad for business and for the broader economy," explains Evan Mills, a staff scientist at the Lawrence Berkeley National Laboratory and an expert on the insurance industry's response to climate change. Yet while environmentalists may gladly claim actuaries as allies, profits, not politics, are driving insurers' interest in limiting carbon emissions and promoting clean energy. Industry representatives openly concede that their interest in combating global warming is mercenary: climate change is bad for their bottom line.

Though the long-term effects of global warming threaten the future of much of the world's economy, the insurance industry is already feeling the pinch. With $3 trillion in yearly revenues, it is three times the size of the oil industry. And unlike the oil industry, which may be able to ride out the fossil-fuel economy for another 50 years, the insurance industry is sensitive to environmental pressures as they happen. Though the industry is not fighting global warming uniformly—most American companies have been slow to get involved—its efforts are getting attention. Insurers are like the financial canary in the coal mine: When they start gasping for breath, it's time to take notice.

If there's one thing insurers do well, it's number crunching, and their numbers on climate change don't look good. The frequency and impact of weather disasters have been steadily climbing during the past century, with a dramatic uptick in the last 50 years. According to data collected by Munich Re, there were less than 200 weather-related disasters in the 1950s, yet over 1,600 in the 1990s. The economic losses caused by such events increased tenfold during the same four-decade period, from $4 billion in the '50s to $40 billion in the '90s. Meanwhile, the insurance industry's responsibility for covering such losses has risen astronomically. During the 1950s, insurance losses due to weather disasters were negligible; by the 1990s, they were up to $9.2 billion a year. As Lloyd's of London chairman Peter Levine told a recent conference of insurers in San Diego, "The real issue for insurers is natural disasters. . . . [T]he impact of those disasters has been increasing because the climate is changing, which presents some very serious challenges for insurers."

The numbers for the U.S. are similarly disquieting. Between 1985 and 1999, 14 percent of the world's weather catastrophes hit the U.S., causing 58 percent of the world's insurance losses. The Insurance Services Office calculated that a hurricane-sized weather catastrophe hitting a major U.S. city such as Miami could cost insurers $50 billion and would bankrupt more than a third of American insurance companies. Such scenarios aren't entirely hypothetical: Hurricane Andrew, which hit

Florida in 1992, cost insurance companies $17 billion, and put several out of business.

These bleak numbers translate into frightening uncertainty for an industry driven by the assumption that unpredictable risks can be mitigated by plugging reliable information into time-tested formulas that spread those risks around. But the increasing chances of property damage and loss of life due to global climate change make it harder for insurers to be certain that they will be able to cover their assumed risks. As legendary investor Warren Buffet explained in 1992, the possibility of global warming means that "catastrophe insurers can't simply extrapolate past experience." More simply put, the insurance industry is like a casino: The odds are usually on its side. But when those odds suddenly change, it faces the unhappy possibility of a long losing streak.

Some companies are trying to hedge their bets by actively looking for solutions to global warming. Working under the auspices of the United Nations Environment Program Insurance Industry Initiative, over 80 insurance companies from 25 countries are encouraging governmental and corporate efforts to stem carbon emissions. However, American companies have been less active than their Canadian, European, and Asian counterparts. The Chubb Group, for example, is not a member of the UNEP initiative and has resisted calls to be more proactive. Last year, the company blocked a shareholder resolution that might have forced it to take a firm stand against global warming. Such recalcitrance may be due to the success of climate change skeptics in stretching out the "debate" over the existence of global warming. Part of the problem, says Evan Mills, is that some American insurers have yet to see global warming as an opportunity to invest in strategies that might reduce their risks and ultimately save them money.

But the big European insurers' insistence that fighting global warming is good for business has, ironically, caused some free-market climate change skeptics to accuse them of trying to make a buck off of global warming. A recent commentary on *TechCentralStation.com* attacked Swiss Re for hyping the costs of weather disasters so that frightened consumers would flock to buy insurance at higher premiums. The author lamented Swiss Re's "sellout" to the environmental movement: "A company using free enterprise to generate profits through an alliance with a movement that has on its agenda the elimination, or at least a profound restructuring, of the system that has allowed the company to prosper."

While their assessment of the insurers' motivations may be off base, the skeptics are right that consumers may wind up paying more for insurance. "As losses rise, so too will premiums," explains Mills. "We need to remember that, like any industry, insurers need to cover their losses and generate a reasonable profit for their shareholders. With the patterns of extreme weather events becoming more intense and more variable, the actuarial challenge will grow, and this will, in turn, put pressure on prices." Another risk to consumers is that nervous insurance companies will stop covering property that's at particular risk for climate-related disasters. This may not seem like a big concern if you don't live in a seaside village in the South Pacific or Alaska. But if you live somewhere that ever experiences hurricanes, droughts, flooding, windstorms, blizzards, or heat waves, at some point you may find you're no longer in good hands.

The Corpse on Union Street

from the *New York Times* (9/8/05)

Dan Barry

NEW ORLEANS—In the downtown business district here, on a dry stretch of Union Street, past the Omni Bank automated teller machine, across from a parking garage offering "early bird" rates: a corpse. Its feet jut from a damp blue tarp. Its knees rise in rigor mortis.

Six National Guardsmen walked up to it on Tuesday afternoon and two blessed themselves with the sign of the cross. One soldier took a parting snapshot like some visiting conventioneer, and they walked away. New Orleans, September 2005.

Hours passed, the dusk of curfew crept, the body remained. A Louisiana state trooper around the corner knew all about it: murder victim, bludgeoned, one of several in that area. The police marked it with traffic cones maybe four days ago, he said, and then he joked that if you wanted to kill someone here, this was a good time.

Night came, then this morning, then noon, and another sun beat down on a dead son of the Crescent City.

That a corpse lies on Union Street may not shock; in the wake of last week's hurricane, there are surely hundreds, probably thousands. What is remarkable is that on a downtown street in a major American city, a corpse can decompose for days, like carrion, and that is acceptable.

Welcome to New Orleans in the post-apocalypse, half baked and half deluged: pestilent, eerie, unnaturally quiet.

Scraggly residents emerge from waterlogged wood to say strange things, and then return into the rot. Cars drive the wrong way on the Interstate and no one cares. Fires burn, dogs scavenge, and old signs from les bons temps have been replaced with hand-scrawled threats that looters will be shot dead.

The incomprehensible has become so routine here that it tends to lull you into acceptance. On Sunday, for example, several soldiers on Jefferson Highway had guns aimed at the heads of several prostrate men suspected of breaking into an electronics store.

A car pulled right up to this tense scene and the driver leaned out his window to ask a soldier a question: "Hey, how do you get to the interstate?"

Maybe the slow acquiescence to the ghastly here—not in Baghdad, not in Rwanda, here—is rooted in the intensive news coverage of the hurricane's aftermath: floating bodies and obliterated towns equal old news. Maybe the concerns of the living far outweigh the dignity of a corpse on Union Street. Or maybe the nation is numb with post-traumatic shock.

Wandering New Orleans this week, away from news conferences and search-and-rescue squads, has granted haunting glimpses of the past, present, and future, with the rare comfort found in, say, the white sheet that flaps, not in surrender but as a vow, at the corner of Poydras Street and St. Charles Avenue.

"We Shall Survive," it says, as though wishing past the battalions of bulldozers that will one day come to knock down water-corrupted neighborhoods and rearrange the Louisiana mud for the infrastructure of an altogether different New Orleans.

Here, then, the New Orleans of today, where open fire hydrants gush the last thing needed on these streets; where one of the many gag-inducing smells—that of rancid meat—is better than MapQuest in pinpointing the presence of a market; and where images of irony beg to be noticed.

The Mardi Gras beads imbedded in mud by a soldier's boot print. The "take-away" signs outside restaurants taken away. The corner kiosk shouting the August 28 headline of New Orleans's *Times-Picayune*: "Katrina Takes Aim."

Rush hour in downtown now means pickups carrying gun-carrying men in sunglasses, S.U.V.'s loaded with out-of-town reporters hungry for action, and the occasional tank. About the only ones commuting by bus are dull-eyed suspects shuffling two-by-two from the bus-and-train terminal, which is now a makeshift jail.

Maybe some of them had helped to kick in the portal to the Williams Super Market in the once-desirable Garden District. And who could blame them if all they wanted was food in those first desperate days? The interlopers took the water, beer, cigarettes, and snack food. They did not take the wine or the New Orleans postcards.

On the other side of downtown across Canal Street in the French Quarter, the most raucous and most unreal of American avenues is now little more than an empty alley with balconies.

The absence of sweetly blown jazz, of someone cooing "ma chère," of men sporting convention nametags and emitting forced guffaws—the absence of us—assaults the senses more than any smell.

Past the famous Cafe du Monde, where a slight breeze twirls the overhead fans for no one, past the statue of Joan of Arc gleaming gold, a man emerges from nothing on Royal Street. He is asked, "Where's St. Bernard Avenue?"

"Where's the ice?" he asks in return, eyes narrowed in menace. "Where's the ice? St. Bernard's is that way, but where's the ice?"

In Bywater and the surrounding neighborhoods, the severely damaged streets bear the names of saints who could not protect them. Whatever nature spared, human nature stepped up to provide a kind of democracy in destruction.

At the Whitney National Bank on St. Claude Avenue, diamond-like bits of glass spill from the crushed door, offering a view of the complementary coffee table. A large woman named Phoebe Au—"Pronounced 'Awe,'" she says—materializes to report that men had smashed it in with a truck. She fades into the neighborhood's broken brick, and a thin woman named Toni Miller materializes to correct the record.

"They used sledgehammers," she said.

Farther down St. Claude Avenue, where tanks rumble past a smoldering building, the roads are cluttered with vandalized city buses. The city parked them on the riverbank for the hurricane, after which some hoods took them for fare-free joy rides through lawless streets, and then discarded them.

On Clouet Street, where a days-old fire continues to burn where a warehouse once stood, a man on a bicycle wheels up through the smoke to introduce himself as Strangebone. The nights without power or water have been tough, especially since the police took away the gun he was carrying—"They beat me and threatened to kill me," he says—but there are benefits to this new world.

"You're able to see the stars," he says. "It's wonderful."

Today, law enforcement troops began lending muscle

to Mayor C. Ray Nagin's vow to evacuate by force any residents too attached to their pieces of the toxic metropolis. They searched the streets for the likes of Strangebone, and that woman whose name sounds like Awe.

Meanwhile, back downtown, the shadows of another evening crept like spilled black water over someone's corpse.

FACTS

The hottest month since 1890 for seawater in the Gulf of Mexico: August 2005
(*Washington Post*, 10/12/05)

Factor increase since the 1970s in the percentage of hurricanes that are category four or five: 2
(*New York Times*, 9/27/05)

Factor by which average hurricane intensity has increased during the past 30 years: 2
(*New York Times*, 9/27/05)

Date as of which Hurricane Wilma became the most intense Atlantic storm ever recorded: October 19, 2005
(Associated Press, 10/19/05)

The Rebellion of the Tools

from *A Short History of Progress* (2004)

Ronald Wright

I have a weakness for cynical graffiti. One relevant to the hazards of progress is this: "Each time history repeats itself, the price goes up." The collapse of the first civilization on earth, the Sumerian, affected only half a million people. The fall of Rome affected tens of millions. If ours were to fail, it would, of course, bring catastrophe on billions.

So far we've looked at four ancient societies—Sumer, Rome, the Maya, Easter Island—which, in roughly a thousand years each, wore out their welcome from nature and collapsed. I've also mentioned two exceptions, Egypt and China, who achieved a run of 3,000 years or more.

Joseph Tainter, in his book on past collapses, nicknames three kinds of trouble the Runaway Train, the Dinosaur, and the House of Cards. These usually act together. The Sumerians' irrigation was certainly a runaway train, a disastrous course from which they could not deviate; the rulers' failure to tackle the problem qualifies them as dinosaurs, and the civilization's swift and irreparable fall shows it to have been a house of cards.

Much the same can be said of the other failures. We are faced by something deeper than mistakes at any particular time or place. The invention of agriculture is itself a runaway train, leading to vastly expanded populations but seldom solving the food problem because of two inevitable (or nearly inevitable) consequences. The first is biological: the population grows until it hits the bounds of the food supply. The second is social: all civilizations become hierarchical; the upward concentration of wealth ensures that there can never be enough to go around. The economist Thomas Malthus explored the first dilemma, and thinkers from Christ to Marx have touched on the second. As the Chinese saying has it: "A peasant must stand a long time on the hillside with his mouth open before a roast duck flies in."

Civilization is an experiment, a very recent way of life in the human career, and it has a habit of walking into what I am calling progress traps. A small village on good land beside a river is a good idea; but when the village grows into a city and paves over the good land, it becomes a bad idea. While prevention might have been easy, a cure may be impossible: a city isn't easily moved. This human inability to foresee—or to watch out for—long-range consequences may be inherent to our kind, shaped by the millions of years when we lived from hand to mouth by hunting and gathering. It may also be little more than a mix of inertia, greed, and foolishness encouraged by the shape of the social pyramid. The concentration of power at the top of large-scale societies gives the elite a vested interest in the status quo; they continue to prosper in darkening times long after the environment and general populace begin to suffer.

Yet despite the wreckage of past civilizations littering the earth, the overall experiment of civilization has continued to spread and grow. The numbers (insofar as they can be estimated) break down as follows: a world population of about 200 million at Rome's height, in the second century A.D.; about 400 million by 1500, when Europe reached the Americas; one billion people by 1825, at the start of the Coal Age; 2 billion by 1925, when the Oil Age gets under way; and 6 billion by the year 2000. Even more startling than the growth is the acceleration. Adding 200 million after Rome took thirteen centuries; adding the last 200 million took only three years.

We tend to regard our age as exceptional, and in many ways it is. But the parochialism of the present—the way our eyes follow the ball and not the game—is dangerous. Absorbed in the here and now, we lose sight of our course through time, forgetting to ask ourselves Paul Gauguin's final question: *Where are we going?* If so many previous ages ran into natural limits and crashed, how has our runaway train (if that's what it is) been able to keep on gathering speed?

I suggested earlier that the Chinese and Egyptian civilizations were exceptionally long-lived because nature gave them lavish subsidies of extra topsoil, brought in by wind and water from elsewhere. But some credit must go to human ingenuity. The number of mouths an acre of land can support, and the length of time it can go on supporting them, does not depend only on natural fertility. Civilization did get better at farming as it went along. The mixed farm, with the use of animal and human dung on ploughed land, proved endlessly sustainable on the heavy loams of northern Europe. Crop rotation and use of "green manure" (the ploughing under of nitrogen-fixing plants) raised yields considerably in early modern times. The Asian development of wet rice cultivation was highly productive, and its precisely levelled paddy fields encouraged sustainable tillage of hillsides. The Islamic civilization of Spain not only handed down Classical learning to late-medieval Europe, it also repaired the eroded landscape Rome had left by building olive terraces and advanced irrigation schemes. In the Andes, the Incas and pre-Incas built an efficient mountain agriculture on flights of stone terraces watered by glacial streams and fertilized with guano, which they mined from ancient seabird rookeries on arid coastal islands. Studies of Andean terracing in use for the past 1,500 years show no loss of fertility.

Such steady improvements in farming methods can explain a steady rise in population, but not the great boom of the past few centuries. Mechanization and sanitation may account for later stages of the boom, but not its beginnings, which pre-date farm machinery and public health. The take-off point was about a century after Columbus. This was when the strange fruits of the Spanish conquest began to be digested. Europe received the greatest subsidy of all when half a planet, fully developed but almost unprotected, fell suddenly into its hands.

If America had been a wilderness, the invaders wouldn't have got much out of it for a long time. Every field would have had to be won from the forest, every crop imported and adapted, every mine discovered, every road cut across trackless desert and ranges. But this unknown world had had its own Neolithic Revolutions, and had built a series of civilizations on a rich agrarian base.

The three Americas formed a complex world much like Asia, teeming with 80 to 100 million people—between a fifth and a fourth of the human race. The most powerful polities in 1500 were the Aztec Empire, a city-state system dominated by the conurbation known as Mexico, and the Inca Empire, or Tawantinsuyu, stretching three thousand miles down the spine of the Andes and Pacific coast. Each of these had roughly 20 million people—midway in scale between ancient Egypt and Rome. With a quarter-million citizens, the Aztec capital was then the biggest city in the Americas and one of the half dozen biggest in the world. The Inca Empire was less urban but tightly organized, with 14,000 miles of paved roads, a command economy, and vast terracing and irrigation projects built by a labor-tax system, rather than slavery. Though hardly a workers' paradise, it soon began to look like one to survivors under Spanish rule. Both these empires were young, the heirs of others, and might have had centuries ahead of them if no outsiders had arrived. But they awaited intruders like orchards of ripe fruit.

The environmental historians Alfred Crosby and William McNeill showed in the 1970s that the New World's true conquerors were germs: mass killers such as smallpox, bubonic plague, influenza, and measles. These arrived for the first time with the Europeans (who had resistance to them) and acted like biological weapons, killing the rulers and at least half the populations of Mexico and Peru in the first wave. "The miraculous triumphs" of the conquistadors, Crosby wrote, "are in large part the triumphs of the [smallpox] virus." Despite their guns and horses, the Spaniards did not achieve any major conquests on the mainland until *after* a smallpox pandemic had swept through. Before that, the Maya, Aztecs, Incas, and Floridians all repelled the first efforts to invade them.

Some years ago, the Pentagon came up with plans for a Strangelovian weapon called the neutron bomb, to be let off high over Russian cities so that a searing blast of radiation would kill all the people but leave the property unharmed. The European invaders of America had a weapon of exactly this effect in disease. Let nobody say the New World went down without a fight: the battles for Mexico and Cusco were among the hardest fought in history. But once the epidemiological veil was torn, the people became too few to defend what their ancestors had built up for 10,000 years. "They died in heaps like bedbugs," wrote a Spanish friar in Mexico.

Except for the Great Plains and its cold regions, even North America was not wild in 1500. Hollywood may have persuaded us that the "typical" Indian was a buffalo hunter. But all temperate zones of the United States, from the Southwest to the Southeast and north to Missouri, Ohio, and the Great Lakes, were thickly settled by farming peoples. When the Pilgrims arrived in Massachusetts, the Indians had died out so recently that the whites found empty cabins, winter corn, and cleared fields waiting for their use: a foretoken of the settlers' parasitic advance across the continent. "Europeans did not find a wilderness here," the American historian Francis Jennings has written, "they made one."

For the Spanish, disease was a better weapon than a neutron bomb because just enough Amerindians survived to work the mines. The Aztec and Inca treasures were only a down payment on all the gold and silver that would flow across the Atlantic for centuries. Karl Marx was among the first economists to see that, financially, the Industrial Revolution begins with Atahuallpa's gold. "An indispensable condition for the establishment of manufacturing industry," he said in 1847, "was the accumulation of capital facilitated by the discovery of America and the importation of its precious metals." The Genoese and German bankers who underwrote Spain's empire were awash in bullion looking for something to do. Much found its way to northern Europe, financing shipbuilding, gun foundries, and other imperial ventures. Much also went on European wars—and wars between peers are mothers of invention. In a way Mao Zedong didn't intend, power would indeed grow from the barrel of a gun: from the cannon's "reeking tube" descends the cylinder of the steam and petrol engines.

Gold and silver formed just one side of a transatlantic triangle of loot, land, and labour. The New World's widowed acres—and above all its crops—would prove far more valuable than its metal in the long run. At their Thanksgiving dinners, devout Americans thank their God for feeding them in a "wilderness." They then devour a huge meal of turkey, maize, beans, squash, pumpkin, and potatoes. All these foods had been developed over thousands of years by New World civilizations. It is also hard to imagine curry without chiles, Italian food without tomatoes, the Swiss and Belgians with no chocolate, Hawaiians without pineapples, Africans without cassava, and the British with fish but no chips.

Besides their effect on diet, the new crops brought a dramatic rise in output—in Africa and Asia, as well as in Europe. Maize and potatoes are about twice as productive as wheat and barley, needing only half the land and workforce to yield the same amount of food. Populations rose and large numbers of people left the farm, generating labour surpluses from Britain to the Gold Coast. In the north these people ended up in mills and factories, while in Africa they became foreign exchange for manufactured goods, especially guns.

Europeans shipped Africans across the Atlantic to

replace indigenous Americans, and made them grow sugar, cotton, and coffee for European cities. Later, Europe also began exporting surplus people—to fill the prairies and pampas, which proved ideal for growing wheat and barley. With the invention of farm machinery, the Old World grains became less labor-intensive. And with the rediscovery and worldwide use of guano—another gift of Inca agriculture—crop yields soared. When the guano deposits and other natural fertilizers were exhausted, commercial farming became almost entirely dependent on chemical fertilizers made from oil and gas. Fossil energy not only powers but feeds the modern world. We are literally eating oil.

In 1991 William McNeill concluded: "The modern surge of population, sustained in large part by the new crops, is still going on, with drastic but unforeseeable ecological results." In the thirteen years since he wrote that, a billion more people have appeared on earth—the same as the whole population at the beginning of mechanization in 1825. One billion may be close to the number who could feed themselves indefinitely by muscle power if industrial civilization were to fail.

We will never know when, where, or even whether the Industrial Revolution would have happened had America not existed. My guess is that it would—but later, more gradually, and in a different way. It might have begun in China rather than in Europe, or in both. But that is for the "what if" school of history. All we can say is that things would have moved more slowly and been very different. The world we have today is the gift of the New World.

The New World, then, really was Eldorado. It was also

Utopia. Early reports of Amazonian societies had influenced Sir Thomas More's book of that name, published in 1516. A century later, the bestselling writer Garcilaso de la Vega, who was half Inca, promoted his mother's fallen empire as the ideal state. In North America, the influence was more direct, a matter of daily example. The early frontier culture was a hybrid, a place where Indians grew orchards and whites took up scalping. Settlers fought, traded, and intermarried with self-governing native peoples who practised social equality, free debate in council, and the rule of consensus. "Their whole constitution breathes nothing but liberty!" wrote James Adair, of the Cherokees, in 1775. Benjamin Franklin had made similar observations about the Iroquois Confederacy, which he urged the Thirteen Colonies to emulate. The whites were particularly impressed by the way dissenters would simply leave the rest of their nation and form an independent group. Here—spread before the eyes of colonists resentful of a distant crown—were freedom, democracy, and the right of secession.

It was, and still is, not well known that these native democracies were largely a post-Columbian development, blooming in the open spaces left by the great dying of the 1500s. Most of the eastern farming "tribes" were remnants of once-powerful chiefdoms. Had the English come to America before the demographic collapse, they would have found a more familiar social structure: lords who lived in great houses atop hundred-foot earthen pyramids, were carried about on litters, and were buried with slaves and concubines. The smallpox virus, having overthrown such societies along with the Aztec and Inca empires, therefore played a precursory role in the American Revolution.

Most uprisings are sparked by want; the American rebels were inspired by plenty—by Indian land and Indian ideals. In more than one way, Franklin's countrymen became, as he called them, "white savages."

The American Revolution in turn influenced the French Revolution, which had its own white savagery known as the Terror. Governments keen to avoid more of the same began broadening the franchise throughout the following century. A measure of participation filtered grudgingly down the social pyramid, while the new industrial economy nourished a growing middle class.

We in the lucky countries of the West now regard our two-century bubble of freedom and affluence as normal and inevitable; it has even been called the "end" of history, in both a temporal and teleological sense. Yet this new order is an anomaly: the opposite of what usually happens as civilizations grow. Our age was bankrolled by the seizing of half a planet, extended by taking over most of the remaining half, and has been sustained by spending down new forms of natural capital, especially fossil fuels. In the New World, the West hit the biggest bonanza of all time. And there won't be another like it—not unless we find the civilized Martians of H. G. Wells, complete with the vulnerability to our germs that undid them in his *War of the Worlds.*

The experiment of civilization has long had its doubters, even in times when change moved too slowly for most people to remark. The tales of Icarus, Prometheus, and Pandora illustrate the risks of being too clever by half, a theme also known to Genesis. Perhaps the most insightful ancient story of this kind—particularly as it comes from a civilization that had suffered collapse—is the "Rebellion of the Tools" in the Maya creation epic, the *Popol Vuh,* where human beings are overthrown by their farm and household implements:

> And all [those things] began to speak. . . . "You . . . shall feel our strength. We shall grind and tear your flesh to pieces," said their grinding stones. . . . At the same time, their griddles and pots spoke: "Pain and suffering you have caused us. . . . You burned us as if we felt no pain. Now you shall feel it, we shall burn you."

As the Cuban writer Alejo Carpentier pointed out, this is our first explicit warning of the threat in the machine.

Such warnings became common in the nineteenth century, when, for the first time ever, wrenching technical and social change was felt within a single lifetime. In 1800, the cities had been small, the air and water relatively clean—which is to say that it would give you cholera, not cancer. Nothing moved faster than by wind or limb. The sound of machinery was almost unknown. A person from 1600 transported to 1800 could have made his way around quite easily. But by 1900, there were motor cars on the streets and electric trains beneath them; movies were flickering on screens; earth's age was reckoned in millions of years, and Albert Einstein was writing his Special Theory of Relativity.

Early in the century, Mary Shelley pondered the new science with her *Frankenstein.* And Charles Dickens gave the social costs of industry a scalding and prescient critique in *Hard Times,* asking whether "the Good Samaritan was a Bad Economist," and foreseeing the new religion of the bottom line: "Every inch of the existence of mankind, from birth to death," he wrote in 1854, "was to be a bargain across a counter."

In his 1872 novel, *Erewhon* (an anagram of "nowhere"), Samuel Butler created a remote civilization that had industrialized long before Europe, but where the effects of progress had sparked a Luddite revolution. The great danger, wrote an Erewhon radical, was not so much the existing machines as the speed at which they were evolving: if not stopped in time, they might develop language, reproduce themselves, and subjugate mankind. Butler was sending up Darwinism here, but the anxieties stirred by the panting monsters of the Steam Age were real enough. Years before he became prime minister, the young Benjamin Disraeli had anticipated *Erewhon*'s fears in his novel *Coningsby*: "The mystery of mysteries," he wrote, "is to view machines making machines, a spectacle that fills the mind with curious and even awful speculation."

As the Victorian age rushed on, many writers began to ask, "Where are we going?" If so much was happening so quickly in *their* century, what might happen in the next? Butler, Wells, William Morris, Richard Jefferies, and many others mixed fantasy, satire, and allegory, creating a genre known as the scientific romance.

In *The Time Machine* of 1895, Wells sent a traveller to a distant future where the human race has split into two species, the Eloi and the Morlocks. The Eloi are a sybaritic upper class living brainlessly on the industrial toil of the Morlocks, never guessing that these underground subhumans—seemingly their slaves—are in fact raising them for meat.

In his *News from Nowhere,* William Morris dreamt up a post-industrial New Age—a pre-Raphaelite Utopia of honest workmanship, good design, and free love—from which he attacked the first great wave of globalization, the world market ruled by the steamship, the telegraph, and the British Empire:

> The happiness of the workman at his work, his most elementary comfort and bare health . . . did not weigh a grain of sand in the balance against this dire necessity of "cheap production" of things, a great part of which were not worth producing at all. . . . The whole community was cast into the jaws of this ravening monster, the World-Market.

While we may learn from the past, we don't seem to learn much. That last generation before the First World War—the time of the young Einstein, Oscar Wilde, and Joseph Conrad's novel of terrorism, *The Secret Agent*—was in many ways a time like ours: an old century grown tired; a new century in which moralities and certainties were withering, bombers were lurking in the shadows and industrialists declaiming from their mansions that unfettered free enterprise would bring a New Jerusalem to all.

More thoughtful observers sensed that change was running out of control, and began to fear that with the powers of industry, mankind had found the means to suicide. They saw jingoistic nation-states engaged in an arms race. They saw social exploitation and vast urban slums, contaminated air and water, and "civilization" being conferred on "savages" through the barrels of machine guns.

What if those guns were turned not on Zulus or Sioux

but on other Europeans? What if the degradation of the slums caused degeneration of the human race? What, exactly, was the *point* of all this economic output if, for so many people, it meant deracination, misery, and filth? By the end of his voyage, Wells's Time Traveller regards civilization as "only a foolish heaping that must inevitably . . . destroy its makers in the end."

No doubt many will say that we stand here to prove those gloomy Victorians wrong. But do we? They may have been wrong on the details they imagined for our times, but they were right to foresee trouble. Just ahead lay the Great War and 12 million dead, the Russian Revolution, the Great Slump—leading to Hitler, the death camps, the Second World War (with 50 million dead), the atom bomb. And these in turn to the Korean War, the Cold War, the near-fatal Cuban Missile Crisis, Vietnam, Cambodia, Rwanda. Even the most pessimistic Victorian might have been surprised to learn that the twentieth century would slaughter more than 100 million in its wars—twice the entire population of the Roman Empire. The price of history does indeed go up.

The Victorian scientific romances had two modern descendants: mainstream science fiction, and profound social satire set in nightmare futures. The latter includes several of the last century's most important books: Aldous Huxley's *Brave New World,* George Orwell's *Nineteen Eighty-four,* J. M. Coetzee's *Waiting for the Barbarians,* and a number of post-nuclear wastelands, of which Russell Hoban's *Riddley Walker* has to be the masterpiece.

With the nuclear threat fading (maybe), modern apocalyptic novels have revisited concerns first raised before Hiroshima—especially the risks of new technology, and how our species might survive without abandoning its humanity for antlike order. (Perhaps the most disturbing aspect of *Brave New World* was the strong case Huxley made for the devil of order, a case harder to answer now than in 1932.) The clanking monsters of Erewhon have taken subtler forms that threaten the whole biosphere: climate disruption, toxic waste, new pathogens, nano-technology, cybernetics, genetic engineering.

One of the dangers of writing a dystopian satire is how depressing it is when you get things right. Ten years ago I began work on my novel *A Scientific Romance,* a title I chose because I wanted to acknowledge the Victorians, and because my theme was our *amour fou* with science. For satirical purposes, I made what I thought were wild extrapolations from things in the news. I had a character die of mad cow disease, thinking that in the final draft I would probably have to kill her off with something less far-fetched. By the time the book was published in 1997, dozens of people really had died of mad cow. Other elements of the satire—climate change that turns wintry London into a tropical swamp, a race of genetically modified survivors, and a GM grass that doesn't need mowing because it has the self-limiting properties of pubic hair—no longer seem quite the funhouse mirrors they were when I began. Just a few months ago, something more specific came to haunt me. In the jungly ruins of London, my protagonist finds a street blocked off and buildings fortified with concrete slabs. Here, he deduces, an embattled British government must have spent its final days in the 2030s. Earlier this year [2005], I read in the paper that Tony Blair's government is planning to surround the Houses of Parliament with a fifteen-foot concrete wall and razor wire.

I don't want to be a prophet, and I certainly don't claim to be. It doesn't take Nostradamus to foresee that walls will go up in times of crisis—though the thickest walls are in the mind. A telling feature of the real mad cow disaster was how long the British government did nothing except hope for the best. In her recent dystopia, *Oryx and Crake,* which concentrates on biotechnology, Margaret Atwood also portrays the collapse of civilization in the near future. One of her characters asks, "As a species we're doomed by hope, then?" By *hope?* Well, yes. Hope drives us to invent new fixes for old messes, which in turn create ever more dangerous messes. Hope elects the politician with the biggest empty promise; and as any stockbroker or lottery seller knows, most of us will take a slim hope over prudent and predictable frugality. Hope, like greed, fuels the engine of capitalism.

John Steinbeck once said that socialism never took root in America because the poor see themselves not as an exploited proletariat but as temporarily embarrassed millionaires. This helps explain why American culture is so hostile to the idea of limits, why voters during the last energy shortage rejected the sweater-wearing Jimmy Carter and elected Ronald Reagan, who scoffed at conservation and told them it was "still morning in America." Nowhere does the myth of progress have more fervent believers.

Marx was surely right when he called capitalism, almost admiringly, "a machine for demolishing limits." Both communism and capitalism are materialist Utopias offering rival versions of an earthly paradise. In practice, communism was no easier on the natural environment. But at least it proposed a sharing of the goods. Capitalism lures us onward like the mechanical hare before the greyhounds, insisting that the economy is infinite and sharing therefore irrelevant. Just enough greyhounds catch a real hare now and then to keep the others running till they drop. In the past it was only the poor who lost this game; now it is the planet.

Those who travelled in their youth, and have gone back to old haunts after twenty or thirty years, can't fail to observe the massive onslaught of progress, whether it be the loss of farms to suburbs, jungles to cattle ranches, rivers to dams, mangroves to shrimp farms, mountains to cement quarries, or coral reefs to condominiums.

We still have differing cultures and political systems, but at the economic level there is now only one big civilization, feeding on the whole planet's natural capital. We're logging everywhere, fishing everywhere, irrigating everywhere, building everywhere, and no corner of the biosphere escapes our haemorrhage of waste. The twentyfold growth in world trade since the 1970s has meant that hardly anywhere is self-sufficient. Every Eldorado has been looted, every Shangri-La equipped with a Holiday Inn. Joseph Tainter notes this interdependence, warning that "collapse, if and when it comes again, will this time be global. . . . World civilization will disintegrate as a whole."

Experts in a range of fields have begun to see the same closing door of opportunity, begun to warn that these years may be the last when civilization still has the wealth and political cohesion to steer itself towards caution, conservation, and social justice. In 1993, just before the Rio environmental summit that led to the Kyoto Accord on climate change, more than half the world's Nobel laureates warned that we might have only a decade or so left to make our system sustainable. Now, in a report unsuccessfully hushed up by the Bush administration, the Pentagon predicts worldwide famine, anarchy, and warfare "within a generation" should climate change fulfill the more severe projections. And in his 2003 book, *Our Final Century*, Martin Rees of Cambridge University, Astronomer Royal and former president of the British Association for the Advancement of Science, concludes: "The odds are no better than fifty-fifty that our present civilisation . . . will survive to the end of the present century . . . unless all nations adopt low-risk and sustainable policies based on present technology."

Sceptics point to earlier predictions of disaster that weren't borne out. But that is a fool's paradise. Some of our escapes—from nuclear war, for one—have been more by luck than judgment, and are not final. Other problems have been side-stepped but not solved. The food crisis, for example, has merely been postponed by switching to hybrid seed and chemical farming, at great cost to soil health and plant diversity.

Following the attacks of September 11th, 2001, the world's media and politicians focused understandably on terrorism. Two things need to be said here.

First, terrorism is a small threat compared with hunger, disease, or climate change. Three thousand died in the United States that day; 25,000 die *every* day in the world from contaminated water alone. Each year, 20 million children are mentally impaired by malnourishment. Each year, an area of farmland greater than Scotland is lost to erosion and urban sprawl, much of it in Asia.

Second, terrorism cannot be stopped by addressing symptoms and not the cause. Violence is bred by injustice, poverty, inequality, and other violence. This lesson was learnt very painfully in the first half of the twentieth century, at a cost of some 80 million lives. Of course, a full belly and a fair hearing won't stop a fanatic; but they can greatly reduce the number who *become* fanatics.

After the Second World War, a consensus emerged to deal with the roots of violence by creating international institutions and democratically managed forms of capitalism based on Keynesian economics and America's New Deal. This policy, though far from perfect, succeeded in Europe, Japan, and some parts of the Third World. (Remember when we spoke not of a "war on terror" but of a "war on want"?)

To undermine that post-war consensus and return to archaic political patterns is to walk back into the bloody past. Yet that is what the New Right has achieved since the late 1970s, rewrapping old ideas as new and using them to transfer the levers of power from elected governments to unelected corporations—a project sold as "tax-cutting" and "deregulation" by the right's courtiers in the media, of which Canada certainly has its share. The conceit of laissez-faire economics—that if you let the horses guzzle enough oats, something will go through for the sparrows—has been tried many times and has failed many times, leaving ruin and social wreckage.

The revolt against redistribution is killing civilization from ghetto to rainforest. Taxes in most countries have not, in fact, been lowered; they were merely shifted down the income pyramid, and diverted from aid and social programs towards military and corporate ones. The great

American judge Oliver Wendell Holmes once said, "I don't mind paying taxes; they buy me civilization." Public confidence in a basic social safety net is essential for lowering birth rates in poor nations, and for a decent society in all nations. The removal of that confidence has set off a free-for-all that is stripping the earth.

During the twentieth century the world's population multiplied by four and the economy by more than forty. If the promise of modernity was even treading water—in other words, if the gap between rich and poor had stayed proportionally the same as it was when Queen Victoria died—all human beings would be ten times better off. Yet the number in abject poverty today is as great as all mankind in 1901.

By the end of the twentieth century, the world's three richest individuals (all of whom were Americans) had a combined wealth greater than that of the poorest forty-eight countries. In 1998, the United Nations calculated that US$40 billion, spent carefully, could provide clean water, sanitation, and other basic needs for the poorest on earth. The figure may be optimistic, and it may have grown in the past six years. But it's still considerably less than the funds already set aside for the obscenely wasteful fantasy of a missile shield that won't work, isn't needed, yet could provoke a new arms race and the militarization of space.

Consider Tainter's three aspects of collapse: the Runaway Train, the Dinosaur, the House of Cards. The rise in population and pollution, the acceleration of technology, the concentration of wealth and power—all are runaway trains, and most are linked together. Population growth is slowing, but by 2050 there will still be 3 billion more on earth. We may be able to feed that many in the short run, but we'll have to raise less meat (which takes ten pounds of food to make one pound of food), and we'll have to spread that food around. What we can't do is keep consuming as we are. Or polluting as we are. We could help countries such as India and China industrialize without repeating our mistakes. But instead we have excluded environmental standards from trade agreements. Like sex tourists with unlawful lusts, we do our dirtiest work among the poor.

If civilization is to survive, it must live on the interest, not the capital, of nature. Ecological markers suggest that in the early 1960s, humans were using about 70 percent of nature's yearly output; by the early 1980s, we'd reached 100 percent; and in 1999, we were at 125 percent. Such numbers may be imprecise, but their trend is clear—they mark the road to bankruptcy.

None of this should surprise us after reading the flight recorders in the wreckage of crashed civilizations; our present behaviour is typical of failed societies at the zenith of their greed and arrogance. This is the dinosaur factor: hostility to change from vested interests, and inertia at all social levels. George Soros, the reformed currency speculator, calls the economic dinosaurs "market fundamentalists." I'm uneasy with this term because so few of them *are* true believers in free markets—preferring monopolies, cartels, and government contracts. But his point is well taken. The idea that the world must be run by the stock market is as mad as any other fundamentalist delusion, Islamic, Christian, or Marxist.

In the case of Easter Island, the statue cult became a

self-destructive mania, an ideological pathology. In the United States, market extremism (which one might expect to be purely materialist, and therefore open to rational self-interest) has cross-bred with evangelical messianism to fight intelligent policy on metaphysical grounds. Mainstream Christianity is an altruistic faith, yet this offshoot is actively hostile to the public good: a kind of social Darwinism by people who hate Darwin. President Reagan's secretary of the interior told Congress not to bother with the environment because, in his words, "I don't know how many future generations we can count on until the Lord returns." George W. Bush surrounded himself with similar minds and pulled out of the Kyoto Accord on climate change.

Adolf Hitler once gleefully exclaimed, "What luck for the rulers that the people do not think!" What can we do when the rulers *will* not think?

Civilizations often fall quite suddenly—the House of Cards effect—because as they reach full demand on their ecologies, they become highly vulnerable to natural fluctuations. The most immediate danger posed by climate change is weather instability causing a series of crop failures in the world's breadbaskets. Droughts, floods, fires, and hurricanes are rising in frequency and severity. The pollution surges caused by these—and by wars—add to the gyre of destruction. Medical experts worry that nature may swat us with disease: billions of overcrowded primates, many sick, malnourished, and connected by air travel, are a free lunch waiting for a nimble microbe. "Mother Nature always comes to the rescue of a society stricken with . . . overpopulation," Alfred Crosby sardonically observed, "and her ministrations are never gentle."

The case for reform that I have tried to make is not based on altruism, nor on saving nature for its own sake. I happen to believe that these are moral imperatives, but such arguments cut against the grain of human desire. The most compelling reason for reforming our system is that the system is in no one's interest. It is a suicide machine. All of us have some dinosaur inertia within us, but I honestly don't know what the activist "dinosaurs"—the hard men and women of Big Oil and the far right—think they are doing. They have children and grandchildren who will need safe food and clean air and water, and who may wish to see living oceans and forests. Wealth can buy no refuge from pollution; pesticides sprayed in China condense in Antarctic glaciers and Rocky Mountain tarns. And wealth is no shield from chaos, as the surprise on each haughty face that rolled from the guillotine made clear.

There's a saying in Argentina that each night God cleans up the mess the Argentines make by day. This seems to be what our leaders are counting on. But it won't work. Things are moving so fast that inaction itself is one of the biggest mistakes. The 10,000-year experiment of the settled life will stand or fall by what we do, and don't do, now. The reform that is needed is not anti-capitalist, anti-American, or even deep environmentalist; it is simply the transition from short-term to long-term thinking. From recklessness and excess to moderation and the precautionary principle.

The great advantage we have, our best chance for avoiding the fate of past societies, is that we know about those past societies. We can see how and why they went wrong. *Homo sapiens* has the information to know itself for what it is: an Ice Age hunter only half-evolved towards intelligence; clever but seldom wise.

We are now at the stage when the Easter Islanders could still have halted the senseless cutting and carving, could have gathered the last trees' seeds to plant out of reach of the rats. We have the tools and the means to share resources, clean up pollution, dispense basic health care and birth control, set economic limits in line with natural ones. If we don't do these things now, while we prosper, we will never be able to do them when times get hard. Our fate will twist out of our hands. And this new century will not grow very old before we enter an age of chaos and collapse that will dwarf all the dark ages in our past.

Now is our last chance to get the future right.

The Global Struggle for Energy

from TomDispatch.com (5/9/05)

Michael T. Klare

From Washington to New Delhi, Caracas to Moscow and Beijing, national leaders and corporate executives are stepping up their efforts to gain control over major sources of oil and natural gas as the global struggle for energy intensifies. Never has the competitive pursuit of untapped oil and gas reserves been so acute, and never has so much money as well as diplomatic and military muscle been deployed in the contest to win control over major foreign stockpiles of energy. To an unprecedented degree, a government's success or failure in these endeavors is being treated as headline news, and provoking public outcry when a rival power is seen as benefiting unfairly from a particular transaction. With the officials of numerous governments coming under mounting pressure to satisfy the needs of their individual countries—at whatever cost—the battle for energy can only become more inflamed in the years ahead.

This struggle is being driven by one great inescapable fact: the global supply of energy is not growing fast enough to keep up with skyrocketing demand, especially from the United States and the developing nations of Asia. According to the U.S. Department of Energy (DoE), global energy consumption will grow by more than 50 percent during the first quarter of the 21st century—from an estimated 404 to 623 quadrillion British thermal units (BTUs) per year. Oil and natural gas will be in particular demand. By 2025, global oil consumption is projected to rise 57 percent, from 157 to 245 quadrillion BTUs, while gas consumption is projected to have a 68 percent growth rate, from 93 to 157 quads. It appears increasingly unlikely, however, that the world's energy firms will actually be able to deliver such quantities of oil and gas in the coming decades, whether for political, economic, or geological reasons. With prices rising all over the world and serious shortages in the offing, every major consuming nation is coming under increasing pressure to maximize its relative share of the available energy supply. Inevitably, these pressures will pit one state against another in the competitive pursuit of oil and natural gas.

Frenzied Search

In the past, such zero-sum contests between major powers over valuable resources have often led to war. Whether that will prove to be true in the case of oil and gas remains to be seen. But the pressure to maximize supplies is already shaping the foreign policy decisions of many states and generating fresh international tensions. Consider, for example, the following recent developments:

• A decision by Japan to initiate natural gas production in a disputed area of the East China Sea sparked massive anti-Japanese protests in China on April 16, the worst outpouring of such animosities in over 30 years. Although leaders of both countries sought to diffuse the crisis by promising fresh efforts at reconciliation, neither side has backed off its claims to the offshore territories. While other issues also fed into Chinese popular discontent, notably Japan's reluctance to express regret for atrocities committed by its forces in China during World War II, Tokyo's unilateral move to extract natural gas from the East China Sea was the precipitating factor. At stake potentially is the ownership of a vast undersea gas field in disputed waters lying between China's central coast and Japan's Ryukyu island chain. Because the offshore boundary between China and Japan has not been established, neither side is willing to countenance the extraction of gas by the other in the disputed "national territory." Thus, when Tokyo announced on April 13 that it would allow drilling by Japanese companies in waters claimed by China, Beijing had no compunctions about allowing an unprecedented, weekend-long display of nationalistic fervor.

• During her first visit to India as Secretary of State, Condoleezza Rice called on New Delhi to back away from a plan to import natural gas by pipeline from Iran, claiming that any such endeavor would frustrate U.S. efforts to isolate the hard-line clerical regime in Tehran. "We have communicated to the Indian government our concerns about the gas pipeline cooperation between Iran and India," she said on March 16 after meeting with Indian Foreign Minister Natwar Singh in New Delhi. But the Indians let it be known that their desire for additional energy supplies trumped Washington's ideological opposition to the Iranian regime. Declaring that the proposed pipeline will be necessary to meet India's soaring energy needs, Singh told reporters, "We have no problem of any kind with Iran."

• One month after her meetings in New Delhi, Rice flew to Moscow and pressured President Vladimir Putin to open up Russia's energy industry to increased investment by American firms. Noting that Moscow's crackdown on the privately owned energy giant, Yukos, along with proposed restrictions on foreign investment in Russian energy projects would discourage U.S. companies from collaborating in the development of Russia's vast oil reserves, Rice implored Putin to adopt a more inviting posture. "What Russia can do is to adopt policies in its energy sector in terms of the development of its energy sector that will increase the supply of oil both in the short term . . . and the long term," she avowed. But while embracing Rice's call for enhanced U.S.-Russian relations, Putin evinced no inclination to back off from his plans to bolster state control over Russian energy companies and to use this authority to advance Moscow's geopolitical objectives.

• On April 25, President George W. Bush met with Crown Prince Abdullah of Saudi Arabia at his ranch in Crawford,

Texas, and exhorted him to substantially expand Saudi petroleum output so as to bring down American gasoline prices. "The Crown Prince understands that it is very important to make sure that the price is reasonable," Bush observed before the meeting. "A high oil price will damage markets, and he knows that." Bush and Abdullah also discussed the Israeli-Palestinian conflict and the continuing threat of terrorism, but it was oil demand that dominated the Crawford summit.

Highlighting the degree to which energy issues had come to overshadow more traditional security concerns, both Secretary of State Condoleezza Rice and National Security Adviser Stephen Hadley emphasized the importance of boosting world oil output in their comments on the meeting. "Obviously, with the states like China, India, and others coming on line, there is concern about demand and supply," Rice observed. "And these issues have to be addressed."

Developments like these, and Rice's comments on the Bush-Abdullah meeting, capture the essence of the current energy equation: Demand is rising around the world; supplies are not growing fast enough to satisfy global requirements; and the global struggle to gain control over whatever supplies are available has become more intense and fractious. Because the first and second of these factors are not likely to abate in the years ahead, the third can only grow more pronounced.

Insatiable Demand

Economies—all economies—run on energy. Energy is needed to produce food and manufacture goods, power machines and appliances, transport raw materials and finished products, and provide heat and light. The more energy available to a society, the better its prospects for sustained growth; when energy supplies dwindle, economies grind to a halt and the affected populations suffer.

Since World War II, economic growth around the world has been fueled largely by abundant supplies of hydrocarbons—that is, by petroleum and natural gas. Since 1950, worldwide oil consumption has grown eightfold, from approximately 10 to 80 million barrels per day; gas consumption, which began from a smaller base, has grown even more dramatically. Hydrocarbons now satisfy 62 percent of the world's total energy demand, approximately 250 quadrillion BTUs out of a total supply of 404 quads. But no matter how important they may be today, hydrocarbons are sure to prove even more critical in the future. According to the Department of Energy, oil and gas will account for 65 percent of world energy in 2025, a larger share than at present; and because no other source of energy is currently available to replace them, the future health of the global economy rests on our ability to produce more and more of these hydrocarbons.

The future availability of oil and gas also affects another key aspect of the global economic equation: the growing challenge to the older industrialized nations posed by dynamic new economies in East Asia, South Asia, and Latin America. At present, the industrialized countries account for approximately two-thirds of total world energy use. Because these countries, for the most part, possess mature and efficient economies, their demand for energy is expected to increase by a relatively modest 35 percent between 2001 and 2025, a conceivably manageable rate.

But demand in the developing world is soaring. By 2025, developing countries are projected to hold a startling half-share in total world energy consumption. When their added demand is combined with that of the industrialized countries, the net world increase jumps 54 percent over the same set of years, a far more demanding challenge for the global energy industry.

The competition for hydrocarbon supplies will be particularly intense. According to the Department of Energy, oil consumption by the developing world will increase by 96 percent between 2001 and 2025, while consumption of natural gas will rise by 103 percent. For China and India, the rate of growth is even more dramatic: China's oil consumption is projected to jump by 156 percent over this period and India's by 152 percent. The struggle these countries, and other developing powerhouses like South Korea and Brazil, face in obtaining additional oil and gas for their growing economies will naturally pit them against the older industrialized countries in the competitive pursuit of energy. As suggested by Rice, "with the states like China, India, and others coming on line, there is concern about demand and supply."

Questionable Supply

Accommodating the growing Chinese and Indian demand would not be a significant problem if we had great confidence that the energy industry is capable of generating the necessary additional amounts. In fact, the Department of Energy wants us to believe that this is indeed the case. Future oil and gas supplies, DoE claims, will be more than adequate to satisfy anticipated world demand. But many experts dispute this view. World oil and gas supplies, they argue, will never achieve such elevated levels. This is true because much of the world's known hydrocarbon reserves have already been exhausted and not enough new fields have been discovered in recent years to make up for the depletion of older reservoirs.

Take the case of oil. The DoE predicts that global petroleum output will reach 120.6 million barrels per day in 2025—44 million barrels more than at present and just a tad shy of the anticipated world demand of 121 million barrels per day. For this to occur, however, the major oil firms must discover massive new reserves and substantially increase their output from existing fields. However, few new large fields have been discovered during the past 40 years, and only one, the Kashagan field in the Caspian Sea, has been found in the past decade. At the same time, many older fields in North America, Russia, and the Middle East have experienced significant declines in daily production. As a result, many geologists now believe not only that the global petroleum industry will *not* be capable of rising to the 120 million barrel level but will fall far below it.

Predictions that global oil output will peak between now and 2025, far short of the DoE's projections, are highly controversial. This is not the place to consider clashing assessments in detail. But one way to get at this issue is to consider the all-important case of Saudi Arabia, the world's leading supplier and the most likely prospect for higher production in the future. According to the DoE, Saudi Arabian oil output will more than double between 2001 and 2025, jumping from 10.2 to 22.5 million barrels per day. If Saudi Arabia could, in fact, raise its output by this amount we would have some degree of confidence that total world supplies could satisfy anticipated demand even at the end of this period. But there are growing indications that Saudi Arabia is *not* capable of coming anywhere close to that figure. In a much-discussed 2004 article in the *New York Times*, business analyst Jeff Gerth reported that "[o]il executives and government officials in the United States and Saudi Arabia . . . say capacity will probably stall near current levels, potentially creating a significant gap in the global energy supply."

In response to Gerth's assertions, Saudi officials insisted that their country is fully capable of boosting daily production by a sufficient amount to satisfy anticipated world requirements. "Should [higher world demand] actually materialize . . . we're going to be ready to meet it," Saudi Oil Minister Ali I. Al-Naimi declared in February 2004. In particular, "we have looked at scenarios of 12 million [barrels per day] capacity, we have looked at 15 million capacity, and those are all feasible." Such pronouncements have provided some relief to those alarmed by Gerth's report. But note that Al-Naimi spoke only of "scenarios" for reaching 12 to 15 million barrels per day—hardly an ironclad guaranty—and even an increase of that size would fall far short of the 22.5 million barrels projected by the Department of Energy. Many energy analysts have suggested, moreover, that any drive by Saudi Arabia to boost its daily output above 10 million barrels for any length of time will cause irreparable harm to its fields and result in an inevitable long-term drop in production. As noted by one senior Saudi oil executive, an attempt to reach 12 million barrels per day would "wreak havoc within a decade."

The question of Saudi Arabia's future oil output is terribly important to this discussion because it is highly unlikely that any other supplier, or combination of suppliers, can make up the difference between Saudi Arabia's sustainable yield of 10–12 million barrels per day and the DoE's 22.5 million-barrel goal for Saudi output in 2025. Other big suppliers—Iran, Iraq, Kuwait, Nigeria, Russia, and Venezuela—are expected to have a hard enough time maintaining their own output at current levels, let alone filling in for the "missing" Saudi oil. This being the case, it appears highly unlikely that the global oil industry will be capable of satisfying anticipated world demand in the years ahead; instead, we should expect chronic petroleum shortages, higher prices, and persistent economic hardship.

Precisely because of this prospect, many national leaders are now placing greater emphasis on the acquisition of increased natural gas supplies. Because gas was developed later in the industrial cycle than oil, its principal sources of supply have not yet been fully exhausted, and new fields—such as those in Iran and the East China Sea—await full-scale development. Like oil, natural gas will eventually reach a global peak in output, but this is not likely to occur for a decade or so after oil has peaked. As petroleum output declines, therefore, natural gas is expected to take up some of the slack—but only some, because there is not enough gas in the world to fully replace petroleum in all its myriad uses. And it is for this reason that many governments seek to gain control over or access to major gas reserves *now*, before they are locked up by someone else.

Intensifying Struggle

What can we expect from this intensifying struggle over

valuable energy resources? Certainly, national leaders are placing ever greater emphasis on the competitive pursuit of energy as Condoleezza Rice made clear in her recent jaunts around the world. Whether in India, Russia, or Latin America, she has raised the energy issue at every turn, pressing America's allies and business partners both to supply us with more oil and to ignore the appeal of "rogue" producers like Iran and Venezuela. Other world leaders like Vladimir Putin of Russia and Junichiro Koizumi of Japan have behaved in a similar fashion. Striking, in fact, is the degree to which the quest for energy has been elevated into the realm of national security, on an equal plane with efforts to combat nuclear proliferation and international terrorism. Thus, it was the President's adviser for national security affairs, Stephen Hadley, who briefed reporters on the outcome of the Crawford summit between Bush and Abdullah. "The news that came out of the meeting today ought to be good news for the [energy] markets," he declared on April 25—not good news in the war against terror or in the drive to promote peace between Israel and the Palestinians.

Secretary of State Rice, however, offered the most telling observations after the April 25 meeting. The problems arising from insufficient supply to meet rising world oil demand, she said, "have to be addressed, not by jawboning, but by having a strategic plan for dealing with the problem." Anyone familiar with the Bush administration lexicon cannot help but be troubled by this call for a "strategic plan" to obtain additional energy, redolent as it is of the administration's bellicose, pre-emptive strategy for dealing with terrorism, "rogue states," and weapons of mass destruction. Just exactly what Rice means is not yet entirely clear, but it certainly suggests that energy issues will be paramount in U.S. foreign and military policy in a Bush second term.

And what is true for the United States is also likely to prove the case for other major oil-importing countries. Warning that China has outperformed India in the pursuit of new oil and gas reserves, Indian Prime Minister Manmohan Singh declared in January that New Delhi would have to accelerate its efforts in this area. "I find China ahead of us in planning for the future in the field of energy security," he told a convention of Indian oil and gas executives. "We can no longer be complacent and must learn to think strategically, to think ahead, and to act swiftly and decisively."

Japanese leaders, too, have stressed the need for decisive action. Energy-poor Tokyo's decision to proceed with drilling in contested areas of the East China Sea is just one indication of this outlook. Equally striking is Japan's effort to convince the Russians to extend a new Siberian oil pipeline to Nakhodka on the Sea of Japan. Originally, Moscow had expected to terminate the pipeline at Daquing in China as part of a plan to strengthen Sino-Russian energy cooperation. But after Prime Minister Koizumi flew to Moscow and offered billions of dollars in additional aid and technology to Russia, President Putin indicated a preference for the Nakhodka route, which will, of course, facilitate oil deliveries to Japan. This has not deterred Chinese leaders from seeking a reversal of this decision, claiming that the "strategic partnership" between Moscow and Beijing outweighs the purely mercantile interests of Japan.

So far, none of these efforts has led to more than verbal

sparring—"jawboning," to use Rice's term—along with high-stakes bidding wars and the occasional outbreak of street protests, as in Shanghai and Beijing. But if history is any guide, such friction—when combined with other sources of animosity like China's smoldering resentments over Japanese atrocities during World War II—can lead to more violent forms of competition. This is certainly the case in the East China Sea, where Chinese and Japanese planes and gunboats have already made threatening passes at one another.

Tensions are sure to rise, moreover, if Japan actually commences drilling in waters claimed by China. "If real exploration starts, we cannot totally exclude the possibility of Japanese private company ships having to face Chinese military ships," Junichi Abe, an analyst at the Kazankai Foundation in Tokyo, told a reporter for the *New York Times*. And if this were to occur, the Japanese government would come under enormous political pressure to protect those private vessels with planes and warships of its own, thereby setting the stage for an armed confrontation with China, whether intended or not.

Similar escalation could occur in other cases of disputed energy claims. In the Caspian Sea, for example, Iran seeks control over offshore oil and gas fields also claimed by Azerbaijan, an ally of the United States. In July 2001, an Iranian gunboat steamed into the contested area and chased off an oil-company exploration vessel operating there under Azerbaijani auspices. In response, the United States has pledged to help Azerbaijan build a small Caspian navy, to better protect its offshore energy claims. On April 11, John J. Fialka of the *Wall Street Journal* revealed that the U.S. Department of Defense will spend

$100 million over the next few years to establish the "Caspian Guard," a network of police forces and special-operations units "that can respond to various emergencies, including attacks on oil facilities." Russia is also expanding its Caspian Fleet, as it too presses its claims to offshore fields in the region. Under such circumstances, it is all too easy to imagine how a minor confrontation could erupt into something much more serious, involving the U.S., Russia, Iran, and other countries.

Territorial disputes of this sort with significant energy dimensions can be found in the Red Sea, the South China Sea, the Persian Gulf, the Gulf of Guinea, and the Bakassi Peninsula (a narrow stretch of land claimed by both Nigeria and Cameroon) among other regions. In each of these areas, opposing claimants have employed military force on occasion to assert their control or to drive off the forces of a challenger. None of these incidents has led to a full-scale conflict, but lives have been lost and the risk of renewed fighting persists. As the global struggle for energy intensifies, therefore, the danger of escalation will grow.

It is important to recognize that energy-related pressures are bound to increase as global demand continues its upward course and the supply of oil and natural gas fails to keep pace. The Bush administration, in particular, is aware of these pressures, having analyzed the global energy equation in its May 2001 report on U.S. energy requirements. While administration officials have repeatedly denied that oil played any role in the 2003 decision to invade Iraq, they clearly believed that control of the country would provide the United States with enormous advantages in any coming struggle with competitors like China over Persian Gulf energy.

Indeed, once a problem like energy security has been tagged as a matter of national security, it passes from the realm of economics and statecraft into that of military policy. Then, the generals and strategists get into the act and begin their ceaseless planning for endless "contingencies" and "emergencies." In such an environment, small incidents evolve into crises, and crises into wars. Expect a hot couple of decades ahead.

FACTS

Year in which U.S. oil production peaked: 1971
(U.S. Geological Survey)

Year in which worldwide oil discoveries peaked: 1964
(Oil Depletion Analysis Centre)

Body Burden: The Pollution in Newborns

The Environmental Working Group (7/14/05)

Jane Houlihan, Timothy Kropp,
Richard Wiles, Sean Gray, Chris Campbell

In the month leading up to a baby's birth, the umbilical cord pulses with the equivalent of 300 quarts of blood each day, pumped back and forth from the nutrient- and oxygen-rich placenta to the rapidly growing child cradled in a sac of amniotic fluid. This cord is a lifeline between mother and baby, bearing nutrients that sustain life and propel growth.

Not long ago scientists thought that the placenta shielded cord blood—and the developing baby—from most chemicals and pollutants in the environment. But now we know that at this critical time when organs, vessels, membranes, and systems are knit together from single cells to finished form in a span of weeks, the umbilical cord carries not only the building blocks of life, but also a steady stream of industrial chemicals, pollutants, and pesticides that cross the placenta as readily as residues from cigarettes and alcohol. This is the human "body burden"—the pollution in people that permeates everyone in the world, including babies in the womb.

In a study spearheaded by the Environmental Working Group (EWG) in collaboration with *Commonweal*, researchers at two major laboratories found an average of 200 industrial chemicals and pollutants in umbilical cord blood from 10 babies born in August and September of

2004 in U.S. hospitals. Tests revealed a total of 287 chemicals in the group. The umbilical cord blood of these 10 children, collected by Red Cross after the cord was cut, harbored pesticides, consumer product ingredients, and wastes from burning coal, gasoline, and garbage.

This study represents the first reported cord blood tests for 261 of the targeted chemicals and the first reported detections in cord blood for 209 compounds. Among them are eight perfluorochemicals used as stain and oil repellants in fast food packaging, clothes, and textiles—including the Teflon chemical PFOA, recently characterized as a likely human carcinogen by the EPA's Science Advisory Board—dozens of widely used brominated flame retardants and their toxic by-products; and numerous pesticides.

Of the 287 chemicals we detected in umbilical cord blood, we know that 180 cause cancer in humans or animals, 217 are toxic to the brain and nervous system, and 208 cause birth defects or abnormal development in animal tests. The dangers of pre- or post-natal exposure to this complex mixture of carcinogens, developmental toxins, and neurotoxins have never been studied.

Chemical exposures in the womb or during infancy can be dramatically more harmful than exposures later in life. Substantial scientific evidence demonstrates that children face amplified risks from their body burden of pollution; the findings are particularly strong for many of the chemicals found in this study, including mercury, PCBs, and dioxins. Children's vulnerability derives from both rapid development and incomplete defense systems:

- A developing child's chemical exposures are greater pound-for-pound than those of adults.

- An immature, porous blood-brain barrier allows greater chemical exposures to the developing brain.
- Children have lower levels of some chemical-binding proteins, allowing more of a chemical to reach "target organs."
- A baby's organs and systems are rapidly developing, and thus are often more vulnerable to damage from chemical exposure.
- Systems that detoxify and excrete industrial chemicals are not fully developed.
- The longer future life span of a child compared to an adult allows more time for adverse effects to arise.

The 10 children in this study were chosen randomly, from among 2004's summer season of live births from mothers in Red Cross' volunteer, national cord blood collection program. They were not chosen because their parents work in the chemical industry or because they were known to bear problems from chemical exposures in the womb. Nevertheless, each baby was born polluted with a broad array of contaminants.

U.S. industries manufacture and import approximately 75,000 chemicals, 3,000 of them at over a million pounds per year. Health officials do not know how many of these chemicals pollute fetal blood and what the health consequences of in utero exposures may be.

Had we tested for a broader array of chemicals, we would almost certainly have detected far more than 287. But testing umbilical cord blood for industrial chemicals is technically challenging. Chemical manufacturers are not required to divulge to the public or government health officials methods to detect their chemicals in humans. Few

Chemicals and pollutants detected in human umbilical cord blood

Mercury (Hg)—tested for 1, found 1
Pollutant from coal-fired power plants, mercury-containing products, and certain industrial processes. Accumulates in seafood. Harms brain development and function.

Polyaromatic hydrocarbons (PAHs)—tested for 18, found 9
Pollutants from burning gasoline and garbage. Linked to cancer. Accumulates in food chain.

Polybrominated dibenzodioxins and furans (PBDD/F)—tested for 12, found 7
Contaminants in brominated flame retardants. Pollutants and byproducts from plastic production and incineration. Accumulate in food chain. Toxic to developing endocrine (hormone) system.

Perfluorinated chemicals (PFCs)—tested for 12, found 9
Active ingredients or breakdown products of Teflon, Scotchgard, fabric and carpet protectors, food wrap coatings. Global contaminants. Accumulate in the environment and the food chain. Linked to cancer, birth defects, and more.

Polychlorinated dibenzodioxins and furans (PBCD/F)—tested for 17, found 11
Pollutants, by-products of PVC production, industrial bleaching, and incineration. Cause cancer in humans. Persist for decades in the environment. Very toxic to developing endocrine (hormone) system.

Organochlorine pesticides (OCs)—tested for 28, found 21
DDT, chlordane and other pesticides. Largely banned in the U.S. Persist for decades in the environment. Accumulate up the food chain, to man. Cause cancer and numerous reproductive effects.

Polybrominated diphenyl ethers (PBDEs)—tested for 46, found 32
Flame retardant in furniture foam, computers, and televisions. Accumulates in the food chain and human tissues. Adversely affects brain development and the thyroid.

Polychlorinated Naphthalenes (PCNs)—tested for 70, found 50
Wood preservatives, varnishes, machine lubricating oils, waste incineration. Common PCB contaminant. Contaminate the food chain. Cause liver and kidney damage.

Polychlorinated biphenyls (PCBs)—tested for 209, found 147
Industrial insulators and lubricants. Banned in the U.S. in 1976. Persist for decades in the environment. Accumulate up the food chain, to man. Cause cancer and nervous system problems.

Source: Chemical analyses of 10 umbilical cord blood samples were conducted by AXYS Analytical Services (Sydney, BC) and Flett Research Ltd. (Winnipeg, MB).

labs are equipped with the machines and expertise to run the tests or the funding to develop the methods. Laboratories have yet to develop methods to test human tissues for the vast majority of chemicals on the market, and the few tests that labs are able to conduct are expensive. Laboratory costs for the cord blood analyses reported here were $10,000 per sample.

A developing baby depends on adults for protection, nutrition, and, ultimately, survival. As a society we have a responsibility to ensure that babies do not enter this world pre-polluted, with 200 industrial chemicals in their blood. Decades-old bans on a handful of chemicals like PCBs, lead gas additives, DDT, and other pesticides have led to significant declines in people's blood levels of these pollutants. But good news like this is hard to find for other chemicals.

The Toxic Substances Control Act, the 1976 federal law meant to ensure the safety of commercial chemicals, essentially deemed 63,000 existing chemicals "safe as used" the day the law was passed, through mandated, en masse approval for use with no safety scrutiny. It forces the government to approve new chemicals within 90 days of a company's application at an average pace of seven per day. It has not been improved for nearly 30 years—longer than any other major environmental or public health statute—and does nothing to reduce or ensure the safety of exposure to pollution in the womb.

Because the Toxic Substances Control Act fails to mandate safety studies, the government has initiated a number of voluntary programs to gather more information about chemicals, most notably the high production volume (HPV) chemical screening program. But these efforts have been largely ineffective at reducing human exposures to chemicals. They are no substitute for a clear statutory requirement to protect children from the toxic effects of chemical exposure.

In light of the findings in this study and a substantial body of supporting science on the toxicity of early life exposures to industrial chemicals, we strongly urge that federal laws and policies be reformed to ensure that children are protected from chemicals, and that to the maximum extent possible, exposures to industrial chemicals before birth be eliminated. The sooner society takes action, the sooner we can reduce or end pollution in the womb.

Tests show 287 industrial chemicals in 10 newborn babies. Pollutants include consumer product ingredients, banned industrial chemicals and pesticides, and waste byproducts.

Sources and uses of chemicals in newborn blood	Chemical family name	Total number of chemicals found in 10 newborns	Range in number of chemicals found in each newborn
Common consumer product chemicals *(and their breakdown products)*		47 Found:	(23–48)
Pesticides, actively used in U.S.	Organochlorine pesticides (OCs)	7	(2–6)
Stain and grease resistant coatings for food wrap, carpet, furniture (Teflon, Scotchgard, Stainmaster . . .)	Perfluorochemicals (PFCs)	8	(4–8)
Fire retardants in TVs, computers, Furniture	Polybrominated diphenyl ethers (PBDEs)	32	(13–29)
Chemicals banned or severely restricted in the U.S. *(and their breakdown products)*		212 Found:	(111–185)
Pesticides, phased out of use in U.S.	Organochlorine pesticides (OCs)	14	(7–14)
Stain and grease resistant coatings for food wrap, carpet, furniture (pre-2000 Scotchgard)	Perfluorochemicals (PFCs)	1	(1–1)

Electrical insulators	Polychlorinated biphenyls (PCBs)	147	(65–114)
Broad use industrial chemicals—flame retardants, pesticides, electrical insultators	Polychlorinated naphthalenes (PCNs)	50	(22–40)
Waste byproducts		**28 Found:**	**(6–21)**
Garbage incineration and plastic production wastes	Polychlorinated and Polybrominated dibenzo dioxins and furans (PCDD/F and PBDD/F)	18	(5–13)
Car emissions and other fossil fuel combustion	Polynuclear aromatic hydrocarbons (PAHs)	9	(1–10)
Power plants (coal burning)	Methylmercury	1	(1–1)
All chemicals found		**TOTAL = 287 chemicals**	**(154–231)**

Source: Environmental Working Group analysis of tests of 10 umbilical cord blood samples conducted by AXYS Analytical Services (Sydney, BC) and Flett Research Ltd. (Winnipeg, MB).

Acknowledgments

Many people made this anthology.

At Thunder's Mouth Press and Avalon Publishing Group: Thanks to Will Balliett, John Oakes, Mike Walters, Michael O'Connor, Nancy Stair, Catheline Jean-Francois, Shaun Dillon, Linda Kosarin, Susan Reich, David Riedy, and Maria Fernandez for their support, dedication, and hard work.

We are especially grateful to J. M. Berger, who contributed original writing to this anthology. We also would like to thank Sean Donahue, John McGrath, and Dave Sheehan of the pioneering Web log worldgonewrong.com (now defunct) for their inspiration. And thanks are due to the many people who helped us with research and permissions.

Finally, we are grateful to the writers and artists whose work appears in this book.

Permissions

We gratefully acknowledge everyone who gave permission for material to appear in this book. We have made every effort to contact copyright holders. If an error or omission is brought to our attention, we will be pleased to correct the situation in future editions of this book. For further information, please contact the publisher.

"War of the Future" by David Morse. Copyright © 2005 by David Morse. Reprinted by permission of the author. • "In the Driver's Seat" by Tom Engelhardt. Copyright © 2004 by Tom Engelhardt. Reprinted by permission of the author. • "New, Advanced Technologies Pose Potential Terrorist Risks of Misuse" by Mike Narkter. Copyright © 2005 by Global Security Newswire. Reprinted by permission of Global Security Newswire. • "How Do I Look?" by Robert Kaplan. Copyright © 2004 by Robert Kaplan. Reprinted by permission of the author. • "Loose Nukes of the West" by Alan J. Kuperman. Copyright © 2003 by Alan J. Kuperman. Reprinted with permission of the author. • "Of Mice, Men, and In Between" by Rick Weiss. Copyright © 2004 by the *Washington Post.* Reprinted by permission of the *Washington Post.* • "The Coming Death Shortage" by Charles C. Mann. Copyright © 2005 by Charles C. Mann. Reprinted by permission of the author. • "We Are Not Immune" by Ronald J. Glasser. Copyright © 2004 by Harper's Magazine. Reproduced from the July issue by special permission. • "The Next Plague?" by Michael Slenske. Copyright © 2005 by Michael Slenske. Reprinted by permission of the author. • "What Will Become of Africa's AIDS Orphans?" by Melissa Fay Green. Copyright © 2002 by Melissa Fay Green. Reprinted by permission of the David Black Literary Agency. • "The Media's Labor Day Revolution" by Russ Baker. Copyright © 2005 by Russ Baker. Reprinted by permission of the author. • "Desperately Seeking Disclosure" by Dianne Farsetta. Copyright © 2005 by PR Watch. Reprinted by permission of PR Watch. • "What Are You Going to Do with That?" by Mark Danner. Copyright © 2005 by Mark Danner. Reprinted by permission of the author and the *New York Review of Books.* • "For Richer" by Paul Krugman. Copyright © 2002 by Paul Krugman. Reprinted by permission of the New York Times Syndication Corp. • "Gouging the Poor" by Barbara Ehrenreich. Copyright © 2004 by Barbara Ehrenreich. Reprinted by permission of *The Progressive,* 409 E. Main St., Madison, WI 53703. www.progressive.org. • "A Passage from India" by Suketu Mehta. Copyright © 2005 by Suketu Mehta. Reprinted by permission of the New York Times Syndication Corp. • "Corruption in the Republic" by Joshua Holland. Copyright © 2005 by Joshua Holland. Reprinted with permission of AlterNet.org. • "Countdown to a Meltdown" by James Fallows. Copyright © 2005 by James Fallows. Reprinted by permission of the author. • "The Great Tom Cruise Backlash" by Mark Morford. Copyright © 2005 by SF Gate. Reprinted by permission of Copyright Clearance Center. • "I Hate *The Passion of the Christ*" by Rob Rummel-Hudson. Copyright 2004 by Rob Rummel-Hudson. Reprinted by permission of the author. • "The New Sex Ed" by Ken Kegan. Copyright © Rolling Stone LLC 2003. All rights reserved. Reprinted by permission. • "Top Ten Reasons Not to Buy a Hummer" by Anonymous. Copyright © 2005 by Code Pink. Reprinted by permission of Code Pink. • "It's Not Just Eskimos in Bikinis" by Chip Ward. Copyright © 2005 by Chip Ward. Reprinted by permission of the author. • "Profits of Doom" by Dave Gilson. Copyright © 2005 by Foundation for National Progress. Reprinted by permission of Foundation for National Progress. • "The Corpse on Union Street" by Dan Barry, copyright © 2005 by the New York Times Company. Reprinted with permission. • Excerpt from *A Short History of Progress* by Ronald Wright. Copyright © 2004 by Ronald Wright. Reprinted by permission of Carroll & Graf. • "The Global Struggle for Energy" by Michael T. Klare. Copyright © 2005 by Michael T. Klare. Reprinted by permission of the author. • "Body Burden: The Pollution in Newborns" by Jane Houlihan, Timothy Kropp, Richard Wiles, Sean Gray and Chris Campbell. Copyright © 2005 by the Environmental Working Group. Reprinted by permission of the Environmental Working Group.

Bibliography

Baker, Russ. "The Media's Labor Day Revolution." Originally published by TomPaine.com, September 6, 2005.

Barry, Dan. "The Corpse on Union Street." Originally published by the *New York Times,* September 8, 2005.

Code Pink. "Top Ten Reasons Not to Buy a Hummer." Originally published by Code Pink, codepink4peace.org.

Danner, Mark. "What Are You Going to Do with That?." Originally published by *The New York Review of Books,* June 23, 2005.

Ehrenreich, Barbara. "Gouging the Poor." Originally published by *The Progressive,* February 2004.

Engelhardt, Tom. "In the Driver's Seat." Originally published by TomDispatch.com, July 7, 2004.

Fallows, James. "Countdown to a Meltdown." Originally published by *The Atlantic Monthly,* July/August 2005.

Farsetta, Dianne. "Desperately Seeking Disclosure." Originally published by *PR Watch,* second quarter, 2005.

Gilson, Dave. "Profits of Doom." Originally published by MotherJones.com, April 18, 2005.

Glasser, Ronald J. "We Are Not Immune." Originally published by *Harper's,* July 2004.

Green, Melissa Fay. "What Will Become of Africa's AIDS Orphans." Originally published by *The New York Times Magazine,* December 22, 2002.

Holland, Joshua. "Corruption in the Republic." Originally published by AlterNet, www.alternet.org, August 22, 2005.

Houlihan, Jane, Timothy Kropp, Richard Wiles, Sean Gray, and Chris Campbell. "Body Burden: The Pollution in Newborns." Originally published by the Environmental Working Group, July 14, 2005.

Kaplan, Robert. "How Do I Look?" Originally published by *The Atlantic Monthly,* May 2004.

Kegan, Ken. "The New Sex Ed." Originally published by *Rolling Stone,* September 18, 2003.

Klare, Michael T. "The Global Struggle for Energy." Originally published by TomDispatch.com, May 9, 2005.

Krugman, Paul. "For Richer." Originally published by *The New York Times Magazine,* October 20, 2002.

Kuperman, Alan J. "Loose Nukes of the West." Originally published by *The Washington Post,* May 7, 2003.

Mann, Charles C. "The Coming Death Shortage." Originally published by *The Atlantic Monthly,* May 2005.

Mehta, Suketu. "A Passage from India." Originally published by the *New York Times,* July 12, 2005.

Morford, Mark. "The Great Tom Cruise Backlash." Originally published by *SF Gate,* July 6, 2005.

Morse, David. "War of the Future." Originally published by TomDispatch.com, August 18, 2005.

Narkter, Mike. "New, Advanced Technologies Pose Potential Terrorist Risk of Misuse, Expert Tells U.S. Lawmakers." Originally published by Global Security Newswire, February 3, 2005.

Rummel-Hudson, Rob. "I Hate *The Passion of the Christ.*" Originally published by Darn-Tootin.com, September 17, 2004.

Slenske, Michael. "The Next Plague?" Originally published by *The Atlantic Monthly,* June 2005.

Ward, Chip. "It's Not Just Eskimos in Bikinis." Originally published by TomDispatch.com, June 6, 2005.

Weiss, Rick. "Of Mice, Men, and In Between." Originally published by *The Washington Post,* November 20, 2004.

Wright, Ronald. *A Short History of Progress.* New York: Carroll & Graf, 2004.

Don't Laugh, Joe

Keiko Kasza

PUFFIN BOOKS

For Yoshiyuki, Chiaki, and Ami

PUFFIN BOOKS
Published by the Penguin Group
Penguin Putnam Books for Young Readers, 345 Hudson Street, New York, New York 10014, U.S.A.
Penguin Books Ltd, 27 Wrights Lane, London W8 5TZ, England
Penguin Books Australia Ltd, Ringwood, Victoria, Australia
Penguin Books Canada Ltd, 10 Alcorn Avenue, Toronto, Ontario, Canada M4V 3B2
Penguin Books (N.Z.) Ltd, 182-190 Wairau Road, Auckland 10, New Zealand

Penguin Books Ltd, Registered Offices: Harmondsworth, Middlesex, England

First published in the United States of America by G. P. Putnam's Sons, a division of The Putnam & Grosset Group, 1997
Published by Puffin Books, a member of Penguin Putnam Books for Young Readers, 2000

1 3 5 7 9 10 8 6 4 2

THE LIBRARY OF CONGRESS HAS CATALOGED THE G. P. PUTNAM'S SONS EDITION AS FOLLOWS:
Kasza, Keiko.
Don't laugh, Joe!/Keiko Kasza.
p. cm.
Summary: Mother Possum is in despair because her son cannot learn to play dead without laughing.
[1. Opossums—Fiction. 2. Laughter—Fiction. 3. Mothers and sons—Fiction.] I. Title.
PZ7.K15645Do 1997 [E]—dc20 95-25534 CIP AC
ISBN 0-399-23036-X

This edition ISBN 0-698-11794-8

Printed in the United States of America
Set in Adminster

Mother Possum dearly loved her little son Joe, but he was always giggling. Lately his giggling made her worry. Mother Possum was about to teach Joe the most important lesson a possum can learn.

JOE

"Joe," said Mother Possum, "you must learn how to play dead."

"Why?" asked Joe.

"Because we possums escape our enemies by playing dead," Mother Possum explained. "When you learn this trick, Joe, I'll bake you the possums' favorite dessert—a bug pie!"

They started to practice.

"No giggling, Joe," Mother Possum warned.

"No problem, Mom," Joe answered.

Joe played dead, and his mother sniffed his fur like a hungry fox.

Sniff, sniff, sniff.

Joe laughed so hard that his stomach hurt. "Can I have my pie now?" he asked.

"No way, Joe," Mother Possum scolded. "Dead possums don't laugh!"

No Laughing!
A B C

Joe practiced playing dead again. This time his mother poked him like a nasty coyote.

Poke, poke, poke.

Joe laughed so hard that he screamed for her to stop. "Can I have my pie now?" he asked.

"No way, Joe," Mother Possum scolded. "Dead possums don't scream!"

Joe practiced playing dead once more. This time his mother shook him like a scary wildcat.

Shake, shake, shake.

Joe laughed so hard that he wiggled loose and fell on the floor.

"How about some bug pie, Mom?" he asked.

"No way, Joe," Mother Possum scolded. "Dead possums don't wiggle!"

One day, Mother Possum took Joe outside to practice. "This time," she said, "I'll be a grumpy old bear. When I growl at you, you play dead. Okay, Joe?"

"Nothing to it, Mom," Joe said.

But just as Mother Possum was about to growl …

... a real grumpy old bear came out of the woods. He let out the fiercest growl Joe had ever heard. Joe and his mother immediately fell to the ground to play dead.

The grumpy old bear sniffed Joe's fur.
Sniff, sniff, sniff.

The grumpy old bear poked Joe's tummy.
Poke, poke, poke.

Finally, the grumpy old bear shook Joe up and down.
Shake, shake, shake.

Joe didn't laugh. Joe didn't scream. Joe didn't wiggle. For the first time, he played dead perfectly. Mother Possum was very proud of him. But the grumpy old bear wouldn't go away. He sat and sat and sat.

Suddenly, the bear started to cry big tears. "This is terrible," he moaned. "I'm always so grumpy. I thought that if anyone could make me laugh, it would be little Joe the possum. But when I find him, poor Joe drops dead before my eyes! Oh, this is awful!"

When he heard the bear's story, Joe was relieved. He even began to feel sorry for the sobbing bear. "Hey, Mr. Bear," he called, "I'm not dead. I was just playing dead."

The bear was so surprised he almost jumped out of his fur. "Playing dead?" he cried. "Boy, you're good at that! Oh, please, Joe," he begged, "teach me how to laugh."

"It's easy," said Joe. "Lots of things are funny, Mr. Bear. What happened just now is funny," and he started to giggle. Soon his laughter spread to everyone around him, even to the grumpy old bear.

Before long, the animals were laughing so hard that the whole forest shook.

"Oh, Joe," the bear howled, "thank you for teaching me to laugh."

"Thank you, Mr. Bear," Joe answered, "for teaching me how to play dead."

"Now can I have my pie?" Joe asked his mother.

"Absolutely," Mother Possum answered. "Everyone, please come and join us for some delicious bug pie."

"With grasshoppers!" Joe shouted gleefully. "And beetles and yummy cockroaches, too!"

The other animals suddenly stopped their giggling. "Bug pie??? Cockroaches!!!" One by one, they fell to the ground ...

... and played dead.

S0-BSV-441

THE LEGEND OF

Illustrated by Lisbeth Zwerger

Translated by Anthea Bell

PICTURE BOOK STUDIO USA

The Duke of Rosery had a very beautiful sister whom he loved more than all the world, and he would do anything to please her. She was extraordinarily fond of flowers, particularly roses, so her brother made almost all his dukedom into one great rose garden. She had another great passion too, for the combing and braiding of her lovely hair. For this purpose she had a number of lady's maids, who were really braiding maids, and who always had golden combs pinned to their dresses.

The princess did nothing all day long but have her hair combed, and then go running about in the garden with her braiding maids until it was untidy again, when they combed it for her once more.

One morning, as she was sitting in the garden with her six maids busy about her, plaiting her six braids of hair, her brother the Duke of Rosery came up to her, leading Prince Evermore by the hand.

"Dear sister," said the Duke, "I have often told you about my dearest friend, Prince Evermore, and you know I have always hoped you would marry him, so that he would stay with me for evermore. Here he is now, and I ask you to give him your heart."

Just at that moment one of the braiding maids pulled at a tangle in Princess Rosalina's hair, which made the Princess very cross, and she cried, "Oh, must you be pulling my hair evermore?"

The maid thought of a clever excuse. "Why, yes, Princess," she said, "it was indeed Prince Evermore who pulled your hair, because the sudden sight of him distracted me."

The Prince was starting to make his own excuses when another of the maids pulled the Princess's hair too, so that Rosalina quite lost her temper, and said to poor Prince Evermore, "Noble Prince, and you too, dear brother, let me tell you that I will no more wed Prince Evermore than a rosebush will marry a pumpkin!" And so saying, she walked away with the braiding maids after her, still plaiting her hair.

The Duke could not offer his friend any comfort. "For she always keeps her word," said he.

"In that case," said Prince Evermore, "I'll be off to seek my fortune." And he embraced the Duke and went away to see his aunt, Lady Nevermore, who was a great enchantress, to ask her advice.

One day, several weeks later, Rosalina happened to be walking in the garden when she saw an old woman looking at all the rosebushes one by one, shaking her head over each of them. Rosalina went over to her and asked why she kept shaking her head.

"Because there are so many roses here, yet the loveliest of all is missing," said the old woman, — "the monthly rose that flowers for evermore."

"Who owns it?" asked Rosalina. "I must have that rose at any price!"

"Why," said the old woman, "it is yours for the asking!" And she took the cover off the basket she was carrying, and showed the Princess a pumpkin with a little rosebush in flower stuck into it. She had put the rosebush in the pumpkin to keep it fresh.

Rosalina was delighted with the little rosebush, and said, "It is the very loveliest rosebush I have ever seen, and I must have it for my own. Tell me what you want for it."

"Two things," said she. "First, I want you to be my guest at my midday meal, and second, when the rosebush comes into flower once a month, you and your braiding maids must hold a festival, and you must all jump over the rosebush. But mind you don't brush off any petals with your skirts, for none of them must fall to the ground. If one of you does cause a petal to drop, she must be struck on the hands with rose twigs.

The rosebush itself will give the blows if you speak these words to it:

"LITTLE ROSE,
STRIKE YOUR BLOWS!
STRIKE ME AS YOU WILL,
BECAUSE I JUMPED SO ILL!
I WILL TAKE CHASTISEMENT GLADLY,
ROSE, BECAUSE I JUMPED SO BADLY."

That made the Princess laugh, and she agreed to everything. Then the old woman took a wooden spoon out of her pocket, divided the pumpkin in half with it, took out a spoonful of its seeds and gave them to the Princess to eat. The Princess made a face at first, but when she tried the seeds she thought they tasted delicious, and she ate a good many of them. After that the old woman planted the rosebush under her window, and as it was already bearing a full-blown rose, she said, "Now, Princess Rosalina, call for your braiding maids and hold the first festival of jumping the rose."

So then Rosalina went and told her brother the Duke the whole story, and he summoned drummers and trumpeters and made ready for the festival. When Rosalina and her maids came out, they drew lots to see who was to jump first, and it happened that Rosalina herself was last of all. Most of the girls jumped over the rosebush easily, but the maids who had pulled the Princess's hair while Prince Evermore was asking for her hand in marriage brushed a couple of petals off the rose with the long trains of their dresses, and they had to hold out their hands to the bush, saying:

"LITTLE ROSE,
STRIKE YOUR BLOWS!
STRIKE ME AS YOU WILL,
BECAUSE I JUMPED SO ILL!
I WILL TAKE CHASTISEMENT GLADLY,
ROSE, BECAUSE I JUMPED SO BADLY."

At that, to the amazement of all present, the rosebush struck them on their fingers a couple of times, so hard that the tears came into their eyes. When it was Rosalina's turn to jump, she took a good run and she too would have jumped the rose quite easily, if her braids of hair had not come undone just as she was jumping and brushed a petal off the rose. But she caught it as she jumped and swallowed it, before it could fall to the ground. The whole company clapped and applauded.

Then there was much merriment, with feasting and dancing, and towards the end of the banquet, when all kinds of toasts were being drunk, the old woman raised her glass and told Rosalina:

"PETAL AND SEED – YOU'VE EATEN BOTH.
NOW YOU'RE FORCED TO KEEP YOUR OATH!
SINCE ROSE AND PUMPKIN NOW ARE ONE,
WHAT YOU HAVE PROMISED MUST BE DONE.
PRINCE EVERMORE WINS YOUR HAUGHTY HAND!
FAREWELL! I VANISH FROM YOUR LAND."

And with these words, she suddenly vanished away before all eyes. But Rosalina, at whom everyone turned to look, uttered a loud cry and fell down in a faint. She was taken to her room, and she remembered, with great dismay, how she had told the Prince she would have him if rose and pumpkin married.

That night she had very strange dreams. She dreamed that roses were growing out of her mouth, and she had pains in her stomach. Such dreams came to her often, and they grew more and more alarming.

When the little rosebush that bore the monthly roses came into flower again, and she jumped over it once more, she felt melancholy and sick, and she had lost her appetite for food and drink.

At the time of the third festival of the rose, she dreamed she was a pumpkin, and her brother had difficulty in persuading her she was not. But as the fourth festival of the rose approached, she took the idea of being a pumpkin into her head more firmly than ever, and she utterly refused to jump over the rosebush again.

When the fifth festival of the rose came, she could not be induced to leave her room, and she spent all day weeping and wailing because, she said, she turned into a pumpkin. The Duke was much distressed by her delusion, and he called in every doctor in the land, but there was no talking her out of it now.

The sixth festival of the rose came around, and by now the rosebush had grown so large that jumping over it was quite out of the question, all the more so when she was grieving all day long because she was a pumpkin. At the seventh festival of the rose, the rosebush came looking in at her window, by the eighth festival of the rose its branches were growing around her bed, and by the ninth it formed a bower of roses over her. Then she had so vivid a dream that she was a pumpkin, and must die, that she had her brother summoned, and he came into her room with a light. But imagine her surprise next morning when she saw half a great golden pumpkin standing by her bed, with a lovely little girl sleeping in it as if it were a cradle.

Then the Princess was deeply moved. "Ah," she said, "if only good Prince Evermore were here now, I would gladly be his wife!" Then the roses around her bed rustled, and she heard a voice:

A ROSE I DIED, A ROSE I BORE,
A ROSE I LIVE FOR EVERMORE."

At that the Princess was in great distress, realizing that good Prince Evermore had become a rosebush for her sake. She called the little girl Rosepetal, and carried her and the cradle into her own most secret chamber, intending to bring her up there, for she loved the child so much she did not want any other human being to set eyes on her. Rosalina soon became merry again, and she stayed in bed for the next few days and told the braiding maids to plait her hair in a different way, for she used to wear the braids around her head like a wreath, but now she wanted to set a golden cap on it. No sooner had the combing of her hair begun than there came a knock at her door, and they told her the old woman who had brought the pumpkin and the rosebush was outside, wanting to see little Rosepetal. However, the Princess sent back word that the old woman must wait until her hair was combed.

Quarter of an hour later the old woman knocked again, and got the same answer. Another quarter-hour passed, and again she knocked and was told to wait. This happened four times more. The seventh time, the old woman grew very angry and called in through the keyhole:

"SEVEN QUARTERS YOU'VE MADE ME WAIT!
SEVEN QUARTERS! NOW IT'S TOO LATE.
SO COMB AWAY FOR SEVEN YEARS MORE,
AND THEN GREAT DANGER LIES IN STORE.
YOU'LL COMB AWAY YOUR OWN CHILD'S BREATH;
YOU'LL COMB ROSEPETAL TO HER DEATH."

And with these angry words, the old woman disappeared. Rosalina took very little notice of them. She thought of nothing but her little Rosepetal who grew bigger and more delightful every day. Like her mother, she had remarkably long and lovely hair, and it was Rosalina's greatest pleasure to shut herself up in the secret room, alone with Rosepetal and comb it. The child grew to be almost seven years old, and the time was near when the old witch woman's curse was to come true:

"YOU'LL COMB AWAY YOUR OWN CHILD'S BREATH;
YOU'LL COMB ROSEPETAL TO HER DEATH."

But Rosalina did not think of that. She went on combing Rosepetal's hair, just as before.

Now one day, when she had the little girl clasped between her knees and was passing a golden comb through her long golden hair, she suddenly felt a great surge of envy, because the child's hair was so much prettier than her own, and she said crossly:

"I WISH THE HAIR WAS OFF YOUR HEAD,
AND BRAIDED UP ON MINE INSTEAD!"

No sooner had she said these words, however, than punishment was sent from Heaven. Down came an invisible pair of scissors and cut all the hair off her head — snip, snap! She started in such amazement that her hand jerked, driving the sharp comb into poor Rosepetal's little head so hard that the child uttered a cry and fell down dead at her feet.

Then poor unhappy Rosalina remembered the old woman's magical curse, but it was too late now. There lay her beloved Rosepetal, dead upon the floor, and her own beautiful hair, of which she had been so vain and which she had combed so long, was all cut off and lay around her. She wrung her hands in despair over her shorn head.

She wept for a long time, and then she stuffed a little mattress with her long hair, filled a pillow with rose petals and laid dead Rosepetal on them with her hands folded, inside a coffin of crystal glass, with six more crystal coffins over it. Then she locked them all away in her secret chamber, which was known to no one but herself and one faithful serving maid.

So she lived on for several years, in constant mourning. The rosebush in her room withered away, and when she felt the hour of her death draw near she asked her brother, the Duke of Rosery, to come to her and told him, "Dear brother, the end of my life has come. I wish I had not been so willful and so vain, but it is too late to mend matters now,

and I pray to God to have mercy on me. All I owned is yours now. But promise me one thing, so that I can die in peace."

The Duke in tears, promised to do all she asked, for he loved her more than anything in the world.

So she gave him a key, saying, "This is the key to the innermost chamber of my apartments. Take great care of it, and never unlock that room."

Her brother assured her once again that he would keep his word.

"Farewell," said Rosalina, "and pray for me." Then she turned over and died, and the Duke had her buried with great pomp and ceremony beside the bush that bore the monthly roses.

A few months later, the Duke married a lady who was beautiful but ill-natured. One day he had to go away on a brief journey, and he asked his wife to look after the castle, warning her, whatever she did, not to unlock the innermost chamber, whose key he kept in his desk.

She promised to do as he said, but as soon as his back was turned curiosity drove her to fetch the key and open the forbidden chamber.

When she saw Rosepetal lying on her mattress inside the glass coffins, she was consumed with fury! Ever since her mother had locked Rosepetal in the room, thinking she was dead, the child had been growing, and the glass coffins with her.

Now she looked like a lovely young girl of fourteen lying there asleep, for the old witch woman had kept her alive in her slumbers all these years.

Angrily, the wicked Duchess flung open the coffins. "Oho!" said she.

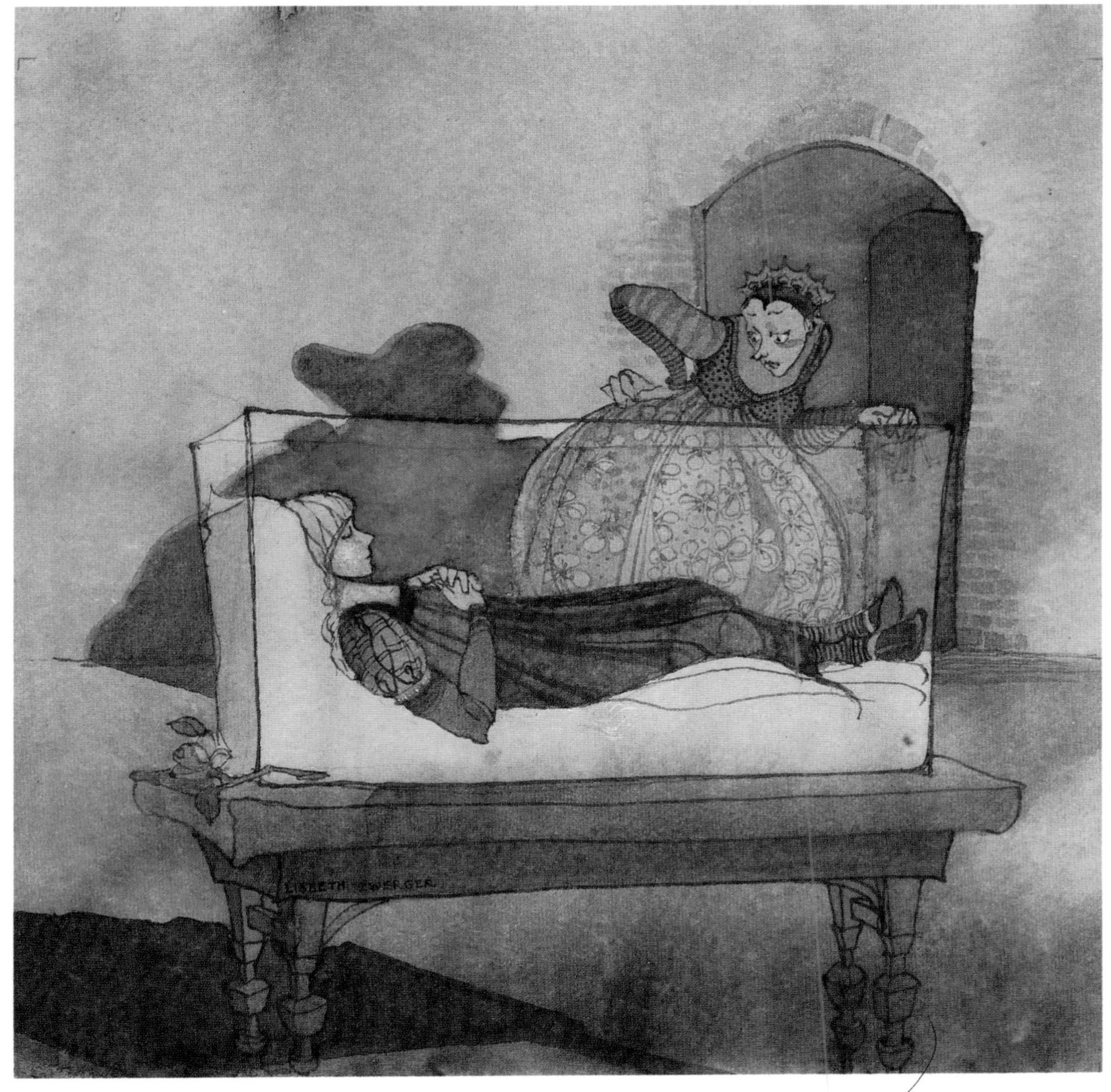

"So that's why I am not allowed into this room — so that this fine young lady here can sleep in peace! We'll soon see about that. I'll wake you, my sleeping beauty!" And she hauled Rosepetal's head up by the hair so roughly that the comb, which was still sticking in her head, fell out and the poor little girl awoke from her magical sleep, crying out, "Oh, Mother, dear Mother, how you hurt me!"

"I'll mother you and father you!" said the Duchess. "And I'll see you don't forget it either!" She pulled Rosepetal, weeping and trembling, out of her crystal coffin, and beat and ill-treated her in all kinds of ways, threatening to drown her if she ever breathed a word to anyone about what had happened to her in this room. Then she cut off the girl's beautiful long hair, gave her a short dress made of sacking, and forced her to fetch firewood and carry water, light the stoves and scour the rooms. She gave her so many blows and cuffs daily, boxing her ears and slapping her, that poor Rosepetal's face was all black and blue, as if she had been eating blueberries.

When the Duke of Rosery came home and asked his Duchess about the poor girl whom he saw her ill-treating so harshly every day, she said, "Oh, she's a slave girl my aunt sent me, but she is so vicious and stupid and lazy that I have to keep punishing her."

Well, after a while the Duke went away to a great fair, and according to his custom he summoned everyone who lived in the castle, down to the very cats and dogs, and asked them all what presents he should bring them home. One asked for this, another for that, and finally poor Rosepetal stepped forward too, in her coarse servant's dress. The Duke was about to speak to her when his wicked wife interrupted him.

"Must we have this dirty wench always about the place?" said she. "Are the rest of us to be put on a footing with this common, lazy slave girl? Send the wretched creature away! I don't know how you can show so low a wretch such honor!"

Tears of grief ran down poor Rosepetal's cheeks, and the kindhearted Duke was touched. "Don't cry, my poor child," he said. "Just say what you would like, for I intend to please you, and no one will stop me!"

"Oh, sir," said Rosepetal, "bring me a doll, and a little knife and a whetstone, and if you forget, I wish you may not be able to cross the first river you come to on your way home."

So the Duke went off to the fair, and he bought everything else, but he forgot Rosepetal's doll and her little knife and whetstone.

On his way back he came to a river, and such a storm arose that no boatman dared ferry him over, and then he remembered Rosepetal's curse. He turned back at once and bought the things she wanted, and then he traveled home to his castle safe and sound, and gave all his presents.

Once Rosepetal had her own gifts she took them into the kitchen, put the doll upon the kitchen range, sat down in front of it, weeping bitterly, and began talking to it as if it were a living person, telling it all the torments she had to suffer at the Duchess's hands. "Do you hear me?" she kept saying. "Do you understand? Are you listening? Isn't it a sad story? What do you think?" But when the doll made no reply, Rosepetal took her little knife and sharpened it on her whetstone, saying, "Little doll, if you won't answer me I'll stab myself to the heart with this knife, for I have no friend on earth but you."

Then the doll began to swell up slowly, like bagpipes when the piper is blowing into them, and at last there was a whirring sound and words came out. "I understand, I understand, I hear, I hear, I understand."

Now the Duke had a room next door to the kitchen, and when he overheard the doll's song and Rosepetal's weeping and wailing several days running, he made a hole in the door so that he could see and hear Rosepetal sitting in front of her doll in tears, telling her story.

She told the tale of Prince Evermore and the pumpkin seeds, the festival of jumping the rose, the rose petal, the golden pumpkin that had been her cradle, her mother's combing of her hair, the witch woman's curse, the driving of the comb into her head, her enchanted sleep as she lay inside the seven glass coffins, the giving of the key to the Duke, who was forbidden to enter the chamber, the death of Princess Rosalina, the Duke's journey and the Duchess's curiosity, the unlocking of the forbidden chamber, the falling out of the comb, the cutting of her own hair, and the harsh treatment she had suffered every hour of the day.

Then she said, once again, "Answer me or I will kill myself!" And she set the point of the knife to her heart. But the Duke burst in through the doorway and snatched the knife from her hand. He embraced his niece lovingly, and took her out of the castle and away to the wife of his chief minister, who dressed her in fine clothes and cared for her well.

A few months later, when she had quite recovered from all her hard work and the ill-treatment given by the wicked Duchess, the Duke held a magnificent banquet in his castle and introduced Rosepetal as his niece. No one knew her in all her splendor. At the end of the meal a model of a house made of sugar was brought in, and everyone wanted to know what was inside it.

LISBETH ZWERGER

"Will you open the sugar house?" the Duke asked the Duchess.

So she opened it, and there was the little doll inside, lying in seven glass coffins just as Rosepetal had lain. The Duchess was afraid, and so angry that she broke the coffins open and snatched out the doll. But the doll ran away from her and perched on Rosepetal's shoulder, where she puffed herself up and up like a pair of bagpipes, and whirred, and spoke, accusing the Duchess of all her cruelties to her face.

And still the doll grew bigger and bigger, until at last, there on the table stood the old enchantress who has played many a part in this story. When she finished her speech, she flew away out of the window.

Then the Duke had his wicked wife put into a coach and driven back to her parents' house, where he had once gone to fetch her.

Rosepetal married a handsome prince, and had the whole dukedom of Rosery for her dowry, and the rosebush Evermore flowered again.

One night, as Rosepetal was breathing in its sweet scent, she and her husband went to the window, and she saw her mother and the braiding maids jumping over the rosebush, and Prince Evermore was also there.

"God bless you, dear Mother and Father!" she cried.

"God bless you, dear children!" they called up from down below, and then they vanished into thin air.

Then Rosepetal became very quiet and gentle in her ways. She had a cradle made, just like a golden pumpkin, and Heaven soon sent her a little prince to lay in the cradle, and he told me this tale for a piece of gingerbread I gave him.

Original title: DAS MÄRCHEN VON ROSENBLÄTTCHEN

Published in USA by Picture Book Studio USA,
an imprint of Neugebauer Press USA Inc.
Distributed by Alphabet Press, Natick, MA.
Distributed in Canada by Vanwell Publishing, St. Catharines, Ont.
Published in U.K. by Neugebauer Press Publishing Ltd., London.
Distributed by A & C Black PLC, London.
Distributed in Australia by Hutchinson Group Australia Pty. Ltd.

Printed in Austria.

LIBRARY OF CONGRESS CATALOGING IN PUBLICATION DATA

Brentano, Clemens, 1778–1842.
The legend of the rose petal.

Translation of: Das Märchen von Rosenblättchen.
Summary: A lover of roses with most of her kingdom
made into a rose garden, Princess Rosalina makes a pact
with an old enchantress to obtain the most beautiful
rosebush of all.
1. Children's stories, German. [1. Fairy tales]
I. Zwerger, Lisbeth, ill. II. Title.
PZ8.B674Le 1985 [E] 84-27386
ISBN 0-907234-71-2